The
Training in Counselling & Psychotherapy Directory
2000
16th Edition

Pass me on when you've finished reading me

Healthy Planet
www.healthyplanet.org

Edited by
Denise Chaytor
BAC Information Office

British Association for Counselling
1 Regent Place • Rugby • Warwickshire • CV21 2PJ
Office 01788 550899 • Information Line 01788 578328 • Fax 01788 562189
Minicom 01788 572838 • e-mail bac@bac.co.uk • http://www.counselling.co.uk

The information contained in this directory has been compiled from material supplied by the individuals and organisations offering training in counselling, therapy or guidance. Every effort has been made to ensure the accuracy of the information but the fact that there is an entry or advertisement in this directory is in no way a recommendation or endorsement of the course concerned.

16th edition 2000

Produced by: British Association for Counselling, 1 Regent Place, Rugby, Warwickshire CV21 2PJ. Company limited by guarantee 2175320 registered in England & Wales. Registered Charity 298361.

Printed by: Hobbs the Printers Ltd, Totton, Hampshire.

Contents

Page   Page

Notes

Foreword

'Begin at the beginning and end at the end', but as anyone who has considered training to become a counsellor has found, it is far from that simple. There is an enormous proliferation of counselling courses offering a wide variety of qualifications, ranging from introductory courses of 10 hours up to Masters or PhD courses of several years duration. In between the extremes there are dozens of other certificates and diplomas of varying length.

The purpose of this directory is to enable you, as a potential student, to make informed decisions as to which courses are the most appropriate for your needs and it is hoped that by the time you have read the section 'Essential Information for Students', you will feel confident about doing so.

About the directory

The information about the courses

Information about the counselling courses provided by the institutions includes brief details of the duration of the course and entry requirements. Full details can be gained by contacting the institution.

Validation

Some counselling courses are validated by the university responsible for the course. Otherwise, the validating body is listed in brackets after the title of the course. If it is not listed, there may be an internal validation and this can be checked with the institution. A list of the most commonly used validations is given in Appendix 1.

A number of training organisations are members of the United Kingdom Council for Psychotherapy, having demonstrated a satisfactory standard of training. These organisations are expected to abide by approved codes of ethics. Their successful trainees can apply for inclusion on the UKCP National Register of Psychotherapists. UKCP may be contacted at 167-169 Great Portland Street, London W1N 5FB, tel: 0207 436 3002.

Where information regarding the Credit Accumulation Transfer Scheme (CATS) has been offered, it has been included within the title section. Points accrued on the CATS scheme may be transferred to appropriate courses at other colleges.

Facilities for disabled students

Institutions have been asked to offer information about their facilities for those who have disabilities and where this information is available it has been included.

Other types of counselling training available

Where institutions offer in-house/tailor-made training, or short course and specialist training it has been noted.

While we have tried to include as many courses as possible, there are always new courses being devised so it is worth checking with local colleges, nursing schools, etc. Please let BAC know if there are courses running which are not listed in the directory. If you want to set up in-house training, an alternative source of trainers is to be found in the U.K Counselling & Psychotherapy Directory obtainable from BAC.

No suitable courses in your area?

For those who have difficulty in finding a course, or who have difficulty in attending a course on a regular basis, there is also a 'National' section. This includes courses run as a series of modules, often at weekends and which may be residential, for those who are able to travel out of their area. It also includes organisations which offer training from venues throughout the UK.

Note:
BAC can only vouch for courses which are marked (BAC Acc) and which are marked by a shaded area.

Please refer to section 'Essential Information for Students'.

Careers in Counselling

Counselling is usually embarked upon as a second career or an avenue for career development. People wishing to work in counselling, other than in a voluntary capacity, will frequently have gained professional qualifications and experience in a related area of work. The initial training for their first occupation may well include some training in counselling skills and these need to be further developed by taking an appropriate course when counselling becomes the main focus. The most obvious professions acting as a first stage to a career in counselling are teaching, careers and advisory work, youth and community work, social work, the church, human resources, nursing and medicine.

Though the number of posts in counselling is increasing, they do not meet the number of professionally trained counsellors available. Positions are advertised in the Guardian (Tuesdays and Wednesdays), the Independent (Thursdays), Times Higher Educational Supplement (weekly), Times Educational Supplement (weekly), Nursing Times (weekly) and Community Care (weekly). BAC also produces the Jobfile, available on subscription (contact BAC for further details).

Counsellor vacancies may be in a variety of settings such as schools, further education, the workplace, youth work, alcohol, drugs and AIDS agencies, general practice and other general counselling services. Counsellors in these jobs will expect to be dealing with a wide range of presenting problems. Frequently, full time posts are advertised where the counsellor is required to fill a dual role as counsellor and teacher, welfare and advice worker, co-ordinator or nurse.

There is much scope for both part-time and voluntary work in counselling. Agencies like Relate (marriage guidance), Cruse (bereavement), Phobic Action and many others select and train volunteers for counselling work within their counselling organisations. However, such agencies may require a commitment of several years from their volunteers. It may be useful to have a basic skills training before offering yourself for this work. People gain valuable experience in these roles and may move on from these voluntary positions to further training and paid work. In looking for voluntary work it can be helpful to approach the local branch of the Council for Voluntary Services, this will be listed in the Phone Book. The Directory of Social Change also produces the Directory of Volunteer & Employment Opportunities and a number of other books concerned with volunteering. They may be contacted at 24 Stephenson Way, London NW1 2DP tel: 0171-435 8171.

It is also possible to work in private practice. Waiting lists for free or low cost counselling can be long. As the general public becomes more aware of the benefits of counselling, people are turning increasingly to private practitioners for help. This private work can combine neatly with part-time or voluntary work.

Counselling Training

Your questions answered

BAC is receiving an increasing number of requests for information about courses for counselling. Many come from those who want to train as a counsellor but even more come from people who want to improve the quality of the work they do, for example in their medical, educational, social or management positions.

This publication offers information for all those who are looking for counselling or counselling skills training. To this end it:

- maps the current counselling field in order that prospective students can better identify their needs

- indicates what they may expect from courses of differing lengths and content

- suggests the kind of questions prospective course members should be asking.

What can be expected from the training on offer?

The information given to you on application should make clear the course objectives and what you can expect to learn by the completion of the course. However, as a rough guide you might expect:

* A brief introduction of, say, 1-5 hours which will allow you to think about counselling skills and how they differ from other forms of helping.

* A one term evening course, or a 4-5 day block course (approximately 25 hours) which should, in addition, allow you to practise briefly some basic skills, discuss and explore the implications of your learning for you in your work/life.

* A one year, part-time evening course or a course consisting of 3-4 one week blocks (75-100 hours) which can constitute a very solid introduction to

the use of counselling skills in your work, providing it includes elements of systematic skills practice, as well as some theory with safe and challenging opportunity to reflect on your learning and its implications for you and your work.

* A two or three year, part-time course which will almost certainly include all the above plus an opportunity (or requirement) that you have supervision of your ongoing practice. In that case it can act as a good basis for practising in your current work setting and training others there in basic counselling skills: as well as for influencing organisations to become more 'person-centred'. It should also allow you to convert to becoming a formal counsellor with the subsequent addition of supervised ongoing counselling practice.

What is the difference between counselling and counselling skills?

Counselling Skills

The term 'counselling skills' does not have a single definition which is universally accepted. For the purpose of the BAC Code of Ethics & Practice for Counselling Skills, 'counselling skills' are distinguished from 'listening skills' and from 'counselling'. Although the distinction is not always a clear one, because the term 'counselling skills' contains elements of these other two activities, it has its own place in the continuum between them. What distinguishes the use of counselling skills from these other two activities are the intentions of the user, which is to enhance the performance of their functional role, as line manager, nurse, tutor, social worker, personnel officer, voluntary worker, etc., the recipient will, in turn, perceive them in that role.

Counselling skills are used alongside other skills and the client will identify the helper as their nurse, teacher, personnel officer and so on.

Counselling

Counselling is an activity with clear boundaries and the client will identify the helper as their counsellor.

BAC as an organisation has a commitment to promote and develop the quality of counselling wherever it is offered – formally or informally; by voluntary, statutory or private sector organisations by volunteers, paid counsellors or by human service workers who have responsibility to consumers at times of choice, change, confusion or distress. This latter category would include the counselling offered by a wide range of workers in health, education, youth and social work settings, as well as those with pastoral or personnel roles.

The Association defines counselling as an interaction in which the counsellor offers another person the time, attention and respect necessary to explore, discover and clarify ways of living more resourcefully, and to his or her greater well-being.

This process differs from other equally valid forms of helping by the emphasis placed on:

- confidentiality
- respect for the client's own perception of their experience
- support for the person in finding their own solution to their difficulties.

In the BAC definition, counselling is entered into when one person in the role of counsellor offers, or agrees, to give the necessary time, attention and respect to another person who is temporarily in the role of the 'client'.

The popular image of a counsellor is that of one person sitting with another in a room and agreeing a series of meetings. In some cases, however, counsellors work with couples or groups of people; and there could be two counsellors co-working.

Also, teachers, doctors, nurses and other professionals may offer brief crisis counselling. A counselling process may be entered into and be completed satisfactorily within a short time. The basic skills and principles are the same as those used in long term counselling.

What is experiential learning?

Participants in counselling courses are likely to be involved at times in experiential learning. This learning is designed to heighten awareness of an experience or give consideration to a familiar happening on which workshop members will be asked to reflect, either in their own terms or in the light of an offered framework. Experiential learning can be personally challenging for students in a number of ways.

1. Counsellors attempt to recognise and respect the ways others see and feel about their situation and the sense they make of it. In training, the process of suspending judgement and continuing to listen can raise anxiety, as can being asked to tolerate and encourage the expression of sometimes taboo thoughts and feelings.

2. Most courses expect students to share with other group members some of the difficulties and problems that they face in their lives. This work gives a personal insight into the opportunities and discomforts of sharing (and working to resolve) thoughts, situations and feelings that are problematic. It also provides an opportunity to give and receive direct feedback to each other as counsellors.

3. The process of learning more about our own values and the ways that we communicate with, relate to and cope with others in our life may result in

initial self-consciousness, self-questioning and some discomfort. Beyond that, most students experience new personal understanding and confidence in life and work which is energising. This can affect life outside the course and lead to personal and social reappraisal.

Because of all these factors, it is important to try and discover, before paying money or making a long-term commitment, whether such a course suits you or whether it will be too stressful. The quality of such a course for everyone depends on sufficient commitment to attendance and learning on the part of each participant.

What can be expected from a counselling skills course?

Courses listed as 'Counselling Skills' courses are not usually designed to train you as a counsellor. They will enhance basic skills which may be valuable in a 'caring' profession or setting. These courses should:

- develop the range of your counselling and enabling skills;

- help you to understand the values and ethics which lie behind a person-centred approach to 'choice, change, confusion and distress' in individuals and organisations;

- develop a clearer understanding of when counselling is appropriate;

- help you to become sensitive to situations where the use of counselling skills is appropriate.

What qualifications are needed to practise counselling?

At present there are no legal qualifications necessary and this can lead to considerable confusion when students first begin to examine their options, as there are numerous training courses and many examining bodies validating courses. Some training institutions award internal certificates which are often simply certificates of attendance, and other validations are of variable standard. It is wise to investigate the value of the award with the course organiser. A substantial core training can be used towards BAC Accreditation at a later date (see below).

Is it necessary to complete a BAC Accredited course?

It is not necessary to have undertaken a BAC Accredited course in order to apply for individual accreditation. Any counsellor training undertaken will count towards the requirement of 450 hours formal training in counselling. These hours need not have been all on one course but the applicant will be expected to have completed a course which is substantial enough to be regarded as 'core training'.

What is meant by an Accredited Course?

BAC has created a scheme for the recognition of in-depth counsellor training courses. The criteria and guidelines developed for course accreditation are related to the requirements laid down by the Association for the accreditation of individual counsellors. Successful completion of a BAC Accredited Course will fulfil the training component for BAC Individual Accreditation. The process of course recognition began in 1988 and a number of courses are now able to designate themselves Accredited as a Counsellor Training Course by BAC (BAC Acc).

Courses eligible to apply for Accreditation are in-depth and likely to be of 1 year full-time or 2-3 years part-time duration, with a minimum of 400 contact hours. Participants might reasonably expect to function as counsellors on satisfactory completion. The scheme in operation is for existing courses which have graduated at least one cohort of students and which has been able to develop in the light of that experience. The accreditation scheme checks the course design and looks at the delivery and assessment process in practice. At this time BAC has no facility for accrediting shorter counselling skills courses.

Accreditation is not automatic on application.

Courses are asked not to include in any publicity material the fact that they intend to apply or even that they have actually applied for Accreditation. Prospective students should assure themselves that Accreditation has been granted by contacting BAC.

What makes an Accredited course?

While courses differ in the approach they take to training, BAC believes that the following guiding concepts and assumptions (summarised below) should be reflected in an Accredited course and will form a basis of comparison when considering other course syllabuses.

1. The course should contain eight basic elements: admission, staff development, client work, supervision, skills training, theory, professional development and assessment.

2. The course should provide grounding in a core theoretical model.

3. The course should create a balance between theory, skills components and personal development, consistent with the core theoretical model.

4. The assessment process should include regular ongoing constructive feedback.

5. The course should help students to develop as reflective practitioners, who should also be required to monitor and evaluate their own work and personal development.

6. The course should be appropriately staffed with not less than two core members for any course.

Information regarding the criteria and guidelines and procedure for Course Accreditation may be found in the publication 'Recognition of Counsellor Training Courses' available from BAC. Accreditation may be granted to courses which lead to such diverse qualifications as, for instance, a Counselling Skills Diploma or an MSc in Counselling Psychology or a Diploma in Psychotherapy; or to an 'in-house' validation offered by a counselling service.

What are models of counselling?

Although there is considerable consensus about the core content of a counselling course, there is still a clear variety of methods of counselling. Most courses start from a theoretical base – typically humanistic, psychodynamic, cognitive or behavioural. The training methods used should be consistent with the basic assumptions about human beings which underlie the counselling methods taught. Before enrolling on a course it is advisable to find out about its theoretical emphasis and what that means in terms of the learning experience offered and the skills acquired.

This does not mean you should be involved in lengthy research before joining a counselling course – just a suggestion that you study the information offered and, if you are confused, talk with the course organisers or previous students of the course.

Is it necessary to find a placement?

Full counsellor training courses (2-3 years as above) should have client work as a component of the training. In practice, the provision of suitable client work is an increasing problem and students should discuss this with their chosen training organisation as they may need to find a placement for themselves in preparation for the course.

Finding a Suitable Placement

It is essential that full counsellor training courses include a substantial amount of supervised counselling practice with **real** clients This should be a minimum of 100 hours of counselling – exclusive of missed sessions – within which students should have the experience of making/maintaining and terminating/ counselling contracts. Training Organisations should take responsibility for assessing students, individually, for their 'readiness' to take clients.

It is not appropriate for inexperienced students to gain their client work experience by finding and seeing clients independently in private practice. Students therefore, will normally need a placement with an agency which offers a counselling service. For some courses, access to a placement will be a pre-requisite for admission; in others it may be negotiated during the course. Students should be aware that this process may take some time and that they need to allow for this. Otherwise they may have to prolong their training period and incur extra costs in order to complete the required number of practice hours. Training organisations should take responsibility for approving the placement as suitable for students for its particular course, but courses vary as to whether they or the student finds the placement and/or initiates the contact.

Placements are in considerable demand and they can be very difficult to find. Students may sometimes therefore be tempted to settle for a less than ideal situation, but this can seriously undermine training, and, at worst become an unsafe experience for both clients and students. It is therefore important that students understand what makes for best practice and the sorts of questions that should be asked of prospective placement agencies. The course should itself provide a check list of such questions; indeed the extent to which a course holds that such questions are important may well be a significant factor in the choice of course.

Can the agency provide formal counselling contracts as distinct from opportunities to use counselling skills?

- Does the agency specialise, have limits as to number of sessions etc? Are these compatible with the requirements of the course?
- Do prospective clients have a pre-counselling interview to discern whether it is appropriate to offer them a contract with a practitioner in training?

Is the theoretical orientation of the placement agency compatible with that of the course?

Will the agency provide adequate supervision (one hour presenting time to 8 hours counselling) with a supervisor who is an experienced practitioner? Or will the agency permit client work to be supervised by an 'outside' supervisor?

Do the placement agency's policies and procedures allow a student to meet the assessment requirements of the course? For example, a course may assess partially through audio-tapes of client sessions, but some agencies do not permit this practice.

Is the agency prepared to have such contact with the course as the training organisation requires, and can it make available sufficient time and resources to fulfill this undertaking?

- Is the student required to pay for supervision, reports, visits to and from the course etc and if so how much? Is this made clear from the outset?
- Are the limits of confidentiality between course and placement in relation to students' personal material and circumstances clear?

- Is the agency's Equal Opportunities policy compatible with that of the course?

Who is taking responsibility for the counselling work; what are the arrangements for insurance? Does the agency work to BAC or similar code of ethics?

- Does the agency require counsellors and students to be individual members of BAC? Is it itself an Organisational Member?

If something goes wrong what happens?

- Is there an internal Complaints procedure? Does the agency distinguish between complaints made re aspects of its service delivery and complaints against practitioners re breaches of codes of ethics? Do its procedures reflect awareness of this distinction?

- What will be the procedure and support system if a complaint involves a student on placement?

Is the agency prepared to make a formal written agreement with the training organisation in respect of responsibility issues such as the above, and of other aspects of the placement?

Has the agency got a track record of having students on placements? Not to have is not necessarily a contra-indication, but there could well be teething problems. There will be an especial need for clarification of mutual requirements and expectations, and such a placement may not suit inexperienced students.

- Is it possible to talk to former students about their experience of both course and placement?

Is the placement agency a Registered Sponsoring Organisation of the UK Register of Counsellors or is it working towards this status? (Because the UKRC is in its infancy this may be a more significant issue in future years than it can be at the present time.

CASE STUDY

KEITH

The next session is a supervision session with a trainee counsellor. I am his first supervisor and this is to be his third session. Keith has two clients, both of whom he sees in an agency, dealing specifically with young people. One of them didn't turn up last week and the other said he felt so much better he didn't need to come any more. Keith had come well prepared for his session and had a lot to offer on what he thought might be his part in these two premature terminations. The session offered us the opportunity to look at the counselling 'frame', and the 'contract' made with the client . . .

Further information may be found in 'The Recognition of Counsellor Training Courses', available from BAC.

What is meant by supervision of counselling?

Supervision is a formal arrangement for counsellors to discuss their work regularly with someone who is experienced in counselling and supervision. The task is to work together to ensure and develop the efficacy of the counsellor/client relationship. The agenda will be the counselling work and feeling about that work, together with the supervisor's reactions, comments and confrontations. Thus supervision is a process to maintain adequate standards of counselling and a method of consultancy to widen the horizons of an experienced practitioner.

What should the student/staff ratio be?

A counselling or counselling skills course requires commitment and offers personal, social and emotional learning as well as more academic study. With this in mind, we consider that the overall staff/student ratio of 1:12 is preferable. This does not preclude some lectures being offered to quite large groups but such occasions should be offset by individual and small group contact with tutors, for skills, tutorial or personal development work.

Is it possible to do specialist courses?

Some of the courses in the directory are aimed at helping people develop counselling or helping skills in specialist areas such as AIDS, bereavement, addiction and marital problems, etc.

Before undertaking one of these, it is important to ascertain if it is designed for those who are already familiar with basic counselling skills – a 'top up' course – or if it is an introduction to offering counselling help in that field.

Is it possible to do general training and more specialised training at the same time?

Training can be very intense and considerable time is needed for personal assessment and reflection which could result in students attempting to do too much at once, if more than one training is being done. It is, for example, Relate policy that their trainees should not be undertaking or intend to undertake any other form of counselling or psychotherapeutic training whilst applying for or undertaking Relate training.

How are specialist courses which offer a counselling component valued?

Increasingly, courses which train students in other 'human service' areas, like pastoral studies, careers guidance, youth and community work, etc., include a substantial counselling or counselling skills component. If you are considering taking such a course and are wondering about how it will serve you as a potential counselling or counselling skills qualification, you should scrutinise the length and content of the counselling component and compare it with the information given above about training in counselling and counselling skills.

Are there equal opportunities in counselling training?

BAC is working to promote equal opportunities in counselling training. An attempt has been made in this directory to indicate those courses which are accessible to disabled people. They may, for example, have induction loop or brailling facilities or have paid attention to physical needs such as wheelchair access to the full range of work, study and social facilities.

There are also many points to consider if you are seeking a multi-cultural training in counselling, some of which are examined in the RACE Information Sheet 1: 'Cross-Cultural Counselling: Some points to consider when choosing a training course', available from BAC.

This is one important concern in working towards equal opportunities in counselling training. There are many others which are under consideration for inclusion in future editions of the directory.

How should a course be ensuring equal opportunities?

Access:

- The course membership is representative of the population from which it draws, including women and men, people of different races, cultures, class, physical ability, sexuality and so on.

Curriculum:

- The course seeks to increase understanding of the life experiences of different groups in society.

- The course helps you to work sensitively with people from very different backgrounds from your own.

- The course tutors avoid stereotypes in course material and raise awareness of stereotyping throughout the course.

Policy:

- The course has an equal opportunities policy which it actively seeks to put into practice.

What is the difference between counselling and psychotherapy training?

It is not possible to make a generally accepted distinction between counselling and psychotherapy. There are well founded traditions which use the terms interchangeably and others which distinguish them. All that can be said without fear of contradiction is that the areas of overlap in skills, approach and theoretical understanding of fully trained and experienced counsellors and psychotherapists are substantial. Perhaps the most useful thing to say with regard to training is that BAC would see the systematic development of basic counselling skills as fundamental to all good counselling and psychotherapy training.

Further information is available in a new version of 'Becoming a Counsellor – a Guide for Training in Counselling & Psychotherapy' which will be published in October 2000 and will offer further information about training.

Whilst this Directory covers many psychotherapy courses, further information can be obtained from the United Kingdom Council for Psychotherapy (UKCP).

What are S/NVQs?

NVQ stands for National Vocational Qualification. SVQ stands for Scottish Vocational Qualification. It is the Scottish equivalent of an NVQ.

S/NVQs are work based qualifications, designed to show a person's competence in carrying out specified work related tasks.

BAC has been involved in producing National Occupational Standards for counselling and S/NVQs are based on these.

S/NVQs are offered at different levels. Level 3 is now available and it is anticipated that the S/NVQ Level 4 in Counselling will be launched in the early part of year 2000.

Level 3 is targeted at counsellors conducting one-to-one counselling in a variety of settings. The counselling may be either face-to-face or via the telephone and may be either general or specialist counselling (such as bereavement counselling). These counsellors will have both counselling and management supervision, for whom there will be higher level qualifications.

The units in the Level 3 qualification are:

- Evaluate and develop own work
- Operate referral procedures
- Ensure a structured counselling setting
- Develop the counselling relationship
- Monitor self with the counselling process
- Work in teams
- Make use of supervision.

As training courses increasingly link their qualifications with the National Occupational Standards – in order to gain accreditation towards a full S/NVQ – we would recommend that you check with your chosen training organisation to ensure these links have been made.

An S/NVQ Level 3 Counselling textbook and workbook are now available from BAC.

Does completing an Accredited Course bring BAC Individual Accreditation?

Successful completion of an Accredited course is evidence that the training requirement has been met for BAC Individual Accreditation. Additional information would still be required to demonstrate that all other criteria are met.

Courses occasionally include in their publicity material a reference to BAC individual accreditation (written in many formats) which implies some formal link with BAC and/or automatic acceptance of the course towards the training criterion of the individual accreditation scheme. Please note that these statements can be misleading as *all successfully completed courses, other than BAC Accredited Courses, have the same status in that they can be counted towards an accreditation application but will be assessed as part of the completed submission.*

What is BAC Accreditation?

BAC Accreditation is a national recognition scheme for counsellors and while it is not a statutory requirement to practise as a counsellor, it is nevertheless a valuable target to which potential counsellors might usefully aspire. BAC Accreditation is very frequently a requirement of employers. It is the means by which independent counsellors can become registered.

What are the criteria for BAC Accreditation?

These criteria apply only to counsellors working with individuals or couples. They do not apply to group counselling.

There are **three** routes to Accreditation. The successful applicant will be one who prior to application:

1. i. **Has completed a BAC Accredited Counsellor Training Course**
   and has had at least 450 hours of counselling practice supervised in accordance with paragraph 2, over a minimum period of three years.
   OR
   Has undertaken a total of 450 hours of successfully completed counselling training comprising two elements:
   a)   200 hours of skills development
   b)   250 hours of theory
   and has had at least 450 hours of counselling practice supervised in accordance with paragraph 2, over a minimum period of three years.
   OR
   ii. Is claiming little formal (course based) counselling training, but can provide evidence of ten years experience in counselling as understood by BAC with a minimum of 150 practice hours per year under formal supervision. The last three submitted years must have been supervised in accordance

CASE STUDY

ALISON

Alison arrives exactly on time. She works flexi-time, so takes an early lunch to come and see me. I've been seeing Alison for twelve weeks now and we are in a very productive stage of our work together. It can be difficult coming for counselling in the middle of a working day, but Alison's flexi-time allows her to drive over, have her fifty-minute session and still have time to recover over a sandwich lunch.

This session proves to be a difficult one for Alison; ten minutes in, a word I use to para-phrase what she has been telling me touches something deep inside her and a great feeling of sadness comes to the surface. I say very little during this session, sensing that she needs to be left relatively

with paragraph 2. [NB: This route will no longer be available to applicants after 31 December 2002.]

OR

iii. Can provide evidence of a combination of:
(a) some formal counselling training
   and
(b) several years of practice (of 150 hours minimum per year, under formal supervision). This *includes* a requirement for at least 450 hours of counselling practice supervised in accordance with paragraph 2, over three years.

75 hours of *completed* counsellor training
   =   1 unit
1 year of supervised practice
   =   1 unit

Together, the total must add up to 10 units. Applicants claiming two or more training units must show a balance of theory and skills approximately in line with that stated in 1.i.

In addition to the above, the applicant is required to meet the following criteria:

2. Has an agreed formal arrangement for counselling supervision, as understood by BAC, of a minimum of one and a half hours monthly on the applicant's work, and a commitment to continue this for the period of the accreditation.

3. Gives evidence of serious commitment to ongoing professional and personal development such as regular participation in further training courses, study, personal therapy, etc.

4. Is a current individual member of BAC and undertakes to remain so for the accreditation period.

5. Has a philosophy of counselling which

integrates training, experience, further development and practice. Evidence of at least one core theoretical model should be demonstrated.

6. Demonstrates practice which adheres to the BAC Code of Ethics & Practice for Counsellors and undertakes to continue working within this Code.

7. Can show evidence of having completed a minimum of 40 hours of personal counselling or has engaged in an equivalent activity consistent with the applicant's core theoretical model.

Applicants are asked to give evidence of the above in the form of a written application including two case studies. Assessors will be looking for congruence between all parts of the application as well as checking that the above criteria have been and are being met.

The following *amendment* to criterion 1.i will be implemented from 1 October 2000:

1. i **and** has had at least 450 hours of counselling practice, supervised in accordance with paragraph 2, over not less than three and not more than five years.

The following *additional* criteria will be implemented from 1 October 2000:

1. iv. Can provide evidence of:
   a. Having obtained **S/NVQ Level III in Counselling**
      [This will be seen as equal to 4 units.]
   b. **Four or five years of supervised practice** (of 150 hours minimum per year under formal supervision. This includes a requirement for at least 450 hours of counselling practice supervised in accordance with paragraph 2, over three years).
      At least two years must be subsequent to

undisturbed to face this feeling which we have only glimpsed in previous sessions.

About ten minutes before the end of our session, Alison swallows her tears and takes on again her public face which, by the time she leaves, shows no trace of what lies underneath. She has well-developed defences which, in this situation, work for her rather than against her. This I know has been a significant development in our working relationship and leaves me moved by the depth of feeling she has expressed.

I make a cup of coffee before I sit down to write up my notes on the session.

All Case Studies abstracted from 'A Day in the Life of Robbi Campbell', 'Counselling', Vol 4, No 3.

obtaining the S/NVQ Level III qualification.

c. **One or two units of Continuing Professional Development [CPD]** (of 75 hours each unit), which must be subsequent to obtaining the S/NVQ Level III quailfication. Together the total must add up to 10 units.

One year of supervised practice = 1 unit
75 hours of CPD = 1 unit.

8. Can show evidence of serious commitment to working with issues of difference and equality in counselling practice.

Is it necessary to have personal therapy while training?

Students experience challenge, and at times stress, during their training as counsellors. Counselling is useful at times of change and reappraisal, as well as in times of high confusion or distress. Many counsellor training courses recommend, and a few require, students to have their own counselling as part of the training process as it provides an opportunity to deal creatively with issues as they arise. It is also a unique way of experiencing the process of therapeutic change from the receiving end – a very basic structure for experiential learning. It is a requirement for BAC Accredited Counsellors.

Is there a national Register of Counsellors?

Currently, those who have no qualifications in counselling can call themselves counsellors because there is no statutory regulation for counsellors. BAC, together with a number of major counselling organisations, has established the UK Register of Counsellors.

The Register is accessible to those who are accredited members of BAC or COSCA (Confederation of Scottish Counselling Agencies). It will also be possible to be registered through a Registered Sponsoring Organisation (RSO); counsellors working for an RSO may be sponsored by them during the time they work for that organisation. Registration will cease on leaving that RSO.

There are a considerable number and type of counselling qualifications. The Register offers the possibility that it may only be necessary to ask if a counsellor is UKRC registered rather than whether they are qualified.

Further information is available from BAC.

What is needed to practise in Europe?

Any European-wide system of qualifications will be based on mutual recognition of national qualifications by the member states of the European Union.

Is there any guarantee of quality?

BAC can only vouch for BAC Accredited Counsellor Training Courses.

However, a scheme is in operation to accredit Counselling Skills Trainers and Counsellor Trainers. The purpose of this scheme is threefold:

1. Protection of students: It is in the interests of students of counselling skills and counselling to ensure that their trainers have appropriate training and experience and are working to BAC Codes of Ethics & Practice.
2. Professional development: The intention is that the scheme provides opportunities for professional development for BAC members who work as trainers.
3. Benchmark for the use of employers and trainers: Accreditation can help employers to appoint competent and experienced trainers.

It is important to note that training of counsellors and training people from a wide range of occupations to use counselling skills in their work are two distinct activities. The BAC Accreditation scheme ensures that trainers have an appropriate background for the training they propose to deliver. In addition, all candidates will have to meet criteria relating to the preparation, delivery and evaluation of training.

The aim is that, in due course, the numbers of trainers who have met the standard of BAC Accreditation will meet the demand for high quality provision. A wise student will discuss the trainer's training and qualifications, working experience, appropriate memberships and codes of ethics and practice with the tutor of their preferred course.

If you feel there has been a breach of the Code of Ethics & Practice for Trainers (see Appendix 3) by BAC members, please contact BAC.

So which course to choose?

In the previous section we have outlined your responsibility as a prospective learner for selecting a relevant and suitable course. This may be done by:

- asking questions. Training in counselling will involve personal exploration and a close relationship with the tutor and other course members. Many of the more advanced courses will have selection procedures during which you will have an opportunity to talk to the tutors. If there is no formal arrangement, try and talk to the tutor before you commit yourself to the course.
- satisfying yourself about staffing, objectives, methods, qualifications on offer and also checking that course organisers and tutors belong to a professional organisation and therefore adhere to a high standard set by codes of ethics and practice.
- recognise and make choices about the degree of personal challenge and commitment involved.

Distance Learning Courses

There are a number of Distance Learning courses in counselling now available, which combine written, video and audio material. While these can offer a useful introduction to the use of counselling skills and a little theory, in most cases it is unlikely that they would greatly contribute to the training element required for BAC Accreditation, as they offer little or no counselling practice under supervision and have little opportunity for observation and practice of counselling skills with feedback from both staff and fellow students, all of which are considered to be very important aspects of training. However, the better courses will offer a group tutorial component in them.

The courses listed below have been designed by BAC members, but this in no way denotes recommendation or recognition by BAC.

Institute of Counselling: College of Counselling
0141-204 2230 • email: iofcounsel@aol.com
web site: www.collegeofcounselling.com

Clinical & Pastoral Department, 6 Dixon Street, Glasgow G1 4AX.

The Institute of Counselling operates a distance learning unit called the College of Counselling. The College is accredited by the Open and Distance Learning Quality Council (ODLQC), formerly the CACC. The College of Counselling offers a wide range of counselling courses. The Diploma in Clinical & Pastoral Counselling Skills is accredited by Glasgow Caledonian University. Course participants may earn up to 60 CATS points (15 year one level, 45 year two university level credits) which is equal to a half year of full-time study. This course comprises four distance learning modules and one residential five day component. Other four module Diploma courses offered by the College are also recognised by the Open University and up to 30 credit points (year one) may be awarded through Accreditation of Prior Learning (APL). Shorter courses and individual modules are also offered within a system which allows students to upgrade at a later stage. In addition to counselling skills studies, the following courses are available: Introduction to Counselling Theory, Introduction to Stress Management and Psychology for Counsellors. A Counselling Skills for Disasters course is planned for year 2000. Most courses combine comprehensive course manual, training videos and audio cassettes with written assignments which are individually responded to by an experienced faculty of tutors. Most courses are recognised by the Association for Christian Counselling (ACC) and count towards their counsellor accreditation criteria.

The Institute of Counselling has offices in Glasgow and Bromsgrove. A free course prospectus is available on request from the Glasgow offices and web site.

National Extension College (NEC)
01223 450500 • e-mail: info@nec.ac.uk
18 Brooklands Avenue, Cambridge CB2 2HN.

The NEC is an independent, educational charity established in 1963 to pioneer flexible forms of learning for adults. High quality course materials and a network of expert tutors are backed up by experienced student advisers at NEC. NEC's counselling courses provide student-focused learning materials and constructive tutor support on a range of individual study programmes from 'A Taste of Counselling' to 'Understanding Loss & Grief'. Students benefit from the knowledge and experience of high-calibre authors, who provide a carefully planned mix of background information and practical activities – with an emphasis throughout on developing reflective, client-centred practice. Each distance learning programme uses skilled tutors to provide individual feedback on written assignments, which can complement face-to-face support from supervisors, mentors and other learners. Courses include: A taste of counselling; Help on the line, for those wishing to support others by telephone; Counselling Skills; Introduction to Counselling Theory; Understanding Loss & Grief; Understanding Trauma.

The Open University   01908 653743

School of Health & Social Welfare Information Office, Walton Hall, Milton Keynes MK7 6AA.

The Open University's School of Health & Social Welfare courses are closely related to practice and take a broad, multi-disciplinary approach which contributes to a better understanding of different experiences and perspectives. While these courses do not provide professional training in counselling, they do offer the opportunity to acquire related knowledge, expertise and qualifications to anyone working in or entering the health and social welfare field, or counsellors wishing to extend their understanding in specific areas. For example, courses are offered on a wide range of subjects including community care, health, working with young people, ageing, mental health, health promotion or death and dying. The Open University is open to all, regardless of previous educational background and qualifications, and offers a combination of high quality materials, personal support and distance teaching methods. Flexible home-study arrangements fit with students' work and lifestyle. On successful completion of a course, students are awarded credit (CATS) points which can be counted towards an Open University Diploma in Health & Social Welfare and/or a BA/BSc degree, or transferred (where relevant) into programmes offered by other institutions. Some courses which have a vocational training element (N/SVQs) attract tax relief.

Funding for Counselling Training

Public Funding

Local Authority Grants/Awards

Discretionary awards may possibly be available for full time courses but are extremely scarce. It may be worth asking in case the authority would be prepared to make some contribution, perhaps paying some or all of the fees.

BAC Educational Bursaries

The British Association for Counselling Educational Bursary aims to assist people on low income with paying for counsellor training. Additionally attention is given to people offering counselling to disadvantaged or under-represented groups in our society.

Application Forms can be obtained from the Accredited Course from 1 April each year once a place has been offered. Applications must be received no later than 31 July of each year and must be accompanied with proof of acceptance for one of the BAC Accredited Courses along with supporting documents providing evidence of financial needs.

Department for Education Bursaries

These are made available to some postgraduate courses. Applications are made to the institution running the course. Normally applicants must not be over 40 years of age, nor have undertaken postgraduate studies previously. Information on available grants can be obtained from:

Economic & Social Research Council • Polaris House • North Star Avenue • Swindon • Wiltshire SN2 1UJ • Telephone: 01793 413000.
The Students Awards Agency for Scotland (SAAS) maintains a register of all educational trusts set up in Scotland. Students who do not get a grant can apply

to the SAAS for details of trusts to which they may be able to apply for financial assistance. **To apply for a search of the Register of Educational Endowments, contact: SAAS • Glenview House • 3 Redheughs Rigg • Edinburgh EH12 9HH • Tel: 0131 244 5833.**

Other bursaries

There is a publication listing a whole range of bursaries available in the United Kingdom for all types of qualifications. This is available on request for reference from the library in your careers office.

Secondment by Employer

The majority of places on full time courses are taken by people who are seconded on full salary. Course fees are usually paid by the employer and possibly, in addition, travelling and accommodation allowances. Local Education Authorities second the largest number of students. Teachers intending to apply for secondment need to discover their LEA's policy about conditions, eligibility and courses favoured.

Other employers in the public and private sectors may consider paying the fees for an employee to undertake a part time course, if the employee can show that the course would be of benefit in his/her work.

Self Finance

More and more people are obliged to consider financing themselves by using their own funds, or borrowing from friends, relatives or the bank. This can, of course, be a risky business as finding employment as a counsellor after training cannot be guaranteed. It would be safer to undertake a part time course which enables the student to continue in employment during training.

Career Development Loans

The Department of Employment in conjunction with three banks, Barclays, Co-op and Clydesdale, offers Career Development Loans. You may apply to borrow up to 80% of your course fees from one of the participating banks. The most you can borrow is £5000 and the least £300. You make no repayments at all during your course and for up to three months after you have finished; the Employment Department will pay the interest during that period. It is your responsibility to repay the loan and interest from that point onwards. The participating banks will be able to give more information and a written quotation if you want one.

For a quotation phone:
Barclays   0171 248 9155 ext 3531
Clydesdale   0141 248 7070 ext 2180
Co-operative   0171 480 5171 ext 322

For more information phone:
Freephone 0800 585505
or write to: Freepost Career Development · PO Box 99· Sudbury · Suffolk CO10 6BR

Reference Books

Available from BAC publications list.

1. Training in Counselling & Psychotherapy - A Directory

2. Handbook of Counselling in Britain (2nd ed) *Edited by Stephen Palmer and Gladeana McMahon. Published by Routledge in association with BAC.*

The following should be available for consultation in libraries:

1. *CRAC Graduate Studies Hobsons Press, Cambridge. Details of postgraduate courses.*

2. *The Grants Register Macmillan Press Ltd.*

3. Directory of Grant-Making Trusts *Charities Aid Foundation, 48 Pembury Road, Tonbridge, Kent TN9 2JT*

4. Dictionary of Counselling *Colin Feltham & Windy Dryden. Whurr Publishers.*

5. Dictionary of Psychotherapy *Sue Walrond Skinner. Routledge, Keegan & Paul.*

6. Choosing Counselling or Psychotherapy Training *Sylvie K. Schapira.* Routledge.

Basic Principles of Counselling

1. The aim of counselling is to provide an opportunity for a client to work towards living in a more satisfying and resourceful way.

2. Counselling is voluntarily and deliberately undertaken by counsellor and client. It is different from other ways of helping.

3. Before counselling starts, the counsellor clarifies with the client the basis on which counselling is to be given, including method, duration, fees and confidentiality; changes can subsequently be made only with the agreement of the client.

4. In counselling the right of the client to make his or her own decisions is respected.

5. Counsellors continually monitor their own skills, experience, resources and practice.

6. Counsellors will be properly trained for their roles and be committed to maintaining their competence.

7. Counsellors will not mis-represent their training or experience.

8. Counsellors have regular and appropriate supervision/consultative support.

9. Counsellors must not abuse their position of trust financially or emotionally or sexually.

10. All that takes place between counsellor and client is treated with respect and discretion.

These principles are observed by all BAC members.

The British Association for Counselling has a series of Codes of Ethics & Practice which expand on these principles:
Code of Ethics & Practice for Counsellors
Code of Ethics & Practice for Counselling Skills
Code of Ethics & Practice for Trainers
Code of Ethics & Practice for the Supervision of Counsellors

Members are required to abide by the Codes appropriate to their role.

Organisations within which counselling is offered should be clear about what they mean by counselling, ensure that standards are upheld and that counsellors are trained and supported adequately.

AWARDING BODIES

Appendix I

Names and Addresses of bodies offering Validations for counselling

The organisations listed below, offer validations of counselling training courses at a number of levels including, certificate and diploma levels and where this is known it is noted in brackets following the course title in the directory

Name & Address of Organisation	Telephone number
AEB (Associated Examining Board), Stag Hill House, Guildford, Surrey	01483 506506
AREBT (Association for Rational Emotive Behavioural Therapy), contact Robin Yapp, 49 Wood Lane, Harbourne, Birmingham B17 9AY	0121 427 7292
BPS (British Psychological Society), St Andrews House, 48 Princes Road East, Leicester LE1 7DR	0116 254 9568
British Accreditation Council, Suite 401, 27 Marylebone Road, London NW1 5JS	0171 487 4643
EDEXEL Foundation (BTEC), Stewart House, 32 Russell Square, London WC1B 5DN	0171 393 4444
CENTRA, Duxbury Park, Duxbury Hall Road, Chorley, Lancashire PR7 4AT	01257 241 428
CPCAB (Counselling & Psychotherapy Central Awarding Body)	01458 835333

An independent awarding body specialised in the field of counselling & psychotherapy

City & Guilds of London Institute, 1 Giltspur Street, London EC1A 9DD	0171 294 2468
Institute For Complementary Medicine, PO Box 194, London SE16 1QZ	0171 237 5165
NCFE (Northern Council for Further Education), Portland House, Second floor Block D, New Bridge Street, Newcastle-upon-Tyne NE1 8AL	0191 201 3100

Northern Examinations & Assessment Board
Devas Street, Manchester M15 6EX   0161 953 1180

Qualifications and Curriculum Authority   0171 509 5555
29 Bolton Street, London W1Y 7PD   fax   0171 509 6666

RSA Examining Board (Royal Society of Arts), Progress House,
Westwood Way, Coventry CV4 8HS   01203 470 033

RSH (Royal Society of Health), 38a St. George's Drive,
London SW1V 4BH   0171 630 0121

The Scottish Qualifications Authority,
Ironmills Road, Dalkeith EH22 1LE   0131 663 6601 • fax 0131 654 2664
(has replaced SCOTVEC and Scottish Examinations Board from April 1997)

WJEB (Welsh Joint Education Committee),
245 Western Avenue, Cardiff CF5 2YX 01222 265000 • fax 01222 575894

A number of courses are listed as being recognised by the Department for Education & Employment, Schedule 2 (a). This is a list of vocational qualifications offerred by awarding bodies which attract funding for those institutions offering the qualification. The institution receives funding from the Further Education Council for each person on the course. Schedule 2(a) approves courses of all levels.

The above are the major validating bodies, some of which may only offer this service in a limited, local area. There are a number of others listed in the Directory which relate to specific models of counselling and/or psychotherapy, such as the European Association for Transactional Analysis (EATA) and the addresses of these should be obtainable from the course organiser.

Universities also validate courses and there are now a number of degrees available.

BAC offers a course accreditation scheme and criteria for this are given in the *Recognition of Counsellor Training Courses* booklet price at £4.50 to non members £3.50 to members and available from BAC.

This list of Awarding Bodies has been compiled from a number of sources by the BAC Information Office and in no way denotes recognition or recommendation by BAC. The only validation of which BAC is fully supportive is the BAC Accreditation of Courses scheme.

Appendix II

INTRODUCTORY READING LIST

Brown D, Pedder J	*Introduction to Psychotherapy* Tavistock, 1979
Carkhuff RR	*The Art of Helping* Human Resources Development Trust, 5th ed.
Cooper J, Lewis J	*Who can I talk to? The user's guide to therapy & counselling.*
Dryden W (ed)	*Individual Therapy in Britain* OU Press, 1984
Egan G	*The Skilled Helper: A Systematic Effective Helping* Monterey: Brooks/Cole, 4th ed.
Einzig H	*Counselling & Psychotherapy: Is it for me?* BAC*
Einzig H, Evans R	*Personal Problems at Work: A manager's guide* BAC*
Feltham C, Dryden W	*Dictionary of Counselling* 1993
Jacobs M	*Psychodynamic Counselling in Action* Sage, 1988
Kennedy E	*On Becoming a Counsellor* Gil & Macmillan
Munro A, Manthei R	*Counselling: The Skills of Problem Solving*
Murgatroyd S	*Counselling & Helping* Methuen, 1985
Nelson-Jones R	*Practical Counselling & Helping Skills* Cassell, 2nd ed.
Noonan E, Spurling L	*The Making of a Counsellor* Routledge, 1992
Palmer S, Dainow S, Milner P (eds)	*Counselling: The 'Counselling' Reader* Sage (in association with BAC), 1996*
Palmer S, McMahon G (eds)	*Handbook of Counselling* Routledge (in association with BAC), 2nd ed, 1997*
Worden W	*Grief Counselling & Grief Therapy* Routledge/Tavistock, 1983.

* Publications available from BAC. List available, please send A5 sae.

Appendix III

GLOSSARY OF TERMS

Accreditation (BAC)   Training Courses which BAC has accredited as being of a sufficiently high standard of education for counsellors

APL (Accreditation of Prior Learning)
A system by which training organisations take into account prior experience.

CATS (Credit Accumulation Transfer Scheme)
The scheme by which a number of Universities & Colleges credit prior training, enabling students to transfer more easily between training organisations

Codes of Ethics   The guiding principles by which BAC members are bound. Their main purpose is to inform and protect clients, maintain standards and to provide a consultative framework in which counsellors can work.

Distance Learning   Courses taken by mail. These are not usually useful for BAC Individual Accreditation as there is too little contact with other students and clients.

Experiential Learning   Learning designed to heighten awareness of an experience or give consideration to a familiar happening on which workshop members will be asked to reflect in their own terms or in the light of an offered framework

Individual Accreditation (BAC)
A combination of counselling training and experience which is formally appraised by BAC.

Models of counselling
: The approach that a counsellor uses with their clients. There are many approaches used and students should discuss the core model with the course tutor.

Modular Training
: Training offered in blocks of time over the year e.g. 5 weekends over 1 year.

NVQs (National Vocational Qualifications)
: A system by which skills and competencies can be assessed in order to confer a qualification.

Placement
: A place where student counsellors can obtain supervised counselling practice whilst training.

Supervision
: Consultative support for counsellors. It is a requirement that all BAC members have supervision whilst practising as a counsellor. *Supervisors are listed in the BAC U.K Counselling & Psychotherapy Directory.*

Validating/Awarding Body
: The organisation which sets up the syllabus for a training and subsequently awards the qualification on successful completion of a course.

Appendix IV

CODE OF ETHICS & PRACTICE FOR TRAINERS (1997)

1.   Status of this Code

1.1   In response to the experience of members of BAC, this Code is a revision of the 1996 Code.

Structure of this Code
This code is in four sections:
A.   A Code of Ethics for all Trainers.
B.   A general Code of Practice for all Trainers.
C.   Additional clause for Trainers in Counselling.
D.   Additional clauses for Trainers in Counselling Skills

2.   Introduction

2.1   The purpose of this Code of Ethics and Practice is to establish and maintain standards for trainers who are members of BAC and to inform and protect members of the public seeking training in counselling, counselling skills or counselling-related areas, whatever the level or length of the training programme. Training in counselling-related areas includes training in counselling supervision, group work, interpersonal skills and other topics involving counselling theory and practice.

Sections A and B apply to all trainers. Section C contains an additional clause for trainers in counselling. Section D contains additional clauses for trainers in counselling skills.

2.2   The document must be seen in relation to all other BAC Codes of Ethics and Practice and BAC Course Recognition Procedures.

2.3   There is an important relationship between the agency employing the trainer and the trainee undertaking the training. This Code reinforces the principle that agencies which are organisational members of BAC abide by all BAC codes.

2.4   Ethical standards comprise such values as integrity, impartiality and respect. Anti-discriminatory practice reflects the basic values of counselling and training. Members of BAC, in assenting to this Code, accept their appropriate responsibilities as trainers, to trainees, trainees' clients, employing agencies, colleagues, this Association and to the wider community.

2.5 In the context of this Code, trainers are those who train people in counselling, in counselling skills or in counselling-related areas. They should be experienced and competent practitioners. Trainers have a responsibility to draw the attention of trainees to all BAC Codes of Ethics and Practice.

2.6 Trainers must be aware that there are differences between training in counselling, training in counselling skills and training in counselling-related areas. Trainees must be made aware of this and trainers should endeavour to ensure that their intending trainees join an appropriate training programme.

2.7 There should be consistency between the theoretical orientation of the programme and the training methods and, where they are used, methods of assessment and evaluation (e.g. client-centred courses would normally be trainee-centred).

2.8 Training is at its most effective when there are two or more trainers. Trainers and their employing agencies have a responsibility to ensure this wherever possible.

2.9 The size of the group must be congruent with the training objectives and the model of working. Decisions about staff:student ratios must take account of the learning objectives and methods of assessment and of the importance of being able to give individual attention and recognition to each course member. Where direct feedback between trainer and trainee is an important part of the course a maximum staff to student ratio of 1:12 is recommended best practice.

A. Code of Ethics for All Trainers

A.1 Values

Training is a non-exploitative activity. Its basic values are integrity, impartiality and respect. Trainers must take the same degree of care to work ethically whether the training is paid or unpaid.

A.2 Anti-discrimination

Trainers must consider and address their own prejudices and stereotyping. They must also address the prejudices and stereotyping of their trainees. They must ensure that an anti-discriminatory approach is integral to all the training they provide.

A.3 Safety

All reasonable steps shall be taken by trainers to ensure the safety of trainees and clients during training.

A.4 Competence

Trainers must take all reasonable steps to monitor and develop their competence as trainers and work within the limits of that competence.

A.5 Confidentiality

Trainers must clarify the limits of confidentiality within the training process at the beginning of the training programme.

A.6 Contracts

The terms and conditions on which the training is offered must be made clear to trainees before the start of the training programme. Subsequent revision of these terms must be agreed in advance of any changes.

A.7 Boundaries

Trainers must maintain and establish appropriate boundaries between themselves and their trainees so that working relationships are not confused with friendship or other relationships.

B. General Code of Practice for All Trainers

B.1 Responsibility

B.1.1 Trainers deliberately undertake the task of delivering training in counselling, counselling skills and counselling-related areas.

B.1.2 Trainers are responsible for observing the principles embodied in this Code of Ethics and Practice and all current BAC Codes and for introducing trainees to the BAC Codes of Ethics and Practice in the early stages of the training programme.

B.1.3 Trainers must recognise the value and dignity of trainees, with due regard to issues of origin, status, gender, age, beliefs, sexual preference or disability. Trainers have a responsibility to be aware of, and address their own issues of prejudice and stereotyping, and to give particular consideration to ways in which this may impact on the training.

B.1.4 Trainers have a responsibility to encourage and facilitate the self-development and self-awareness of trainees, so that trainees learn to integrate practice and personal insights.

B.1.5 Trainers are responsible for making explicit to trainees the boundaries between training, counselling supervision, consultancy, counselling and the use of counselling skills.

B.1.6 Trainers are responsible for modelling appropriate boundaries.

1.6.1 The roles of trainee and client must be kept separate during the training; where painful personal issues are revealed, trainers are responsible for suggesting and encouraging further in-depth work with a counsellor outside the training context.

1.6.2 The providers of counselling for trainees during the programme must be independent of the training context and any assessment procedures.

1.6.3 Trainers should take all reasonable steps to ensure that any personal and social contacts between them and their trainees do not adversely influence the effectiveness of the training.

B.1.7 Trainers must not accept current clients as trainees. Former trainees must not become clients, nor former clients become trainees, until a period of time has elapsed for reflection and after consultation with a counselling supervisor.

B.1.8 Trainers are responsible for ensuring that their emotional needs are met outside the training work and are not dependent on their relationships with trainees.

B.1.9 Trainers must not exploit their trainees financially, sexually, emotionally, or in any other way. Engaging in sexual activity with trainees is unethical.

B.1.10 Trainers must ensure that consideration is given to the appropriateness of the settings in which trainees propose to, or are expected to, work on completion of the training programme.

B.1.11 Trainers are expected, when appropriate, to prepare trainees to practice effectively within their work setting.

B.1.12 Trainers have a responsibility to ensure that appropriate counselling supervision arrangements are in place for trainees where working with clients is part of the course.

B.1.13 Visiting or occasional trainers on programmes must ensure that they take responsibility for any former or current pre-existing professional or personal relationship with any member of the training group.

B.1.14 Trainers must acknowledge the individual life experience and identity of trainees. Challenges to the views, attitudes and outlooks of trainees must be respectful, related to the stated objectives of the course, and model good practice.

B.1.15 Trainers are responsible for discussing with trainees any needs for personal counselling and the contribution it might make to the trainees' work both during and after the programme.

B.1.16 Trainers must at all times conduct themselves in their training activities in ways which will not undermine public confidence in their role as trainers, in the work of other trainers or in the role of BAC.

B.2. Competence

B.2.1 It is strongly recommended that trainers should have completed at least one year's post-training experience as practitioners in an appropriate field of work. They should commit themselves to continuing professional development as trainers.

B.2.2 Trainers must monitor their training work and be able and willing to account to trainees and colleagues for what they do and why.

B.2.3 Trainers must monitor and evaluate the limits of their competence as trainers by means of regular supervision or consultancy.

B.2.4 Trainers have a responsibility to themselves and to their trainees to maintain their own effectiveness, resilience and ability to work with trainees. They are expected to monitor their own personal functioning and to seek help and/or agree to withdraw from training, whether temporarily or permanently, when their personal resources are so depleted as to require this.

B.3 Confidentiality

B.3.1 Trainers are responsible for establishing a contract for confidential working which makes explicit the responsibilities of both trainer and trainees.

B.3.2 Trainers must inform trainees at the beginning of the training programme of all reasonably foreseeable circumstances under which confidentiality may be breached during the training programme.

B.3.3 Trainers must not reveal confidential information concerning trainees, or former trainees, without the permission of the trainee, except:

    a. in discussion with those on whom trainers rely for professional support and supervision. (These discussions will usually be anonymous and the supervisor is bound by confidentiality);

    b. in order to prevent serious harm to another or to the trainee

    c. when legally required to break confidentiality;

    d. during selection, assessment, complaints and disciplinary procedures in order to prevent or investigate breaches of ethical standards by trainees;

If consent to the disclosure of confidential information has been withheld, trainees should normally be informed in advance that a trainer intends to disclose confidential information.

B.3.4 Detailed information about specific trainees, or former trainees, may be used for publication or in meetings only with the trainees' permission and with anonymity preserved. Where trainers need to use examples from previous work to illustrate a point to trainees, this must be done respectfully, briefly and anonymously.

B.3.5 If discussion by trainers of their trainees, or former trainees, with professional colleagues becomes necessary, it must be purposeful, not trivialising, and relevant to the training.

B.3.6 If trainers suspect misconduct by another trainer which cannot be resolved or remedied after discussion with the trainer concerned, they should implement any internal complaints procedures that may be available or the BAC Complaints Procedure. Any required breaches of confidentiality should be limited to those necessary for the investigation of the complaint.

B.4 Management of the Training Work

B.4.1 Trainers must make basic information available to potential trainees, in writing or by other appropriate means of communication, before the start of the programme. This should include:

    a. the fees to be charged and any other expenses which may be incurred;

b. the dates and time commitments;

c. information on selection procedures, entry requirements and the process by which decisions are made;

d. basic information about the content of the programme, its philosophical and theoretical approach and the training methods to be used;

e. the relevant qualifications of the trainers;

f. any requirements for counselling supervision or personal counselling which trainees will be expected to comply with while training;

g. guidelines for work experience or placements to be undertaken as part of the training.

h. evaluation and assessment methods to be used during the programme and the implications of these;

i. if the programme carries a qualification, arrangements for appeals should a dispute arise.

B.4.2 Trainers must check whether training is being undertaken voluntarily or compulsorily and, if necessary, draw employers' attention to the fact that a voluntary commitment is the more appropriate.

B.4.3 Trainers should ensure that trainees receive regular feedback on their work and that self and peer assessment are encouraged at regular intervals.

B.4.4 Trainers must be alert to any prejudices and assumptions that trainees reveal and raise their awareness of these issues, so that trainees are encouraged to recognise and value difference.

B.4.5 Trainers should ensure that trainees are given the opportunity to discuss their experiences of the programme and are also invited to evaluate these individually, in groups, or both, at least once in a training programme.

B.4.6 Trainers who become aware of a conflict between their obligation to a trainee and their obligation to an agency or organisation employing them, must make explicit to both the trainee and the agency or organisation employing them the nature and existence of this conflict and seek to resolve it.

B.4.7 Where differences between trainer and trainee, or between trainers, cannot be resolved the trainer and, where appropriate the trainer's line manager, should consult with, and when necessary refer to, an independent expert.

C.   Additional Clause for Trainers in Counselling

C.1 Trainers are encouraged to ensure that:

a. practical experience as a counsellor in an external setting is, where possible, part of the training programme.

b. the setting where trainees propose to practice as counsellors is appropriate, paying particular attention to the need for confidentiality, privacy and counselling supervision.

D.   Additional Clauses for Trainers in Counselling Skills

D.1 Trainers are responsible for ensuring that their trainees consider the appropriateness of the setting in which they use their counselling skills.

D.2 Trainers should ensure that trainees are clear that using counselling skills may lead to conflicting responsibilities. These should be discussed on the training course and in supervision.

Equal Opportunities Policy Statement

The 'British Association for Counselling' (BAC) is committed to promoting Equality of Opportunity of access and participation for all its members in all of its structures and their workings. BAC has due regard for those groups of people with identifiable characteristics which can lead to visible and invisible barriers thus inhibiting their joining and full participation in BAC. Barriers can include age, colour, creed, culture, disability, education, 'ethnicity', gender, information, knowledge, mobility, money, nationality, race, religion, sexual orientation, social class and status.

The work of BAC aims to reflect this commitment in all area including services to members, employer responsibilities, the recruitment of and working with volunteers, setting, assessing, monitoring and evaluating standards and the implementation of the complaints procedures. This is particularly important as BAC is the 'Voice of Counselling' in the wider world.

BAC will promote and encourage commitment to Equality of Opportunity by its members.

HOLWELL INTERNATIONAL CENTRE FOR PSYCHODRAMA & SOCIODRAMA   01271 850 267

East Down, BARNSTAPLE, Devon, EX31 4NZ,
No response received to our enquiries for 2000, course details as of Nov 1998

**   **1) Psychodrama Practicum** (Training for Counsellors

**   **2) Diploma in Competence in Sociodrama**

**   **3) Diploma of Competence in Advanced Psychodrama**

***   **4) Psychodrama & Sociodrama** (UKCP, British Psychodrama Assoc.)

THE CHILD BEREAVEMENT TRUST,   01494 678088

Brindley House, 4 Burkes Road, BEACONSFIELD, Bucks, HP9 1PB,
Short course and in-house training on bereavement skills available. Courses are
offered in a variety of places in UK. Produces books and videos for grieving families.

  Disabled people can be accommodated

Bereavement Counselling Diploma

Duration	Contact the organisation for details.
Apply To:	Jenni Thomas

CLINICAL THEOLOGY ASSOCIATION,   0121 454 1527

Queen's College, Somerset Road, Edgbaston, BIRMINGHAM, B15 2QH,
Seminars held in most parts of the UK. Tailor-made training available.

  Courses base at the CTA Centre, Queen's College, have full facilities for disabled
people.

**   **Pastoral Counselling & Pastoral Care**

Duration	Foundation course in 4 modules, part-time
Entry	For those who wish to further their development for personal and professional reasons, within a faith context.
Apply To:	Alistair Ross, Executive Director

HERM COLLEGE,   01278 653 808

Wayland Farm, Stockland, BRIDGWATER, Somerset, TA5 2PY,
No response received to our enquiries for 2000, entry details as of Nov 1998

*   **1) Introduction to Counselling** (Certificate of Attendance)

continued...

---

*Star System: * Introductory course only • ** 2-3 yr pt-time course to Cert/Dip level •
*** Professional development for trained counsellors*
For added help, see section 'Essential Information for Students', page 1

47

*   **2) Therapeutic Counselling Skills for Complementary Health Practitioners**

*   **3) Certificate in Counselling Skills & Therapeutic Counselling**

**   **4) Diploma in Integrative Therapeutic Counselling** (Skills Theory & Practice)

***   **5) Postgraduate Advanced Diploma in Counselling**

NATIONAL EXTENSION COLLEGE,   01223 450500

18 Brooklands Avenue, CAMBRIDGE, CB2 2HN,

♿ Students with disabilities or caring responsibilities can apply for a grant through the College's scheme 'Equal Access to Open Learning'

*   **1) A Taste of Counselling**
Duration	Study at your own pace
Entry	None
Apply To:	Student Adviser

*   **2) Counselling Skills**
Duration	Study at your own pace
Entry	None

*   **3) Introduction to Counselling Theory**
Duration	Study at your own pace
Entry	You should be a practising or trainee counsellor or have a good general understanding of counselling practice to benefit fully from this course.
Apply To:	Student Advisor

*   **4) Help on Line**
Duration	Study at your own pace
Entry	Access to a telephone, but students will get the most out of the course if they are already using the telephone to provide help or support to others, in a voluntary or professional capacity.
Apply To:	Student Adviser

*   **5) Understanding Loss and Grief**
Duration	Study at your own pace
Entry	None
Apply To:	Student Adviser

---

*Star System: * Introductory course only • ** 2-3 yr pt-time course to Cert/Dip level •*
*** Professional development for trained counsellors*

For added help, see section 'Essential Information for Students', page 1

48

*   **6) Understanding Trauma**
Duration   Study at your own pace
Entry   None
Apply To: Student Adviser

KINHARVIE: COUNSELLING, EDUCATION, TRAINING
TEL/FAX 0141 337 1070 (GLASGOW)
01387 850 433 TEL, 465 FAX (DUMFRIES)

49 Dowanhill Street, GLASGOW, G11 5HB,
Also at Kinharvie House, New Abbey, Dumfries DG2 8DZ. In-house & tailor-made courses: working with groups, counselling skills, Myers Briggs, team-building, leadership training, group facilitation, etc

♿ Ground floor, limited facilities for disabled

*   **1) Certificate in Counselling Skills** (Kinharvie)
Duration   1 yr part-time course, afternoon or eve, plus residential weekend (120 hrs), available in Glasgow & Dumfries
Entry   Details on request

**   **2) Postgraduate Diploma/MSc in Counselling & Supervision** (Glasgow Caledonian Univ)
Duration   Postgraduate Diploma: 2 yrs residential (total 240 hrs) MSc: additional 3rd yr non residential Available in Dumfries only
Entry   Details on request

**   **3) Masters in Effective Leadership**
Duration   Please contact the organisation for further details
Apply To: Course Co-ordinator

COUNSELLING TRAINING INITIATIVES LTD,(CTI)   0345 660 538

Galtee House, 1 Heanor Road, ILKESTON, Derbyshire, DE7 8DY,
No response received to our enquiries for 2000, entry details as of Nov 1998

*   **1) Exploring Counselling/Exploring Counselling Further**

*   **2) Foundation Certificate in Counselling** (NOCN/CTi)

**   **3) Advanced Diploma in Counselling** (NOCN/CTi)

Star System: * Introductory course only • ** 2-3 yr pt-time course to Cert/Dip level •
*** Professional development for trained counsellors
For added help, see section 'Essential Information for Students', page 1

49

REALITY THERAPY CENTRE (UK), 01525 851588
FAX 01525 851800

Green House, 43 George Street, LEIGHTON BUZZARD, Bedfordshire, LU7 8JX,
Course is designed on a modular basis; minimum 145 hrs training. This cannot be
completed in less than 18 months

♿ Access for people with disabilities. Arrangements should be discussed with the
director prior to application

* **Reality Therapy Certificate** (The William Glasser Institute [International])
Duration   Basic workshop (4 days) 27 hrs; Basic Practicum 40 hrs/6 months.
            Adv workshop: (4days); Adv Practicum: 40hrs/6 months
Entry   Certification week/workshop (4 days) 30 hrs
Apply To: John Brickell, Director

ALCOHOL COUNSELLING AND PREVENTION SERVICES
020 7737 3579

34 Electric Lane, Brixton, LONDON, SW9 8JT,
One day workshops offered on a range of subjects.

♿ Induction Loop

* **1) Assessing & Working with Problem Drinking**
Duration   3 days, (18 hrs) full-time (repeated 4-5 times/year)
Entry   Working with problem drinking

2) Basic Alcohol Awareness
Duration   2 days (12 hours)
Entry   None stated

3) Motivational Interviewing
Duration   1 day (6 hours)

4) Solution Focussed Approaches
Duration   2 days (12 hours)

5) Relapse Prevention and Management
Duration   1 day (6 hours)

6) Alcohol Assessment Skills for Professionals
Duration   1 day
Apply To: ACAPS, Training Officer

Star System: ** Introductory course only • ** 2-3 yr pt-time course to Cert/Dip level •*
*** Professional development for trained counsellors
For added help, see section 'Essential Information for Students', page 1

50

THE BRITISH AUTOGENIC SOCIETY   0171 713 6336
WWW.AUTOGENIC-THERAPY.ORG.UK

The Royal London Homeopathic Hospital, Great Ormond Street, LONDON, WC1N 3HR

Venue may vary, usually central London, to be advised.

The above address is for enquiries only to The Administrator, British Autogenic Society

 ♿ Special needs should be discussed with the training organiser

*   **1) Autogenic Therapy** (Leading to Full Membership & Diploma of Autogenic Therapy (Dip AT) (Level 1)

Duration	1 yr, part-time, inc 6 w/end modules, tutorial, supervision (minimum 396 hrs)
Entry	Post graduate; Foundation qualification in Medicine, Psychotherapy, Nursing, Counselling, Clinical Psychology; CV showing relevant clinical experience; 60 hrs self-knowledge of autogenics; in depth interview; 2 prof referees

*   **2) Diploma in Autogenic Therapy**

Duration	1 yr, part-time
Entry	Accreditation of Diploma status by Buckinghamshire Chilterns University

This course is subject to final validation

**   **3) Autogenic Psychotherapy**

Duration	2 yrs part time (details to come) leading to UKCP Registration and Dip AP (Level 2)
Entry	Diploma AT and membership of BAS

**   **4) Advanced Analytic Autogenic neutralisation**

Duration	2 yrs part time (details to come) leading to Dip AAN (Level 3)
Entry	Dip AP; Membership BAC; UKCP Registration

BROADCASTING SUPPORT SERVICES,   020 8735 5042

Union House, Shepherds Bush Green, Ealing, LONDON, W12 8UA,

No response received to our enquries for 2000, entry details as of Nov 1998

*   **1) Introductory Helpline skills**

*   **2) Advanced Telephone Helpline Skills**

*   **3) Facilitating groups by telephone**

*   **4) Stress Management for Helpline Workers**

continued...

Star System: ** Introductory course only • ** 2-3 yr pt-time course to Cert/Dip level •*
*** Professional development for trained counsellors
For added help, see section 'Essential Information for Students', page 1

51

*   **5) Managing and Supervising Helpline Staff**

*   **6) Recruitment & Selection**

CANCERLINK,   020 7833 2818

11-21 Northdown Street, LONDON, N1 9BN,

Runs a variety of workshops concerned with cancer issues. Will also train on client's premises. Apply To: Training and Development Officer

 Premises have disabled access

CENTRAL SCHOOL OF COUNSELLING & THERAPY,
0800 243 463

80 Paul Street, LONDON, EC2A 4UD,

Validated by AEB and recognised by the Department for Education and Employment (1992); Over 200 centres nationwide

 Suitable for people with disabilities.

*   **1) Introduction to Counselling**

Duration	30 hrs, part-time
Entry	Open access, courses are run throughout the year

*   **2) Introduction to Counselling in the Workplace**

Duration	30 hrs, part-time
Entry	Open access

*   **3) Introduction to Counselling Children & Adolescents**

Duration	30 hrs, part-time
Entry	Open

*   **4) Introduction to Cognitive Therapy**

Duration	30 hrs, part-time
Entry	Open access

*   **5) Certificate in Counselling Skills — Level 1**

Duration	75 hrs, over 1 or 2 years, courses start Autumn, New Year and Easter
Entry	Open access

*   **6) Certificate in Counselling Theory — Level 1**

Duration	75 hrs, over 1-2 years, (September — June)
Entry	Open access

Star System: * Introductory course only • ** 2-3 yr pt-time course to Cert/Dip level •
*** Professional development for trained counsellors
For added help, see section 'Essential Information for Students', page 1

52

*   **7) Certificate**(s) in Specialist Counselling Skills — Level 1 (Bereavement; Cancer; AIDS/HIV; Disability; Alcohol/Drugs; Children and Adolescents; in Organisations

Duration	75 hrs, per course, 1-2 years (Sept-June)
Entry	Some relevant experience required

**   **8) Advanced Certificate in Counselling Skills & Theory — Level 2**

Duration	150 hrs, September — June
Entry	Successful completion of Level 1 or APL

**   **9) Diploma in Therapeutic Counselling** (Humanistic or Psychodynamic)

Duration	215 hrs and 100 hrs supervised placement and personal counselling of at least 50 hrs
Entry	Successful coompletion of Levels 1 and 2 and interview or APL; 3 entries/year
Core Model	Psychodynamic and humanistic routes available
Apply To:	Details of APL available from APL Co-ordinator

**   **10) Full-time Diploma in Thearpeutic Counselling**

Duration	475 hrs, full-time, + 100 hrs supervised placement
Entry	By written application and interview, 3 entries/year
Core Model	Psychodynamic and humanistic routes available

***   **11) Diploma in Supervision of Counsellors & Therapists**

Duration	150 hrs
Entry	Diploma in Counselling/Therapy and minimum of 2 years supervised practice. Written application and interview
Apply To:	The Director of Academic Studies

*   **12) Working with Difference**

Duration	30 hrs
Entry	Open access

*   **13) Support in Changing Times**

Duration	30 hrs
Entry	Open access

*   **14) Personal and Professional Development through Creativity**

Duration	30 hrs
Entry	Open access

continued...

Star System: ** Introductory course only • ** 2-3 yr pt-time course to Cert/Dip level •*
*** Professional development for trained counsellors
For added help, see section 'Essential Information for Students', page 1

*   **15) Workline with Mental Health Issues**

Duration   30 hrs
Entry   Open access

*   **16) Dealing with Grief and Loss**

Duration   30 hrs
Entry   Open access

*   **17) Understanding Addiction**

Duration   30 hrs
Entry   Open access — continuing professional development

*   **18) Working with Drugs and Alcohol**

Duration   30 hrs
Entry   Open access

*   **19) Cognitive Therapy**

Duration   30 hrs
Entry   Open access

*   **20) Working with People: Key Skills Development**

Duration   30 hrs
Entry   Open access

*   **21) Working with Child Abuse**

Duration   30 hrs
Entry   Open acces

*   **22) Working with Eating Distress**

Duration   30 hrs
Entry   Counselling Skills necessary

Star System: * Introductory course only • ** 2-3 yr pt-time course to Cert/Dip level •
*** Professional development for trained counsellors
For added help, see section 'Essential Information for Students', page 1

54

CENTRE FOR STRESS MANAGEMENT,

**0181 293 4114,
0181 853 1122
FAX: 0181 293 1441
ADMIN@MANAGINGSTRESS.COM
WEBSITE: WWW.MANAGINGSTRESS.COM**

156 Westcombe Hill, Blackheath, LONDON, SE3 7DH,

Also workshops/short courses in basic/advanced counselling, stress management with various psychotherapeutic approaches.

*   **1) Primary Certificate in Multimodal Therapy** (BPS recognised course for CPD)

Duration	12 hours, 2 days
Entry	Open

*   **2) Primary Certificate in Counselling Skills** (HPA, IMS)

Duration	2 days
Entry	Selection by application, reference and interview

*   **3) Primary Certificate in Rational Emotive Behaviour Therapy** (AREBT, HPA, IMS) (BPS recommended as 1) above)

Duration	18 hours, in extended weekend
Entry	Open

*   **4) Primary Certificate in Cognitive Behavioural Therapy & Training** (BPS recognised above)

Duration	12 hrs, 2 day module
Entry	Open

*   **5) Primary Certificate in Problem Focused Psychotherapy and Training**

Duration	12 hrs, 2 day module
Entry	Open

*   **6) Advanced Certificate in Problem Focused Psychotherapy and Counselling**

Duration	76 hours, modular course
Entry	Open
Apply To:	Dr S Palmer and Gladeana McMahon

*   **7) Primary Certificate in Trauma & PTSD Counselling**

Duration	12 hours, 2 days
Entry	Open

continued...

Star System: ** Introductory course only • ** 2-3 yr pt-time course to Cert/Dip level •*
*** Professional development for trained counsellors
For added help, see section 'Essential Information for Students', page 1

55

** 8) **Advanced Certificate/Diploma in Multimodal Counselling and Therapy** (HPA, IMS)

Duration   Modular course, Advanced Certificate: 92 hours; Diploma: Additional 50-70 hours

Entry   Advanced Cert: Open; Diploma: Experienced Counsellors

Apply To: Dr S Palmer

** 9) **Advanced Certificate/Diploma in Cognitive Behavioural Approaches to Psychotherapy and Counselling** (HPA)

Duration   Modular course; Advanced Certificate: 75 hours; Diploma: Additional 75 hours

Entry   Advanced Certificate: Open; Diploma: Experienced counsellors

Apply To: Dr S Palmer

** 10) **Advanced Certificate in Rational Emotive Behaviour Therapy and Counselling** (HPS, IMS)

Duration   9 months, part-time, 4 modules

Entry   Completion of Certificate in RET and passing of the exam; selection by application, reference and interview.

** 11) **Certificate/Diploma in Stress Management** (IMA + HPA) (Diploma is BPS recognised)

Duration   Modular courses

Entry   Selection by application, reference and interview (Entry is at Advanced Certificate stage initially)

*** 12) **Certificate in Crisis & Trauma Counselling & Critical Incident Debriefing**

Duration   49 hours, modular course

Entry   Experienced counsellors

Apply To: Dr S Palmer and Gladeana McMahon

*** 13) **Primary Certificate in Supervision** (BPS recognised as above)

Duration   Contact the Centre for details

Entry   Experienced counsellors

Apply To: Dr S Palmer

*** 14) **Primary Certificate in Brief Therapy & Time Limited Therapy**

Duration   12 hours, 2 days

Entry   Counsellors with experience of Cognitive Behavioural Therapy. Not suitable for beginners

---

*Star System: * Introductory course only • ** 2-3 yr pt-time course to Cert/Dip level •*
*** Professional development for trained counsellors*
For added help, see section 'Essential Information for Students', page 1

56

***   **15) Primary Certificate in Critical Incident Stress Debriefing**

Duration   12 hours, 2 days
Entry   Experienced counsellors
Apply To: Dr S Palmer, FBAC Director

***   **16) Certificate/Advanced Certificate in Cognitive Behavioural Approaches tp Psychotherapy and Counselling** (Adv Cert BPS recognised for CPD)

Duration   9 months, modular
Entry   Selection buy application, reference and interview
Apply To: Dr S Palmer

***   **17) Certificate/Advanced Certificate in Cognitive Behavioural Therapies with Trauma, PTSD and CISD** (HPA, IMS)

Duration   9 months, modular
Entry   Selection by application, reference and interview
Apply To: Dr S Palmer

CENTRE FOR TRANSPERSONAL PSYCHOLOGY,   0171 937 9090

7-11 Kensington High Street, LONDON, W8 5NP,
No response received to our enquiries for 2000, entry details as of November 1998

*   **1) Certificate in Transpersonal Skills & Perspectives, Stage 1**

**   **2) Professional Preparation in Transpersonal Psychology — Stage 2**

**   **3) Accreditation Stage: As a Transpersonal Psychotherapist**

INSTITUTE FOR ARTS IN THERAPY & EDUCATION
0171 704 2534
INFO@ARTS-THERAPY.DEMON.CO.UK
WWW.ARTS-THERAPY.DEMON.CO.UK

Terpsichore, 70 Cranwich Road, LONDON, N16 5JD,
Please telephone above number for brochure

**   **1) Diploma in Integrative Arts Psychotherapy**

Core Model   Integrative Arts Psychotherapy
Duration   3 years, part-time, 1 day/week + 6 weekends/year. Also modular scheme, running weekends only
Entry   Degree/qualification in a helping profession or teaching. Strong empathetic skills, maturity & life experience. personal therapy for the duration of the course

continued...

Star System: * Introductory course only • ** 2-3 yr pt-time course to Cert/Dip level •
*** Professional development for trained counsellors
For added help, see section 'Essential Information for Students', page 1

57

**   2) Certificate in the Therapeutic & Educational Application of the Arts

Duration	1 year, part-time, 1 day/week + 6 weekends/year. Also modular scheme, weekends only
Entry	A Post-School qualification; strong empathetic skills; maturity & life experience; ability to image; personal therapy for the duration of the course

*   3) Certificate in Creativity and Imagination

Duration	8 weekend days
Entry	Professional experience in education, counselling, a helping profession or in the arts

*   4) Certificate in the Education of the Emotions

Duration	1 term, evening course
Entry	Minimum of 2 'A' levels or equivalent; professional experience in education, counselling or a helping profession

**   5) MEd/BPhil The Arts in Therapy & Education (Exeter)

Duration	2 years, part-time, over 3 weekends a term + a summer school in year 2
Entry	Professional qualification in education, therapy or a helping profession

**   6) Diploma in Child Therapy

Duration	2 yrs/part-time/2.5 days per month.
Entry	Certificate in the Therapeutic and Educational Application of the Arts. Strong empathetic skills, maturity and life experience, personal therapy for duration of course.
Apply To:	Margot Sunderland

LONDON COLLEGE OF CLINICAL HYPNOSIS,   0171 402 9037

229a Sussex Gardens, LONDON, W2 2RL,

No response received to our enquiries for 2000, entry details as of November 1998

*   1) Certificate Course in the use of Clinical Hypnosis (BHHEB)

**   2) Diploma in Clinical Hypnotherapy (BMHEB)

Star System: ** Introductory course only* • *** 2-3 yr pt-time course to Cert/Dip level* •
*** Professional development for trained counsellors

For added help, see section 'Essential Information for Students', page 1

58

NATIONAL SCHOOL OF HYPNOSIS & PSYCHOTHERAPY
0171 359 6991

28 Finsbury Park Road, LONDON, N4 2JX,
Send large SAE + 2x1st class stamps for further information. Member UKCP. Affil.
ICM; venue: Central London

**   Diploma/Advanced Diploma in Therapeutic Hypnosis & Psychotherapy

Core Model	Hypnotherapy
Duration	Diploma: 1 year; min 2 yrs under clinical supervision & inc. Adv Hypnotherapy Practitioner Diploma studies, weekends
Entry	Mature candidates, at a post graduate level of competence or relevant experience
Apply To:	The Registrar, Administrator

PERSON-CENTRED WORKSHOPS,
0181 531 9760

376 Hale End Road, Highams Park, LONDON, E4 9PB,
No response received to our enquiries for 2000. Entry details as of Nov 1998

**   1) Diploma in Working with Survivors of Childhood Abuse (Anglia Univ)

**   2) Diploma in Working with People with Learning and/or Physical Disabilities

---

POST ADOPTION CENTRE,
0171 284 0555

5 Torriano Mews, Torriano Ave, LONDON, NW5 2RZ,
Workshops & in-house/tailor-made training also offered. External Venues; BSL stage 1 available. Course 1) leads to accreditation as pre-adoption counsellor

♿ Toilets for disabled people, groundfloor training room with easy access

***   1) Pre-Adoption Preparation Counselling Training (PREP)

Duration	12 days — variable days
Entry	Qualified counsellor or Therapist with either 3 years post qualifying experience or previous experience in the field of adoption as a professional
Apply To:	Sue Cowling, Course Co-ordinator

***   2) Post Adoption Counselling Training & Skills Course (PACTS)

Duration	3 days monthly (12 days total) Each Autumn
Entry	3 years post qualified or equivalent experience

---

*Star System: * Introductory course only • ** 2-3 yr pt-time course to Cert/Dip level •*
*** Professional development for trained counsellors
For added help, see section 'Essential Information for Students', page 1

PPD PERSONAL DEVELOPMENT,   0181 201 3333
Leroy House, 30a The Loning, Colindale, LONDON, NW9 6DR,
No response received to our enquiries for 2000. Entry details as of Nov 1998

*   1) NLP Introductory Weekends

*   2) NLP 'Free' Introductory evening

*   3) NLP Foundation Skills — Practitioner Part 1

*   4) NLP Practitioner Certification — Practitioner Part 2

**   5) Master Practitioner in NLP

PROFESSIONAL DEVELOPMENT FOUNDATION,   0171 987 2805
Studio 21, Limehouse Cut, 46 Morris Road, LONDON, E14 6NQ,
No response received to our enquiries for 2000. Entry details as of Nov 1998

*   1) Royal Society of Health Certificate in Counselling

**   2) Royal Society of Health Diploma in Counselling, Psychotherapy

***   3) Royal Society of Health Fellowship & linked Masters Degree

***   4) College of Preceptors, Associateship in Supervision/Training

***   5) College of Preceptors, Fellowship

WPF COUNSELLING,   020 7937 6956
23 Kensington Square, LONDON, W8 5HN,
WPF has a network of 23 centres offering training leading to WPF training awards.
Each centre offers some of the courses listed below. For details ring WPF centre/s in
your area.

♿ Facilities for disabled people vary, please enquire at each centre.

*   1) Certificate in Counselling Skills
Duration   90 hours, over 1 year
Entry   No formal entry requirements

**   2) Certificate in Psychodynamic Counselling
Duration   200 hours (approx) over 2 years
Entry   Certificate in Counselling Skills

---

*Star System: * Introductory course only • ** 2-3 yr pt-time course to Cert/Dip level •*
*** *Professional development for trained counsellors*
For added help, see section 'Essential Information for Students', page 1

** 3) Diploma in Counselling Skills

Duration	1/2 day (approx 4.5 hrs/week)
Entry	Certificate in Counselling Skills
Core Model	Psychodynamic

** 4) Diploma in Psychodynamic Counselling

Duration	2 years, 200+ hours (seminars)
Core Model	Psychodynamic
Entry	Certificate in Counselling

*** 5) Advanced Diploma in Psychodynamic Counselling (BAC Acc)

Core Model	Psychodynamic
Duration	2 years, 210+ hours (seminars)
Entry	Certifiicate in Counselling Skills, Diploma in Counselling Skills

YOUTH WITH A MISSION,   0171 370 4424

Earl's Court Project, 24 Collingham Road, LONDON, SW5 0LX,
No response received to our enquiries for 2000. Entry details as of Nov 1998

* 1) Community Counselling School

** 2) Diploma in Christian Counselling

CSS DEVELOPMENTAL STRESS TRAINING,   01908 675 717
FAX 01908 691 288

Exchange House, 494 Midsummer Boulevard, MILTON KEYNES, MK9 2EA,
No response receoved to our enquiries for 2000, entry details as of Nov 1998

* Developmental Stress Training

ICAS — INDEPENDENT COUNSELLING & ADVISORY
SERVICES   019008 285 236

Radlett House,, West Hill, Aspley Guise, MILTON KEYNES, MK17 8DT,
No response received to our enquiries for 2000, entry details as of November 1998

* 1) Career Counselling

* 2) Counselling Skills at Work

* 3) Coaching & Developing

*Star System: * Introductory course only • ** 2-3 yr pt-time course to Cert/Dip level •
*** Professional development for trained counsellors*
For added help, see section 'Essential Information for Students', page 1

61

NATIONAL COLLEGE OF HYPNOSIS AND PSYCHOTHERAPY
01282 699378
FAX 01282 698633
HYPNOSIS_NCHP@COMPUSERVE.COM

12 Cross Street, NELSON, Lancashire, BB9 7EN,

Courses at various centres. Member of UKCP & as a member of BAC is bound by its Codes of Ethics & Practice and subject to its complaints procedure

♿ London/Cheadle venues suitable for disabled people

**   Diploma in Hypnotherapy & Psychotherapy (BACIFHE)

Duration	18 months-2 years, weekends, 3 stages (supplementary training offered if recommendation for UKCP register is required)
Entry	Professional qualification; degree or other evidence of ability to undertake course; progression through course dependent upon successful completion of earlier stages
Apply To:	Enrolment Secretary
Core Model	Hypnotherapy

CAER — CENTRE FOR ALTERNATIVE EDUCATION,
01736 810530
INFO@CAER.CO.UK
WWW.CAER.CO.UK

Rosemerryn, Lamorna, PENZANCE, Cornwall, TR19 6BN,

All courses are residential and repeated throughout the year

♿ Wheelchair access

*   1) Being Present

Duration	3 + 3 day residential
Entry	For those in the helping professions

*   2) Facilitator Training

Duration	5 days + weekend follow-up (residential)
Entry	Some previous experience of personal development or counselling preferable

**   3) Certificate in Personal & Group Facilitation (Facilitator Development Associates)

Duration	Modular, 20 days, self-selected
Entry	Open to all, also as preparation for the Diploma

Star System: * *Introductory course only* • ** *2-3 yr pt-time course to Cert/Dip level* •
*** *Professional development for trained counsellors*
For added help, see section 'Essential Information for Students', page 1

62

** 4) **Diploma in Facilitator Development** (FDA)

Duration 2 years, monthly, 3 day residential modules + 4 weekends/year
Entry   Post graduate level/equivalent
Apply To: Jo May, Administrator

CENTRE TRAINING INTERNATIONAL SCHOOL OF
HYPNOTHERAPY AND PSYCHOTHERAPY   01772 617663
FAX: 01772 614211

145 Chapel Lane, Longton, PRESTON, PR4 5NA,

Venues: Belfast, Birmingham, Bristol, Edinburgh, Inverness, Ipswich, Preston, Manchester, Leeds, Winchester, Aberdeen. Also workshops.

♿ Full facilities available

** **Diploma in Hypnotherapy & Psychotherapy** (ICM) (Training and
 Accrediting member UKCP)

Duration 300 hours, (130 classroom contact — 10 weeks)
Entry   Postgraduate level of competence/work or life experience; selection by
    interview.
Apply To: Don Hatherley, Course Administrator

CRUSE,   020 8940 4818

Cruse — Bereavement Care, Cruse House, 126 Sheen Road, RICHMOND, Surrey, TW9 1UR,

Offers training through local branches; tailor-made training for organisations; occasional bereavement awareness events

* **1) Aspects of Bereavement**

Duration One day and evening events runs in London and regionally throughout
    UK
Entry   Open to interested professionals, counsellors
Apply To: Uk Training Administrator

* **2) Introduction to Bereavement Counselling**

Duration 40-60 hours, part-time evenings or weekend
Entry   By application
Apply To: Branch Administrator

---

*Star System: * Introductory course only ● ** 2-3 yr pt-time course to Cert/Dip level ●
*** Professional development for trained counsellors*
For added help, see section 'Essential Information for Students', page 1

63

SKYROS INSTITUTE,   **0171 267 4424**
SKYROS ISLAND,
No response received to our enquiries for 2000, entry details as of Nov 1998

*   **Fundamentals of Imagework Certificate** (Skyros) 1: Life Choices, Life Changes; 2: Expanding Imagework

Star System: ** Introductory course only* • *** 2-3 yr pt-time course to Cert/Dip level* •
*** Professional development for trained counsellors
For added help, see section 'Essential Information for Students', page 1

64

British
Association of
Psychotherapists

A professional organisation of psychotherapists, established in 1951, with over 400 Members nationwide. Headquarters in London

PROFESSIONAL TRAININGS

Jungian Analytical Psychotherapy • Psychoanalytic Psychotherapy

Psychoanalytic Psychotherapy with Adults for Child Psychotherapists

Trainings lead to National Registration with the BCP or ACP

Active Postgraduate Life - Twice-yearly Journal - Extensive Library

Conference & Seminar Rooms - Consulting Rooms

CLINICAL SERVICES

A prompt assessment and referral system for children, adolescents

and adults requiring psychotherapy

EXTERNAL COURSES - A diverse range of evening and weekend courses for

professionals, from introductory lectures to advanced workshops.

MSc in THE PSYCHODYNAMICS OF HUMAN DEVELOPMENT - a part-time 2-year

MSc/1-year diploma course run jointly with Birkbeck College, University of London

SUPERVISION SERVICE • PUBLIC CONFERENCES

MEDIA CONSULTATION SERVICE

For further information contact:

THE BRITISH ASSOCIATION OF PSYCHOTHERAPISTS

37 Mapesbury Road, London NW2 4HJ

Tel: 0181 452 9823, Fax: 0181 452 5182

Email: mail@bap-psychotherapy.org

or visit our Website: www.bap-psychotherapy.org

Star System: *Introductory course only* • ** *2-3 yr pt-time course to Cert/Dip level* •
*** *Professional development for trained counsellors*
For added help, see section 'Essential Information for Students', page 1

65

SCHOOL OF SOCIAL, HEALTH CARE AND COUNSELLING

The School is a Centre of Excellence in the South West and offers an extensive range of professional counselling training from introductory to diploma level.

Courses offered through the School include:

CPCAB (Counselling and Psychotherapy Central Awarding Body)
Introduction to Communication and
Human Relationship Skills
Certificate in Counselling Skills
Certificate in Therapeutic Counselling
Certificate in Health Counselling
Combined Certificate in Counselling
(Skills and Therapeutic)
Advanced Certificate in Therapeutic Counselling
Diploma in Therapeutic Counselling
Certificate & Diploma in Counselling Supervision
Certificate & Diploma in Group Facilitation

Plus additional short specialist courses

For further information in respect of any of the above, please contact Annette Farley on (01202) 205496

The BOURNEMOUTH AND POOLE
College OF FURTHER EDUCATION

Star System: ** Introductory course only • ** 2-3 yr pt-time course to Cert/Dip level •*
*** Professional development for trained counsellors

For added help, see section 'Essential Information for Students', page 1

66

Charity Reg. No. 326750

BRITISH AUTOGENIC SOCIETY

Diploma Course in Autogenic Therapy
One year part-time starts September annually

Come and train with us and qualify to teach

profound relaxation and stress management to individuals and groups. Autogenic Training is an EASILY TAUGHT AND LEARNT method of balancing the body's autonomic nervous system to resolve old stress patterning into healthier emotional balance with creative and self healing potential.

Autogenic Therapy provides a simple yet flexible non-drug approach to treating a wide clinical spectrum of both organic and psychomatic illness.

Over 3000 scientific papers have been published on its normalising effects on physiological indices, behaviour and also peak performance. The therapy has numerous Medical applications in skin conditions, asthma, hypertension, colitis, arthritis, migraine, irritable bowel, pain-tension syndromes, etc..., and psychological applications in anxiety states, insomnia, depression, unresolved grief reactions, post- traumatic stress disorder, performance anxiety etc...

Course Features
• Must have learnt own Autogenic Training
• Ideal for Doctor's, Nurses, Counsellors, Psychotherapists, Psychologists and allied professional groups
• Six 2-day weekend modules - (Sept, Oct, Nov, Feb, April, June)
• Personal tutorial supervision
• High quality handouts
• Start practice after Module 3

Qualification by continous assessment leads to
a Diploma in Autogenic Therapy
and Membership of the British Autogenic Society

Enquiries to:
The Administrator - Course Application,
The British Autogenic Society,
The Royal London Homœopathic Hospital,
Great Ormond Street,
London WC1N 3HR

The British Autogenic Society is the teaching, research and supervisory body for Autogenic Therapy in the UK. BAS is a member of the UKCP, the EAP and ICAT

Find out more at www.autogenic-therapy.org.uk

Star System: * *Introductory course only* • ** *2-3 yr pt-time course to Cert/Dip level* •
*** *Professional development for trained counsellors*
For added help, see section 'Essential Information for Students', page 1

67

Hadiqa

a centre for creative self-development

Diploma in Counselling
The Body, Gestalt and the Spiritual

*"The road yourself must journey on
lies in tending to your heart – a garden in bloom."*

Hakim Sanai

A two year humanistic and integrative training
starting September, 2000

Hadiqa
16, Victoria Grove, Southsea, Hants. PO5 1NE   Tel. 01705 863266
Hadiqa (pronounced Hadeeka) is a *Sufi* term meaning *'Garden of the Heart'*

*Star System: * Introductory course only •   ** 2-3 yr pt-time course to Cert/Dip level •*
*** Professional development for trained counsellors*
For added help, see section 'Essential Information for Students', page 1

68

Hexagon Training Company

Hypnosis I & II

October 2nd – 6th 2000 • The Haybergill Centre Cumbria • Cost: £595 Full Board

Come and enjoy 5 days of residential trance work in the beautiful Cumbrian hills, studying and experiencing Ericksonian hypnosis at its magical best.

As with other Hexagon courses, our material is at the cutting edge of training and will be of use to anyone seeking to apply hypnosis in the context of healing, training or business.

For further details of this and other courses, please contact

Tina Stacey or Sandra Barber at;
Hexagon Training Company • 78 Ivy Park Road • Sheffield S10 3LD
Telephone/Fax: 0114 230 2753 • E-mail: Staceylon@aol.com

Philadelphia association

PSYCHOTHERAPY COMMUNITIES AND TRAINING

The PA, a charity founded in 1965 by R.D. Laing and others challenging traditional approaches to mental health, offers a phenomenological perspective to theory and practice, emphasising the importance of attending to the individual's unique experience within a particular social context. We provide low cost therapeutic communities, a psychotherapy referral service, and:

- 1 yr introductory course in phenomenology and psychoanalysis
- training in psychoanalytic psychotherapy (UKCP accredited)

Contact: **Philadelphia Association, 4 Marty's Yard, London NW3 1QW. Tel: 0171-794 2652**

Star System: ** Introductory course only • ** 2-3 yr pt-time course to Cert/Dip level •*
*** Professional development for trained counsellors
For added help, see section 'Essential Information for Students', page 1

69

The ASSOCIATION OF INDEPENDENT PSYCHOTHERAPISTS

PSYCHOTHERAPY TRAINING
A training based on Jungian and psychoanalytic concepts for experienced counsellors

PSYCHOTHERAPY REFERRAL SERVICE
Confidential consultation with view to referral to a suitable psychotherapist or analyst

SUPERVISION
Individual or group supervision with qualified supervisors

PO Box 1194
London N6 5PW
Tel 0171-700 1911

Member UKCP

The Association of Independent Psychotherapists Ltd. Registered in England 28431R
Registered Address: Basement Flat, 16 Marlborough Rd, London N19 4NB

*Star System: * Introductory course only • ** 2-3 yr pt-time course to Cert/Dip level •*
**** Professional development for trained counsellors*
For added help, see section 'Essential Information for Students', page 1

70

Masters Degrees in
collaboration with

UNIVERSITY OF
NORTH LONDON

INSTITUTE OF PSYCHOTHERAPY
AND SOCIAL STUDIES

Member of the United Kingdom Council for Psychotherapy

MA/DIPLOMA IN PSYCHOANALYTIC
PSYCHOTHERAPY AND SOCIAL STUDIES

The Institute of Psychotherapy and Social Studies offers a training in psychoanalytic psychotherapy and object relations theory which also takes into account the interpersonal, social and political context within which psychotherapy takes place.

The four year part-time course in conjunction with the **University of North London** is designed to give students the clinical and theoretical experience needed to develop their own understanding and practice of psychoanalytic psychotherapy.

The cost of supervision is included and successful completion of the MA/Diploma entitles graduates to be included on the **UKCP Register of Psychotherapists**. For further details apply to: **IPSS**, West Hill House, 6 Swains Lane, London N6 6QU.

' EXPLORING PSYCHOTHERAPY '
ONE YEAR INTRODUCTORY COURSE

Ideal for those wanting to find out more about psychotherapy but not commit to a full professional training.

Seminars summarise the development of therapeutic theory and practice using a broad psychoanalytic approach which also emphasises the social and political context of psychotherapy.

The evening includes participation in a therapy group.

Contact: David 0181 299 9918 or Bernadette 0181 509 1484

*Star System: * Introductory course only ● ** 2-3 yr pt-time course to Cert/Dip level ●*
*** Professional development for trained counsellors*
For added help, see section 'Essential Information for Students', page 1

71

THE IRON MILL CENTRE
OAKFORD, TIVERTON, DEVON, EX16 9EN
TEL/FAX: 01398 351379
e-mail: juliehewson@ironmill.demon.co.uk

Certificate in Counselling Skills and Theory - 90 hour course, basis for application to professional training.

Advanced Diploma in Integrative Counselling (BAC Accredited) - This two year part-time training also carries Higher Educational Awards up to a Master's Degree.

Supervision Certificate and Diploma - These courses cover skills and methods of Supervision and can lead to UK and European accreditation.

Transactional Analysis Psychotherapy Training - This can lead to UKCP registration and also carries Higher Educational Awards up to a Master's Degree.

Counselling Children and Adolescents - This training carries a Certificate in Advanced Professional Studies.

Trauma workshop - An indepth approach including Though Field Therapy run by Willem Lammers TSTA, Switzerland on 30 & 31 October.

Intervision group - For professionals to provide a forum for the interface between personal and professional lives. A second group will commence in October 99, in Exeter and will meet one evening per month, please apply now for places are limited.

The IMC offers Higher Educational Awards through Bath Spa University College and is affiliated with Strode College of Further Education.

For details please contact Julie Hewson - Centre Director or Maria Phillips - Administrator.

*Star System: * Introductory course only • ** 2-3 yr pt-time course to Cert/Dip level •
*** Professional development for trained counsellors*
For added help, see section 'Essential Information for Students', page 1

72

LINCOLN CLINIC & CENTRE FOR PSYCHOTHERAPY

Reg.Charity No.297990 Reg.England 901650
British Confederation of Psychotherapists

The Lincoln Centre, a founder member of the British Confederation of Psychotherapists, invites applications for the following courses:

ASSOCIATE MEMBERSHIP COURSE (AMC)

A four-year part-time course leading to qualification as Associate Member of the Centre. The course is open to graduates and some non-graduates.

As a student your training will include the treatment of two patients under supervision, a supervised infant observation, three years of conceptual and theoretical teaching, and clinical seminars. Our senior and experienced analysts and therapists will cover the major contributions to clinical thinking from the Contemporary Freudian, Independent and Kleinian schools. In parallel, skilled practitioners from the different orientations will conduct seminars that continue throughout your training.

Your qualification as an Associate Member of the Lincoln provides a variety of opportunities. You can play a full part in the scientific life of the centre: you may join one of our post-graduate seminars, and take advantage of our Clinical Services which provide a comprehensive referral service for students and qualified members.

OBSERVATIONAL STUDIES AND APPLICATION OF PSYCHOANALYTIC CONCEPTS TO WORK WITH CHILDREN, YOUNG PEOPLE AND FAMILIES (MA/Postgraduate Diploma) (OSC)

(Linked with the Tavistock Clinic and University of East London)

This course (minimum two years) is designed for those undertaking work with children, adolescents and families. It will enhance awareness and understanding of human development and interaction. Both professionals and non-professionals wishing to enter the mental health field will be helped to widen their approach to current work through applying a psychoanalytic frame of reference.

The course is based in the Clapham area but small group units may also be arranged in north London.

You may take individual parts of the course, such as Psychoanalytical Theory, Infant Observation, Work Discussion and Child Development Research if you wish. There is no obligation to undertake the course as a whole.

ENQUIRIES WELCOME: Lincoln Training Administrator, 25 Hillcroft Crescent, W5 2SG. Tel. 0181 998 1949, Fax 0181 248 4021

*Star System: * Introductory course only • ** 2-3 yr pt-time course to Cert/Dip level •
*** Professional development for trained counsellors*
For added help, see section 'Essential Information for Students', page 1

73

London Marriage Guidance

Working with Couples

FOUNDATION COURSE IN PSYCHODYNAMIC MARITAL AND COUPLE COUNSELLING

The two term, twenty week, course starts each year in January and takes place one evening a week. It is pre-requisite for the LMG Diploma.

Selection conferences for January start are being held in the autumn. Information sessions are held throughout the year.

DIPLOMA IN PSYCHODYNAMIC MARITAL AND COUPLE COUNSELLING
(This course is BAC Accredited and validated by Roehampton Institute London)

The Diploma is a three year part-time course. It is a specialist couples training which offers integrated theory, case work and supervision from LMG's training team and visiting experts. Applicants must first successfully complete the Foundation Course.

POST GRADUATE CERTIFICATE IN PSYCHODYNAMIC MARITAL AND COUPLE COUNSELLING

This course is designed for those who hold a recognised qualification in psychodynamic therapy or counselling and who wish to develop expertise in working with couples. The course is designed to enable participants to undertake both the training and the clinical work within one working day. The course starts in January and runs for 15 months.

DIPLOMA IN PSYCHOSEXUAL MARITAL AND COUPLE THERAPY

(This course has full approval from the British Association for Sexual and Relationship Therapy)

This course is designed to equip experienced couples workers to be more effective with the psychosexual aspects of their clients' difficulties. It includes working behaviourally and the treatment of particular dysfunctions.

It is for experienced psychodynamic couple counsellors/therapists. It runs for three terms of weekly seminars, supervision groups and 8 day workshops.

For more information and application forms please contact:

Training Department, London Marriage Guidance,
76a New Cavendish Street,
London W1M 7LB
Tel: 020 7637 1318 Fax: 020 7637 4546
e-mail: training@lmg.org.uk

*Star System: * Introductory course only • ** 2-3 yr pt-time course to Cert/Dip level •*
*** Professional development for trained counsellors
For added help, see section 'Essential Information for Students', page 1

74

Is Counselling/Psychotherapy for Me?

METANOIA
INSTITUTE

Metanoia offers nationally and internationally accredited diploma, BA, MSc, Masters/ Doctorate and post-graduate courses in a number of counselling and psychotherapy approaches validated by Middlesex University. All courses are modular and can be studied part-time to fit with other life commitments.

We also hold regular two-hour workshops for people considering training in counselling or psychotherapy so that they can learn more about the profession itself and about the various different training approaches.

INTRODUCTORY WORKSHOPS

A range of two and three-day workshops in each of our training approaches is offered, which gives participants the opportunity to experience Metanoia's teaching style. An Introductory Workshop is a pre-requisite of all programmes.

PERSON-CENTRED COUNSELLING

A 3-4 year course BA/Diploma course (accredited *by BAC*) offering a comprehensive study of the theory and practice of the Person Centred approach, and the opportunity to consider other approaches to Counselling. This course is aimed at individuals wishing to develop their counselling skills and/or those hoping to become professional counsellors. Courses commence through the year. Each years comprises 8 three-day modules.

TRANSACTIONAL ANALYSIS COUNSELLING

A 3-4 year BA/Diploma course exploring TA as a primary theoretical framework for counselling in a variety of settings. Each years comprises 10 two-day modules.

COUNSELLING WORKSHOPS

Open to students and graduates of Metanoia and other training organisations, we offer over 20 two- and three-day workshops.

DIPLOMA/MSC IN PSYCHOTHERAPY VALIDATED BY MIDDLESEX UNIVERSITY

Metanoia offers Diplomas/MScs in Gestalt, Integrative and Transactional Analysis Psychotherapy. Achieving the MSc will include completing both of the Diploma Course and qualification as a psychotherapist.
Graduation from the psychotherapy courses leads to UKCP registration.
The MSc course is open to students who have a psychology degree or equivalent first training in the helping professions and who have completed the foundation year in their chosen discipline. However, in line with UKCP requirements, Metanoia now offers suitably experienced individuals the opportunity to apply to enter any of our psychotherapy training programmes without the above qualifications on the basis of Accreditation of Prior Experiential Learning (APEL). If individuals have completed other training and/or have experience to Foundation or further years standard, they may enter part way through a training programme at the relevant level on an Accreditation of Prior Learning (APL) basis.

For further information on all of Metanoia's courses, please telephone:
(020) 8579 2505
13 North Common Road
Ealing
London
W5 2QB

Metanoia is a member of the UK Council for Psychotherapy   Registered Charity No. 1050175

Star System: * Introductory course only • ** 2-3 yr pt-time course to Cert/Dip level •
*** Professional development for trained counsellors
For added help, see section 'Essential Information for Students', page 1

75

THE MINSTER CENTRE

The Minster Centre has been running training programmes in integrative psychotherapy and counselling since 1978. The Centre's diploma courses are recognised by the BAC and lead towards UKCP registration. Its MA degrees are validated by Middlesex University. All courses are modular and taught part-time to fit in with those with full-time work commitments.

The Minster Centre runs a full referral service for individual and group psychotherapy and counselling. Rooms are also available to rent at hourly, daily and weekly rates.

Training
Foundation Course
A one year certificate course providing an introduction to basic counselling and psychotherapeutic skills. This course is suitable for those wishing to use counselling skills as part of their work or as a basis for further training.

The Diploma/MA in Integrative Psychotherapy is a three/four year course leading towards UKCP registration. The course systematically covers all major theories, philosophies and practices that have been developed in psychotherapy. Students will also work on personal integration and integration in their practice.
The MA in Integrative Psychotherapy is a four year course validated by Middlesex University. The Diploma is a co-requisite of the MA. MA students are assessed by joint Middlesex University-Minster Centre boards.
Graduate Diploma/MSc in Psychological Counselling and Psychotherapy in Health and Social Care (Diploma validated by Roehampton Instititute and MSc awarded by the University of Surrey).

DIPLOMA AND/OR MA IN INTEGRATIVE COUNSELLING

The Diploma in Integrative Counselling is a two year course recognised by the British Association for Counselling. In addition to developing practical counselling skills, students will be introduced to a number of theoretical perspectives.

The MA in Integrative Counselling is a three year course validated by Middlesex University. In addition to the requirements of the Diploma MA students will work on personal integration and integration in their practice and will attend additional modules assessed by joint Middlesex University-Minster Centre boards.

RESEARCH, DEVELOPMENT AND OTHER SPECIALIST TRAINING

Supervision of Masters and Doctoral students.
Ongoing research projects on Refugees, Male Violence and Psychosomatic Illnesses.

PROFESSIONAL DEVELOPMENT COURSES

A number of short courses have been designed for qualified psychotherapists and counsellors who wish to develop their skills further (such as 'Philosophy East & West', Assessment, Bodywork, Experiential Training Groups, Groupwork, Supervision, Object Relations, Personal Integration, Psychiatry Today, Working with Survivors of Organised Violence, etc).

One and two year courses: Diploma in Integrative Supervision (one year) and Certificate or Diploma in Integrative Group Psychotherapy (one or two years).

Summer School - focusing on counselling and the human condition, to cover: conflict, oppression, diversity, etc.

This year we introduced a new one year short course (Theory and Integrated Skills modules):

Conflict, Oppression and Personal Politics -
Working with individuals, families and communities.

The course is suitable for 'Care' Practitioners (childcare, mental health, criminal justices counselling, family work, mediation, education, human resource management, etc.) that work with an appreciation of human difference and diversity. **There will be a another intake for this course in January 2000.**

For further information please contact: The Minster Centre,
1-2 Drakes Courtyard, 291 Kilburn High Rd, London NW6 7JR
Tel: 0171 372 4940 Fax: 0171 372 6816 Email: os94@dial.pipex.com
Website: http://dialspace.dial.pipex.com/minster/index.htm

Registered Charity No. 1042052 Company Registration No. 296 6937

Star System: * *Introductory course only* • ** *2-3 yr pt-time course to Cert/Dip level* •
*** *Professional development for trained counsellors*
For added help, see section 'Essential Information for Students', page 1

76

PSYCHOANALYTICAL PSYCHOTHERAPY TRAINING

Starting in January each year, an **Introductory Course** integrating psychoanalytic thought with contemporary social and cultural ideas. This introductory year offers theoretical and clinical seminars and participation in an ongoing experiential group. Application to the three year training in **Psychoanalytic Psychotherapy** takes place after successful completion of the introductory course. This academic training includes intensive supervised clinical experience in the **Crisis Centre** and the **Residential Communities.**

The Arbours Association founded in 1970, is a London based, mental health charity and a member of the UKCP. Arbours provides personal psychotherapeutic support and places to live for people in emotional distress.

The Arbours operates an Equal Opportunities Policy and welcomes applicants from a wide variety of backgrounds.

Further information:

Jenny Bryant, Courses Administrator, Arbours Training Programme,
6 Church Lane, London N8 7BU
Tel: 0181 341 0916

Psychotherapy Training in Transactional Analysis

A fully accredited four year Training Course, leading to a qualification in Transactional Analysis, recognised by the United Kingdom Council for Psychotherapy (UKCP), also recognised by the Institute of Transactional Analysis (ITA) and is accredited by the European Association of Transactional Analysis (EATA).

The course is structured over ten weekends a year, with the next intake commencing September 2000. It does not have to be taken in consecutive years, each year is complete in itself. A Certificate will be given upon the first year.

Year One   Fundamentals,Theory in Transactional Analysis concepts, personal development & supervised application.

Year Two   Skills application, diagnosis, supervision & technique.

Year Three   Disorders of the Self & pathological disturbances within a TA framework.

Year Four   Transactional Analysis & Integration. Plus exam overview & supervisory application.

The Manchester Institute for Psychotherapy is a member of The European Association of Psychotherapy.

For a detailed prospectus contact: Bob Cooke

THE MANCHESTER INSTITUTE FOR PSYCHOTHERAPY
454 Barlow Moor Road, Chorlton, Manchester, M21 1BQ
Telephone: 0161 862 9456 Fax: 0161 881 8225 www.mcpt.co.uk e-mail bob@mcpt.co.uk

---

*Star System: * Introductory course only • ** 2-3 yr pt-time course to Cert/Dip level •*
*** Professional development for trained counsellors*
For added help, see section 'Essential Information for Students', page 1

77

SYNTHESIS

Synthesis is offering a 15-month professional development course in Psychosynthesis Counselling and Therapy, which will commence in February 2000.

This course is intended for qualified counsellors who wish to add a psycho-spiritual dimension to their work with clients. The course will consist of 14 three-day training modules (Friday, Saturday, and Sunday), which will take place every month from February 2000 to March 2001. Between these modules, the training group will meet on Fridays for supervision and personal development groups.

Topics covered include: Psychosynthesis Models of the Personality; Body and Soul; The Therapeutic Relationship; Self and Self-Realisation; Working with Imagery; Working with Shadow; Working with the Transpersonal; Self-Realisation and Psychological Disturbance.

After successfully completing this course, the student will receive a diploma and can apply for entry into the Psychotherapy Training which will commence in 2001.

For further information, contact Kunderke Kevlin at:

Synthesis, 12 Avon Vale, Stoke Bishop, Bristol BS9 1TB. Tel: 0117 968 7748

*Star System: * Introductory course only • ** 2-3 yr pt-time course to Cert/Dip level •*
*** Professional development for trained counsellors*
For added help, see section 'Essential Information for Students', page 1

78

MSc and POSTGRADUATE DIPLOMA IN COUNSELLING PRACTICE

(Isis Centre (Oxfordshire Mental Healthcare NHS Trust) and Oxford Brookes University)

This part-time programme aims to develop counselling and related professional skills, and a critical approach to research. The course takes a psychodynamic approach and is informed by reflective practice. It offers:

- A range of clinical experience within an NHS setting.

- Intensive clinical supervision

- Professional Development seminars, including the impact of the setting on clinical practice.

- An established theoretical programme, including seminars on Psychodynamic Theory, Mental Health and Research Methods.

- A small student group.

Applications from a range of backgrounds are encouraged, but those with experience in the NHS, Social Services, Education and other public and voluntary settings will be given some preference.

Isis Centre Associate Programme

A limited number of places are also available in the Associate programme for experienced counsellors who wish to consolidate their clinical experience under supervision.

For further information please contact Philip Roys, Coordinator, The Isis Centre, Little Clarendon Street, Oxford OX1 2HS

Telephone (01865) 556648

OXFORD
BROOKES
UNIVERSITY

Star System: * Introductory course only • ** 2-3 yr pt-time course to Cert/Dip level •
*** Professional development for trained counsellors
For added help, see section 'Essential Information for Students', page 1

79

University of
Hertfordshire

COUNSELLING COURSES
- 1999 -
INTRODUCTION TO COUNSELLING

A ten-week course for anyone who wants to help other people more effectively - voluntary workers, nurses, teachers, pastoral care workers. It is also a preparation for those who intend to undertake a more advanced training in this field.

CERTIFICATE IN COUNSELLING

A part-time, two year course for people from professional and non-professional backgrounds. The course provides an introduction to the psychodynamic and person-centred approaches to counselling.

POSTGRADUATE DIPLOMA IN COUNSELLING
(BAC Accredited training programme)

A two year part-time course designed to prepare students theoretically, practically and personally to practise counselling with an emphasis on linking and integrating personal, professional and academic development.

MA IN COUNSELLING INQUIRY/ADVANCED COUNSELLING STUDIES

A part-time, two year scheme of advanced study and professional development for qualified and experienced counsellors. Modules (including Research Methods, Eating Disorders, Children and Adolescents, Psychosomatic Issues, Drug & Alcohol Addiction) are combined for students to develop a research orientation in a specific aspect of counselling or taken individually as part of our Advanced Studies Scheme.

*POSTGRADUATE CERTIFICATE IN SUPERVISION OF COUNSELLING AND THERAPY**

A part-time one year scheme developed to meet the needs for professional development and advanced study of qualified and experienced counsellors and therapists with an emphasis on the distinctiveness, similarities and contrasts between different theoretical approaches.

*Subject to validation.

For further information contact Admissions on 01707 284800 or Admissions@herts.ac.uk

---

Star System: * Introductory course only • ** 2-3 yr pt-time course to Cert/Dip level •
*** Professional development for trained counsellors
For added help, see section 'Essential Information for Students', page 1

UNIVERSITY OF WALES COLLEGE, NEWPORT

COLEG PRIFYSGOL CYMRU, CASNEWYDD

DEPARTMENT OF HEALTH & SOCIAL CARE

POSTGRADUATE COUNSELLING PROGRAMME

POSTGRADUATE CERTIFICATE IN COUNSELLING SKILLS
(Stage 1)

Tuesdays – Full day over one year 9.30 – 4.30 p.m.
Or evening over 2 years

POSTGRADUATE DIPLOMA IN COUNSELLING
(Stage 2)
Wednesday Full day over one year 9.30 – 4.30 p.m.

MA IN COUNSELLING (Cognitive Behavioural)
(Stage 3)
Full day over one year (plus 6 months dissertation) 9.30 – 4.30 p.m.

ENTRY:　　**Stage 1:** Professional qualifications and/or degree and experience in the helping field. Some exceptions. Minimum age 25 years.
　　　　　　Stage 2: University of Wales Certificate in Counselling or equivalent. APA criteria apply
　　　　　　Stage 3: University of Wales Diploma in Counselling or equivalent. APA criteria apply.

Selection Process:　　By interview and references for all stages. Certificate students have to write a short essay.

FOR AN APPLICATION FORM AND PROSPECTUS
Contact the Information Centre on (01633) 432432. E mail : uic@newport.ac.uk

Please send your completed application form to the University Information Centre. All applicants are interviewed for the courses as long as places are available. Interviews for all stages of the course take place after Easter. Please apply early for the stage of the course in which you are interested and bear in mind that most places for the Diploma stage tend to be filled by the end of July.

Star System: * Introductory course only • ** 2-3 yr pt-time course to Cert/Dip level •
*** Professional development for trained counsellors
For added help, see section 'Essential Information for Students', page 1

81

UNIVERSITY OF WALES COLLEGE, NEWPORT

COLEG PRIFYSGOL CYMRU, CASNEWYDD

University of Wales Postgraduate Certificate and Diploma in Mediation

Recognising the need for trained and credibly qualified professionals in this emerging and important field, UWCN is pleased to be offering this programme on a one day a week basis in the *Department of Health and Social Care at Newport.* The Department is already very well known for its Counselling and Social Welfare Courses which have an excellent pedigree.

The new Mediation course combines a solid grounding in the skills and strategies of mediation with a strong academic, ethical and theoretical base. There is, we believe, no existing comparable programme which provides this combination designed to enable professionals to initiate and implement appropriate mediation interventions to facilitate effective and lasting change.

Who should do it ?

Those who use mediation as part of their job and/or who wish to develop in this field. Particularly relevant professions include the Law, Police, Arbitrators, Conciliators, Housing, Probation/ Social work, Human Resources, Trade Union officials, Health workers, Local government officers, Teachers.

The Postgraduate Certificate in Mediation (£990) is achievable in 9 months *(one day a week)* and may be used as a qualification in its own right or as a stepping stone to the **Postgraduate Diploma in Mediation** (£990) which requires a further 9 months of study *(ie 18 months at one day a week in total).* *Some bursaries are available to those in need. Fees are waived for the unemployed and group discounts are available for more than one student who comes from the same organisation.*

Admissions : Normal postgraduate rules apply. A degree in Law or the Social sciences is preferred. Mature students with 2 or more years relevant experience may also apply. Students need to be mature and open to self development both personally and professionally. All applicants are interviewed and final entry is on the professional recommendation of the tutor. References must also be supplied.

For further information, a brochure and an application form please apply to University Information Centre, UWCN **01633 432829**. **E mail :** uic@newport.ac.uk

You may also speak directly with the Course Tutor **Mr Graham Waddington** on 01633 432520 *(Mondays to Wednesdays only).* E-mail : graham.waddington@newport.ac.uk

Star System: * Introductory course only • ** 2-3 yr pt-time course to Cert/Dip level •
*** Professional development for trained counsellors
For added help, see section 'Essential Information for Students', page 1

82

CAROLE SPIERS ASSOCIATES
International Occupational Stress Management Consultancy

ISMA validated
trainer

NATIONWIDE IN-HOUSE STRESS MANAGEMENT TRAINING & COUNSELLING SERVICES

STRESS MANAGEMENT	*EMPLOYEE COUNSELLING*
? Corporate consultancy ? Training the Trainers ? Strategy/policy/procedure ? Audits ? Impartial investigations/Mediation	? Employee Assistance Programmes ? Consultancy ? Telephone/face-to-face stress counselling ? In-house First Contact Counselling Teams
HARASSMENT/BULLYING IN THE WORKPLACE	*POST TRAUMA SUPPORT AND MANAGEMENT*
? Strategy/policy/procedures ? Counselling – training ? First Contact Counselling Teams ? Impartial investigations	? Counselling – Training ? Expert Witness Critical Incident/ Psychological Debriefing Management

**Gordon House,
83-85 Gordon Ave,
Stanmore Middx
HA7 3QR**

**Tel: 020 89541593
Fax: 020 89079290
Email:
CSA@stress.org.uk
Web:
www.stress.org.uk/csa**

*Star System: * Introductory course only • ** 2-3 yr pt-time course to Cert/Dip level •*
*** Professional development for trained counsellors*
For added help, see section 'Essential Information for Students', page 1

83

The Manor House Centre for Psychotherapy and Counselling

IS PSYCHODYNAMIC COUNSELLING TRAINING FOR ME?
One-day workshops to experience the psychodynamic model of counselling.

CERTIFICATE IN COUNSELLING SKILLS
Part-time Counselling Skills Course, enabling people working in the community in whatever capacity, to attain and maintain effective and creative relationships.

DIPLOMA IN PSYCHODYNAMIC COUNSELLING AND THERAPY IN THE COMMUNITY
An established three year vocational training course based on Psychoanalytic constructs offering both practical and theoretical components. ACCREDITED BY THE BRITISH ASSOCIATION FOR COUNSELLING.

ADVANCED DIPLOMA IN COUNSELLING AND THERAPY
A one year part-time Course for experienced counsellors who wish to receive the MHCPC Advanced Diploma.

TRAINING COURSES

THE THEORY AND PRACTICE OF PSYCHODYNAMIC THERAPY
For practitioners of Humanistic Psychology who are interested in the understanding of psychodynamic practice.

SHORT COURSES
Specialist ten-week Courses for Counselling graduates. Topics include:
• Advanced Skills
• Mother and Infant Relationship
• Loss and Bereavement

ADVANCED SUPERVISION GROUPS
Daytime or evening, ongoing supervision for graduates.

For Prospectus send a self-addressed 39p stamped envelope (23cm x 16cm) to The Co-ordinator of Courses MHCPC, 80 East End Road London N3 2SY Tel: 0208 371 0180   Fax: 01708 620858   Registered Charity No. 1054223

*Star System: * Introductory course only ● ** 2-3 yr pt-time course to Cert/Dip level ●*
*** Professional development for trained counsellors*
For added help, see section 'Essential Information for Students', page 1

84

PSYCHOSYNTHESIS UK,   01273 473113
LEWES, BN7 2QP,
Venues in London & West Yorkshire
Please see full entry in Sussex

BRITISH PSYCHO-ANALYTICAL SOCIETY,   020 7580 4952/3/4
Mansfield House, 63 New Cavendish Street, LONDON, W1M 7RD,
No response received to our enquiries for 2000, entry details as of November 2000

** **Training in the Psychoanalysis of Adults & Children**

CENTRE FOR PROFESSIONAL DEVELOPMENT,   0171 209 6592
University College London, Gower Street, LONDON, WC1E 6BT,
No response received to our enquiries for 2000, entry details as of Nov 1998

** **Diploma in Forensic Psychotherapeutic Studies** (in assoc. with Portman Clinic) (UCL)

GESTALT COUNSELLING CENTRE LONDON,   020 7613 4480
62 Paul Street, LONDON, EC2A 4NA,
Member of UKCP. Also offers introductory counselling skills workshops.

* **1) Counselling Skills Certificate**

Duration	Modular, comprising: Foundation — 15 weeks, Gestalt in Action — 5 weeks, Loss & Bereavement — 10 weeks
Entry	Anyone using counselling skills, Foundation course for Diploma in Counselling
Core Model	Gestalt

** **2) Diploma in Counselling with Gestalt as the core model (BAC Accredited)**

Core Model	Gestalt
Duration	2 years, part-time, 1 evening/week + 4 full weekend days/term (450 hrs) then entry to 4) is possible
Entry	Those who have completed 1) or equivalent and working in the caring profession, business or voluntary

continued...

*Star System: * Introductory course only • ** 2-3 yr pt-time course to Cert/Dip level •
*** Professional development for trained counsellors*
For added help, see section 'Essential Information for Students', page 1

85

** **3) Advanced Professional Diploma in Gestalt Studies** (UNL validated — confirmation pending)

Core Model	Gestalt
Duration	36 weeks, part-time, 1 evening/week + 6 weekends
Entry	Min. age 25, relevant professional/voluntary experience, interview

** **4) Gestalt Psychotherapy — Post Graduate Certificate Course**

Core Model	Gestalt
Duration	36 weeks, part-time, 1 evening/week + 6 weekends
Entry	Completion of 3) or similar

** **5) Gestalt Psychotherapy — Post Graduate Diploma Course**

Core Model	Gestalt
Duration	36 weeks, part-time, 1 evening/week + 6 weekends
Entry	Completion of 4) or similar

** **6) MA in Psychotherapy** (Univ of North London)

Core Model	Gestalt
Duration	2 years, part-time, evening, afternoons & weekends OR 19 months modular, 2-3 day sessions/month
Entry	Completion of 5) or similar
Apply To:	A McDonald, Administrator

GUILD OF PSYCHOTHERAPISTS,　　　　0181 540 4454
47 Nelson Square, LONDON, SE1 0QA,

** **Psychotherapy Training in Central London**

Duration	4 years, part-time, 1 evening/week. Leads to UKCP registration
Entry	Over 30, minimum of 1 year, twice weekly personal individual psychotherapy with an appropriate psychoanalytical psychotherapist prior to application; some experience of working with psychologically disturbed people.
Apply To:	Marion Holt

LONDON MARRIAGE GUIDANCE COUNCIL,　　　020 7580 1087
76a New Cavendish Street, Harley Street, LONDON, W1M 7LB,
No response received to our enquiries for 2000, entry details as of November 1998

* **1) The Foundation Course**

** **2) Diploma Course in Psychodynamic Marital & Couple Counselling (BAC Acc; Roehampton Inst)**

*Star System:　* Introductory course only ● ** 2-3 yr pt-time course to Cert/Dip level ●*
*** *Professional development for trained counsellors*
For added help, see section 'Essential Information for Students', page 1

86

***   **3) Diploma in Psychosexual Marital & Couple Counselling** (BASMT approved)

***   **4) Post Graduate Certificate Course in Psychodynamic Marital & Couple Counselling**

PSYCHOTHERAPY CENTRE, THE,   **0171 723 6173**
1 Wythburn Place, LONDON, W1H 5WL,
No response received to our enquiries for 2000. Entry details as of Nov 1998

**   **Psychotherapy**

UNIVERSITY OF WESTMINSTER,   **0171 911 5000 X 2142**
309 Regent Street, LONDON, W1R 8AL,
No response received to our enquiries for 2000. Entry details as of Nov 1998

*   **1) Introductory Certificate in Counselling: Helping Relationships**

**   **2) Certificate Course in Counselling: The Skilled Helper**

**   **3) Diploma in Counselling Skills**

---

*Star System: * Introductory course only • ** 2-3 yr pt-time course to Cert/Dip level •*
*** Professional development for trained counsellors
For added help, see section 'Essential Information for Students', page 1

87

NEWHAM COLLEGE OF FURTHER EDUCATION,   020 8257 4000
FAX 020 8257 4307

Counselling Department, East Ham Campus, High St South, LONDON, E6 6ER,

♿ Access for disabled people and disability & learning support

*   1) Certificate in Integrative Counselling (North East London Access Federation, OCN)

Core Model	Integrative
Duration	5 hrs/week for 34 weeks
Entry	No formal requirements but over 21; initial interview & assessed piece of writing

**   2) Diploma in Integrative Counselling (NELAF, OCN)

Core Model	Integrative
Duration	5 hrs for 34 weeks
Entry	1) above or equivalent
Apply To:	Hugh Clarke

THE PHOENIX CENTRE,   020 8530 8198 ALSO FAX

Bressey Lodge, Bressey Grove, South Woodford, LONDON, E18 2HP,

In-house/tailor made training offerd; also workshops in counselling/counselling skills

♿ Limited access to ground floor lecture rooms and toilet facilities

**   Certificate in Counselling

Duration	360 hrs
Entry	Selection by interview and seminar

**   Diploma in Counselling

Duration	1055 hrs
Entry	Successful completion of certificate level training also selection by interview and Seminar
Apply To:	Jeanette March
Core Model	Integrative using Egan as Core

TOWER HAMLETS COLLEGE,   0171 538 5888

Poplar High Street, LONDON, E14 0AF,

No response received to our enquiries for 2000, entry details as of November 1998

*   1) Introduction to Counselling Skills (Certificate of Attendance)

*   2) RSA Certificate in Counselling Skills

Star System: * Introductory course only • ** 2-3 yr pt-time course to Cert/Dip level •
*** Professional development for trained counsellors
For added help, see section 'Essential Information for Students', page 1

88

** 4) Advanced Diploma in Counselling & Psychotherapy

UNIVERSITY OF EAST LONDON,   020 8590 7722
Dept of Psychology, Romford Road, Stratford, LONDON, E15 4LZ,
2/3 day short courses available eg Basic & Advanced Counselling Skills & Supervision

♿ Toilets with access for disabled people, stairs with handrails, lifts, parking by arrangement, Disability Unit to advise on learning & teaching & to provide support

** 1) Postgraduate Diploma in Therapeutic Counselling (Integrative) (BAC Acc)

Duration	2 years, part-time, 1 afternoon & eve/week + 2 residential weekends/year
Entry	Introductory training, relevant work experience, degree/equivalent professional qualification, own counselling &/or personal growth work, interview(s) + written excercise
Core Model	Integrative
Apply To:	Rowan Bayne, Admissions Tutor

** 2) MSc Counselling Psychology

Duration	2 years, part-time, 1 day/week (October start)
Entry	Psychology degree, basic skills training & experience in counselling
Apply To:	Jill Mytton, Admissions Tutor

*** 3) MA Counselling & Psychotherapy

Duration	1 year, part-time, 1 eve/week, peer study groups as negotiated
Entry	Completed BAC or UKCP accredited course/equivalent
Apply To:	Tony Merry, Admissions Tutor

WALTHAM FOREST ADULT EDUCATION SERVICE,
0181 539 7205
Davis Centre, 192 Vicarage Road, Leyton, LONDON, E10 5DX,
No response received to our enquiries for 2000. Entry details as of Nov 1998

* 1) Introduction to Counselling Skills

* 2) RSA Certificate Counselling Skills in the Development of Learning

Star System: ** Introductory course only • ** 2-3 yr pt-time course to Cert/Dip level •*
*** Professional development for trained counsellors
For added help, see section 'Essential Information for Students', page 1

89

WALTHAM FOREST COLLEGE,   0181 527 2311 X 4267

The Library, Forest Road, LONDON, E17 4JB,
No response received to our enquiries for 2000, entry details as of November 1998

*   **1) Introduction to Basic Counselling Skills**

*   **2) Psychosynthesis Fundamentals**

*   **3) Foundation Course in Psychosynthesis**

*   **4) RSA Certificate in Counselling Skills in the Development of Learning**

*   **5) Certificate in Counselling Skills** (CSCT/AEB)

*   **6) Certificate in Counselling Theory** (CSCT/AEB)

*   **7) Neuro-Linguistic Programming for Professional & Personal Development**

**   **8) Diploma in Counselling** (CSCT/AEB)

**   **9) Diploma in Intercultural Counselling** (Core Model Psychosynthesis)

Star System: * Introductory course only • ** 2-3 yr pt-time course to Cert/Dip level •
*** Professional development for trained counsellors
For added help, see section 'Essential Information for Students', page 1

90

ASSOCIATION FOR GROUP & INDIVIDUAL PSYCHOTHERAPY
0171 272 7013

1 Fairbridge Road, LONDON, N19 3EW,
No response received to our enquiries for 2000, entry details as of November 1998

** **Training in Psychoanalytical Psychotherapy** (Assoc/Full Membership of AGIP)

ASSOCIATION OF INDEPENDENT PSYCHOTHERAPISTS
0171 700 1911

PO Box 1194, LONDON, N6 5PW,

** **Psychotherapy Training**

Duration | 4-8 yrs, part-time, 1 eve/week for 3 yrs, 1 eve/month thereafter + individual & group supervision
Entry | Written application, 2 interviews, previous counselling experience/ training, personal therapy at least twice/week, aged 30-60
Apply To: | Training Co-ordinators

BARNET COLLEGE,
0181 361 5101 X 381

Russell Lane, LONDON, N20 0AX,

♿ Disabled Access, Learning Support

* **1) On Becoming a Counsellor**
Duration | 8 evenings, 2 hrs/week
Apply To: | Mary Williamson

* **2) Foundation Programme in Counselling** (LOCF)
Duration | 85 hours part-time
Apply To: | Social Studies Support Officer

* **3) RSA Certificate in Counselling Skills in the Development of Learning**
Duration | 102 hrs, part-time, 0.5 day or eve/week (2 intakes/year)
Entry | By interview for those interested in developing counselling skills for professional or personal development.

4) Intermediate Year
Duration | Eve 105 hrs
Entry | Foundation Course or RSA Counselling Skills or equivalent. Interviews and personal statement

continued...

---

*Star System: * Introductory course only • ** 2-3 yr pt-time course to Cert/Dip level •*
*** Professional development for trained counsellors*
For added help, see section 'Essential Information for Students', page 1

91

** **5) Diploma in Professional Development in Counselling** (Psychodynamic) (Univ of North London)

Duration	2 years, part-time, either all day or afternoon and evening (annual intake)
Entry	Those who have completed the Intermediate Year or equivalent, over 22 years of age, selection by personal statement and interview
Apply To:	Mary Williamson and Jenny Riddell
Core Model:	Psychodynamic

CITY & ISLINGTON COLLEGE,   0171 700 8600
444 Camden Road, LONDON, N7 0SP,
No response received to our enquiries for 2000, entry details as of November 1998

*   **1) Certificate in Counselling Skills** (CPCAB)

*   **2) Certificate in Therapeutic Counselling**

**   **3) Advanced Certificate in Counselling** (CPCAB)

**   **4) Diploma in Counselling** (CPCAB)

COLLEGE OF NORTH EAST LONDON,   020 8442 3096 X 2717
FAX: 0181 442 3091
Tottenham Green Centre, Townhall Approach Road, LONDON, N15 4RX,

*   **1) Introduction to Basic Counselling Skills**

Duration	12 weeks, 3 hours/week, evening
Entry	Anyone with an interest in/using counselling skills

*   **2) Certificate in Counselling Skills in the Development of Learning**

Duration	32 weeks, part-time, 1 afternoon or evening/week
Entry	Candidates should be using counselling skills in some form of paid or voluntary work; selection by interview

**   **3) Diploma in Counselling** (BAC Acc)

Duration	Modular, minimum 2 years, part-time, day
Entry	Completion of 2) or equivalent and have a formal counselling role in their work; selection by interview.
Apply To:	Sharon Roughan, Lecturer in Counselling

---

*Star System: * Introductory course only • ** 2-3 yr pt-time course to Cert/Dip level •*
*** Professional development for trained counsellors*
For added help, see section 'Essential Information for Students', page 1

92

CPPD SCHOOL OF COUNSELLING LTD,   020 8829 9419
33 Thorald Road, Bowes Park, LONDON, N22 4YE,
In-house/tailor-made training, workshops in counselling and counselling skills

**   **1) Certificate in Humanistic Integrative Counselling**

Duration	120 hrs, 30 weeks, 3.5hrs/week evenings + one weekend
Entry	First degree or relevant previous training or equivalent suitable life experience

***   **2) Diploma in Humanistic Integrative Counselling**

Duration	180 hrs, 30 weeks, 3.5hrs/week evenings + 3 weekends + supervision
Entry	Previous counselling training of 120 hrs + 50 hrs personal development work + an ability to accumulate 120 client hours

***   **3) Advanced Diploma in Humanistic Integrative Counselling (BAC Acc)**

Duration	175 hours, 30 weeks, 3.5 hrs/week evenings + Introductory weekend + 3 additional training days
Entry	Counselling or Psychotherapy training of 290 hours + 50 hours personal development work + 120 hours of client work

***   **4) Diploma in Clinical Supervision**

Duration	130 hours, 9 weekends throughout the year
Entry	For supervisors of counsellors/psychotherapists and other professionals who carry a supervisory role
Apply To:	Lynne Kaye

HARINGEY HEALTHCARE NHS TRUST,   0181 442 6528
                                         FAX: 0181 442 6545
Psychotherapy Department, St Ann's Hospital, St Ann's Road, LONDON, N15 3TH,
No response received to our enquiries for 2000, entry details as of Nov 1998

*   **The Therapeutic Relationship — An Introduction to the Pschodynamic Approach** (North London Univ)

HIGHGATE COUNSELLING CENTRE,   020 8883 5427/8
Tetherdown Halls, Tetherdown, Muswell Hill, LONDON, N10 1ND,
No response received to our enquiries for 2000. Entry details as of Nov 1998

**   **Diploma in Psychodynamic Counselling (BAC Acc)** (includes an addiction counselling options)

Star System: * Introductory course only • ** 2-3 yr pt-time course to Cert/Dip level •
*** Professional development for trained counsellors
For added help, see section 'Essential Information for Students', page 1

93

INSTITUTE OF PSYCHOTHERAPY & SOCIAL STUDIES
0171 284 4762

37 Ashbourne Avenue, LONDON, NW11 0DT,
In-house training

♿ Regrettably the current premises are not suitable for wheelchair users, otherwise committed to equality of opportunity to all sections of the community

*　　**1) Exploring Psychotherapy**
Duration　　　1 year, part-time
Entry　　　　For people who wish to develop a basic understanding of
　　　　　　Psychoanalytic Psychotherapy, selection by intervies

**　　**2) MA/Diploma in Psychoanalytic Psychotherapy & Social Studies**
　　　　(Graduates eligible for UKCP registration)
Duration　　　4 yrs, part-time
Entry　　　　Graduate or equivalent, relevant experience, personal twice-weekly
　　　　　　therapy prior to and throughout the course, 2 interviews

**　　**3) MA in Group Analytic Psychotherapy and Social Studies** (inc. Dip in
　　　　Psychoanalytic Psychotherapy)
Duration　　　3 yrs, part-time
Entry　　　　Graduate or equivalent, relevant experience, personal twice-weekly
　　　　　　therapy prior to and throughout the course, 2 interviews

**　　**4) MA in Psychoanalytic & Social Studies** (non-clinical course)
Duration　　　3 yrs, part-time
Entry　　　　Graduate or equivalent, relevant experience, personal twice-weekly
　　　　　　therapy prior to and throughout the course
Apply To:　　Admissions Secretary, IPSS

ITS (INTERNATIONAL TEACHING SEMINARS),　　020 7247 0252
FAX 020 7247 0242
E-MAIL ITS@NLP-COMMUNITY.COM
WWW.NLP-COMMUNITY.COM

19 Widegate Street, LONDON, E1 7HP,

*　　**1) First Principles of NLP**
Duration　　　3 days
Entry　　　　Open

Star System:　* Introductory course only ● ** 2-3 yr pt-time course to Cert/Dip level ●
*** Professional development for trained counsellors
For added help, see section 'Essential Information for Students', page 1

94

*   **2) NLP Practitioner Programme**

Duration   20 days in 5 x 4day modules
Entry   Open
Apply To: Ian McDermott, Director of Training

LONDON ASSOCIATION OF PRIMAL PSYCHOTHERAPISTS
0171 267 9616 FAX 0171 482 0858

West Hill House, 6 Swains Lane, LONDON, N6 6QU,

**   **Diploma in Primal Psychotherapy** (UKCP)

Duration   4 yrs, part-time, 2 eves/week + occasional weekend
Entry   First degree or professional qualification in a related field
Apply To: Marsha Nodelman, Training Co-ordinator

MANOR HOUSE CENTRE FOR PSYCHOTHERAPY & COUNSELLING
0208 371 0180
FAX 01708 620 858

80 East End Road, LONDON, N3 2SY,

*   **1) Certificate in Counselling Skills**

Duration   30 weeks, part-time, day or evening — 3 hrs/week
Entry   All interested in improving communication; selection by interview

**   **2) Diploma in Psychodynamic Counselling & Therapy in the Community — Modules 1, 2 & 3 (BAC Acc)**

Core Model   Psychodynamic
Duration   Each module consists of minimum 1 year (30 weeks), 8.5 hrs/week, 1 evening/1day (450 hrs theory + 405 hrs practice)
Entry   Completion of 1)/similar; basic understanding of counselling skills; commitment to own emotional development; selection by interview for entry to Module 1 or 2

***   **3) Advanced Diploma in Counselling & Therapy**

Duration   30 weeks, 3x10 academic terms; seven hrs/week
Entry   By selection. Graduates of psychodynamic counselling courses and/or experienced counsellors seeking individual accreditation

***   **4) Advanced Supervision Groups**

Duration   30 weeks each year, 2 hrs/week
Entry   For those who have completed 2) or similar

continued...

Star System: * *Introductory course only* • ** *2-3 yr pt-time course to Cert/Dip level* •
*** *Professional development for trained counsellors*
For added help, see section 'Essential Information for Students', page 1

95

***　5) The Theory and Practice of Psychodynamic Practice

Duration	Please contact the Centre for details
Entry	For practitioners of Humanistic Psychology who are interested in the understanding of psychodynamic practice
Core Model	Psychodynamic
Apply To:	The Course Administrator

SOUTH BANK UNIVERSITY,　　　　　0171 288 3074

School of Counselling &, Psychotherapy, St Mary's Wing, Highgate Hill, LONDON, N19 5NF,

No response received to our enquiries for 2000. Entry details as of 1998

*　1) Certificate in Counselling (Reg. ICM)

**　2) Diploma in Humanistic Counselling (Reg.ICM, South Bank Univ)

**　3) PG Diploma + MSc in Psychotherapy or Psychosexual Therapy (BASMT approved)

SPECTRUM,　　　　　0181 341 2277 FAX 0181 340 0426

7 Endymion Road, Finsbury Park, LONDON, N4 1EE,

Also offers workshops in Gestalt, Child Sexual Abuse, etc. Member of Humanistic & Integrative Section of UKCP

♿ Limited access to building, adapted toilet, dining/waiting room area + one workshop room on lower ground floor

**　1) Foundation Course in Counselling Skills (Certificate)

Duration	1 year, part-time in 3 terms, 1 day/week + 2 x 3 day workshops (180 hrs)
Entry	By interview, for those interested in counselling, including business, voluntary & statutory organisations

**　2) Post-graduate Training in Psychotherapy

Duration	Minimum 3 yrs, part-time, modular course, day/eve/weekend (Leads to UKCP registration)
Entry	By interview
Apply To:	Training Administrator

**　3) One Year Course in Psychotherapy

Duration	1 yr, 35 weekdays over 3 terms (210 hrs)
Entry	Selection by interview

Star System:　* Introductory course only ● ** 2-3 yr pt-time course to Cert/Dip level ●
*** Professional development for trained counsellors

For added help, see section 'Essential Information for Students', page 1

*** 4) Pairs: Practical Application of Intimate Relationship Skills

Duration	100 hrs, 2 terms x 8 eves + 2 weekends
Entry	By application

*** 5) Working with Surivivors of Incest & Sexual Abuse

Duration	6 days, (36 hrs)
Entry	Selection by interview
Apply To:	Oriel Methuen

THE SITE FOR CONTEMPORARY PSYCHOANALYSIS, 0181 374 5934

3 Pilgrims Place, LONDON, NW3 1NG,

** Training in Contemporary Psychoanalysis (UKCP, Psychonalytic Section)

Duration	Min 4 yrs part-time, one evening/week + 1 non-residential w/end. Entry Oct & Jan
Entry	Selection by three interviews, one year personal analysis, relevant work experience and prior learning at graduate level or equivalent
Apply To:	The Secretary, 0181 374 5934

UNIVERSITY COLLEGE LONDON, 0171 263 4130

Nafsiyat, 278 Seven Sisters Road, LONDON, N4 2HY,

No response received to our enquiries for 2000. Entry details as of Nov 1998

** MSc in Intercultural Therapy (London Univ)

UNIVERSITY OF NORTH LONDON, 0171 7537005

166-220 Holloway Road, LONDON, N7 8DB,

Tailor-made training available for organisations inc. voluntary sector. Workshops in counselling skills

♿ Dedicated disabilities Service offering a range of information, facilities+ support eg Needs Assessment consultation, specialist equipment/resources, advice on allowances, adapted rooms etc

* 1) Diploma in Professional Development: Counselling Skills + Perspectives

Duration	1 eve/week + 4 Saturdays/year
Entry	Relevant to professionals & volunteers involved in direct work with people, also those intending to train as a professional counsellor
Apply To:	Jane Stavert, Course Director

continued...

---

*Star System: * Introductory course only • ** 2-3 yr pt-time course to Cert/Dip level •*
*** *Professional development for trained counsellors*
For added help, see section 'Essential Information for Students', page 1

97

** **2) Postgraduate Diploma in Integrative Counselling** (incorporating Person-Centred/Psychodynamic)

Duration	2 years, 1 afternoon + eve/week, 2 hrs supervision grp/fortnight, half day placement/week, 3 Saturdays/year
Entry	100 hrs counselling training, degree or substantial related experience, emotional maturity, paid or unpaid work experience involving use of counselling/interpersonal skills, aged 25+
Apply To:	Paula Collens/Jane Stavert, Course Directors

WOMEN'S THERAPY CENTRE,   0171 263 7860
10 Manor Gardens, Holloway, LONDON, N7 6JS,

Offers a variety of short courses connected with women's issues eg: domestic violence, cross cultural work, incest etc.

♿ Entry ramp for wheelchairs, adapted toilet, supportive staff

* **1) Working with Women**

Duration	5x1.5 hrs sessions (7.5 hrs)
Entry	For women, working in roles which require an understanding of issues influencing women's psychology
Apply To:	Marion Gow

* **2) Containing the Secret**

Duration	2 days, weekend
Entry	For women working with incest survivors

* **3) Working with Women — A Psychodynamic Approach**

Duration	1 year, 30 weeks (90 hrs)
Entry	Aimed at women working in th helping professions including those practising psychotherapy
Apply To:	Abi Franses

---

*Star System: * Introductory course only • ** 2-3 yr pt-time course to Cert/Dip level •*
*** Professional development for trained counsellors*

For added help, see section 'Essential Information for Students', page 1

98

AN-NISA SOCIETY, 0181 838 2882

BACES, 1 Morland Gardens, Hillside, LONDON, NW10,

No response received to our enquiries for 2000. Entry details as of Nov 1998

*   **1) Islamic Counselling Course — Stage 1**

***   **2) Work Discussion Seminars on Therapeutic Work with Asylum Seekers & Refugees**

ANNA FREUD CENTRE, 0171 794 2313
FAX: 0171 794 6506
CRESSIDA.STEVENS@ANNAFREUD.ORG

21 Maresfield Gardens, Hampstead, LONDON, NW3 5SH,

The course is designed for qualification in child psychoanalysis/psychotherapy

♿ Unfortunately there is no easy wheelchair access to the building

***   **Psychoanalytic Study & Treatment of Children & Adolescents** (The Assoc. of Child Psychotherapists)

Duration	Approximately 2 afternoons and 2 evenings/week + time for clinical work, over 4-5 yrs
Entry	An honours degree in psychology (or other equivalent subject) + experience of working with children and adolescents.
Apply To:	Cressida Stevens, Training Secretary

ARBOURS ASSOCIATION, 0181 341 0916
FAX: 0181 341 5822

6 Church Lane, LONDON, N8 7BU,

**   **Certificate in Psychoanalytic Psychotherapy**

Duration	3 years, part-time (January start)
Entry	At postgraduate level of competence and upon completion of the one year Associate Training Programme
Apply To:	Courses Administrator

Star System: * Introductory course only • ** 2-3 yr pt-time course to Cert/Dip level •
*** Professional development for trained counsellors
For added help, see section 'Essential Information for Students', page 1

99

BRENT ADULT & COMMUNITY EDUCATION SERVIC,
0181 838 2882

1 Morland Gardens, LONDON, NW10 8DY

♿ Wheelchair access, disabled toliets, induction loops

*   **1) Counselling Introductory**
Duration   10 weeks, part-time evening
Entry   None stated

*   **2) Certificate in Counselling — Stage 1** (CPCAB) C501
Duration   30 weeks, part-time, 3hrs/wk, daytime or evening or Sunday
Entry   None stated

*   **3) Islamic Counselling — Introductory Stage 1** (CPCAB) C501
Duration   15 weeks, 6 hrs/week + workshops, Sunday

*   **4) Counselling Skills NCFE 3701/2**
Duration   20 weeks 2hrs/week + workshops, evening
Entry   None stated

**   **5) Certificate in Therapeutic Counselling — Stage 2** (CPCAB) TC01
Duration   30 weeks, 3 hrs/week + workshops, evenings and daytime
Entry   Prior training/experience in counselling

**   **6) Certificate in Therapeutic Counselling — Advanced Stage** (CPCAB) TC02
Duration   30 weeks, 3hrs/week (Sundays) + workshops
Entry   Completion of earlier stages

**   **7) Islamic Counselling — Stage 2** (CPCAB) TC01
Duration   15 weeks, 6 hrs/week + workshops, Sunday
Entry   Prior training/experience in Islamic Counselling
Apply To: Courses Co-ordinator

Star System: * Introductory course only • ** 2-3 yr pt-time course to Cert/Dip level •
*** Professional development for trained counsellors

For added help, see section 'Essential Information for Students', page 1

100

BRITISH ASSOCIATION OF PSYCHOTHERAPISTS,   0181 452 9823
FAX: 0181 452 5182

37 Mapesbury Road, LONDON, NW2 4HJ,

♿ Wheel chair access, kitchen and lavatory facilities

*   1) Trauma and Abuse Seminars

Duration	2 terms, weekly seminars (starts Jan 2000)
Entry	Those with a background in social work, medicine, psychology, community care or related profession
Apply To:	External Courses Secretary

*   2) Therapeutic Communication with Children & Adolescents

Duration	2 terms, weekly seminars
Entry	For professionals wanting to understand the contribution psychoanalysis can make to the inner world of the child

*   3) Jungian Thoughts in a modern World

Duration	1 term, 12 weekly seminars
Entry	Basic knowledge of Jung

**   4) Diploma/MSc Psychodynamic of Human Development

Duration	Diploma: 1 year, part-time MSc: 2 years, part-time (seminars, dissertation, infant observation) 1 afternoon or evening/wk
Entry	Those with a background in social work, community care, primary care, or related profession
Apply To:	MSc Secretary

***   5) Jungian Dream Workshops

Duration	6 workshops held monthly
Entry	Professionals wanting to deepen their understanding of dreamwork

***   6) Infant Observation Seminars: A Jungian Approach

Duration	2 years, weekly seminars
Entry	Professionals considering training or wishing to develop skills

***   7) Training in Adult Individual Psychotherapy

Duration	Minimum 4 years, part-time, evenings
Entry	Degree in medicine, psychology or social science and experience of working with disturbed people. Own personal therapy required throughout training.

continued...

Star System: * Introductory course only • ** 2-3 yr pt-time course to Cert/Dip level •
*** Professional development for trained counsellors
For added help, see section 'Essential Information for Students', page 1

101

*** 8) Training in Child & Adolescent Psychotherapy

Duration	Minimum of 4 years
Entry	Degree in medicine, psychology or social science and experience of working with disturbed people. Own personal therapy required throughout training
Apply To:	Secretary

CENTRE FOR ATTACHMENT-BASED PSYCHOANALYTIC PSYCHOTHERAPY　　　　　0171 794 4306

12a Nassington Road, LONDON, NW3 2UD,

No response received to our enquiries for 2000, entry details as of November 1998

** Training in Attachment-Based Psychoanalytic Psychoanalytic Psychotherapy (Emphasis on the Traumatised Child within the Adult) (UKCP)

CENTRE FOR FREUDIAN ANALYSIS & RESEARCH,
0171 267 3003

76 Haverstock Hill, LONDON, NW3 2BE,

No response received to our enquiries for 2000. Entry details as of Nov 1998

* 1) Preliminary Programme in Lacanian Analysis

** 2) Training Programme for Lacanian Analysis

CENTRE FOR PSYCHOANALYTICAL PSYCHOTHERAPY
0181 922 8551

538 Finchley Road, Golders Green, LONDON, NW11 8DD,

In-house/tailor-made training

** 1) Training in Adult Psychoanalytic Psychotherapy

Core Model	Psychoanalytical Psychotherapy
Duration	Minimum 360 hrs over minimum 4 years
Entry	Degree or equivalent
Apply To:	Training Adult Psychoanalytic Psychotherapy

Star System: * *Introductory course only* • ** *2-3 yr pt-time course to Cert/Dip level* •
*** *Professional development for trained counsellors*
For added help, see section 'Essential Information for Students', page 1

102

COLLEGE OF NORTH WEST LONDON,   0181 208 5000

Dept of Arts,Community,Leisure, Willesden Centre, Dudden Hill Lane, LONDON, NW10 1DG,

In-house training and wokhops available on request eg: bereavement, assertion etc.

 ♿ Wheelchair access and appropriate support for those with visual/hearing impairment

*   RSA Certificate, Counselling Skills in the Development of Learning

Duration	1 year, part-time, day or evening
Entry	Those who are either employed in a position where they are using counselling skills or be willing to undertake relevant voluntary work
Apply To:	Tricia Mulcahy or Marion Mathura

CONTEXT,   0171 281 0707

91 Fortress Road, Tufnell Park, LONDON, NW5 1AG,
No response received to our enquiries for 2000. Entry details as of Nov 1998

**   Diploma in Psychotherapy & Movement Therapy

HAMPSTEAD GARDEN SUBURB INSTITUTE,   020 8455 9951

Central Square, LONDON, NW11 7BN,

*   Introduction to Counselling

Duration	2 terms, 1 eve/week
Entry	None stated
Apply To:	Course Administrator

HENDON COLLEGE,   0181 200 8300

Health & Care Programme Area, Corner Mead, Colindale, LONDON, NW9 5RA,
No response received to our enquiries for 2000, entry details as of November 1998

*   1) RSA Certificate in Counselling Skills & the Development of Learning

*   2) Introductory Counselling Skills Course (AEB)

**   3) Diploma in Counselling (proposed course for Sept 1999)

Star System: ** Introductory course only* • *** 2-3 yr pt-time course to Cert/Dip level* •
*** Professional development for trained counsellors
For added help, see section 'Essential Information for Students', page 1

103

INSTITUTE OF FAMILY THERAPY,   0171 391 9150
FAX 0171 391 9169
E-MAIL IFT@PSYC.BBK.AC.UK

24-32 Stephenson Way, LONDON, NW1 2HX,

Workshops: 1) Death talk — working with children in death & dying, 2) Working with black families, 3) Eating disorders. Courses 1, 2, 3 & 5 following in conjunction with Birbeck College (Mem UKCP)

♿ Lift and access available

*   1) Certificate in Systemic Practice with Families & Couples -Yr 1

Duration   1 yr, part-time, Tuesday afternoons
Entry   Professional qualification & able to work with families and/or couples during the course

**   2) Certificate in Systemic Practice with Families & Couples — Yr 2

Duration   1 yr part-time, Wednesday afternoons or eves
Entry   Completion of 1) or similar

***   3) MSc in Family & Systemic Psychotherapy

Duration   2 years, part-time, afternoon & eves
Entry   Completion of 2) above or similar

***   4) Advanced Training in the Supervision of Family and Systemic Psychotherapy

Duration   2 yrs, part-time, 2 days/month
Entry   Completion of 3)

***   5) Doctorate in Family and Systemic Psychotherapy

Duration   3 yrs, part-time, overlaps with 4) above for first 2 years
Entry   Completion of 3)
Apply To: The Training Department

INSTITUTE OF GROUP ANALYSIS,   0171 431 2693 FAX
0171 431 7246
WWW.IGALONDON.ORG.UK

1 Daleham Gardens, LONDON, NW3 5BY,

Group analytic/psychotherapy workshops & trainings, Organisational Counsultancy, Clinical Services

*   1) Introductory General Course in Group Analysis

Duration   1 yr part-time, late Thursday afternoon/eve
Entry   For those from a wide range of backgrounds who wish to develop their understanding of working with group analytic concept

---

*Star System: * Introductory course only • ** 2-3 yr pt-time course to Cert/Dip level •*
*** Professional development for trained counsellors
For added help, see section 'Essential Information for Students', page 1

104

*   **2) Work Discussion Seminars**

Duration   1 yr, part-time, afternoons

Entry   For those conducting or leading groups of various kinds, often those on 1) may attend

*   **3) Advanced Work Discussion Seminars**

Duration   At least 1yr part-time

Entry   For those not intending to proceed to any formal training

*   **4) Seminars on Psychotherapy with Severely Disturbed Patients** (Borderline Psychotic, Psychopathic)

Duration   Held Tuesdays, monthly p.m.

Entry   For sharing experiences and gaining knowledge and skills in difficult areas. Participants come from various settings, prisons, young offender institutions, psychiatric hospitals & community centres

*   **5) Seminars on Management & Leadership**

Duration   1 yr, part-time

Entry   Managers & leaders of staff teams

**   **6) London Qualifying Course in Group Analysis & MSc in Group Analysis**

Duration   4 yrs

Entry   Criteria includes completion of 1) or equivalent (leads to Membership of Institute of Group Analysis), as well as the clinical training required for entry to the MSc in Group Analysis at Birkbeck College

**   **7) UK Diploma in Group Analysis** (Proposed Masters)

Duration   4 yrs part-time, block weekends, based in Manchester Group Analysis North

Entry   Please see separate entry for Group Analysis North

Apply To: Course Administrator

INSTITUTE OF PSYCHOSYNTHESIS,   **0181 202 4525**

65a Watford Way, Hendon, LONDON, NW4 3AQ,

No response received to our enquiries for 2000, entry details as of November 1998

**   **PG Dip in Applied Psychosynthesis & Counselling/MA in Psychosynthesis Psychotherapy** (In assoc with Middlesex Univ)

Star System: * *Introductory course only* • ** *2-3 yr pt-time course to Cert/Dip level* •
*** *Professional development for trained counsellors*
For added help, see section 'Essential Information for Students', page 1
105

LONDON CENTRE FOR PSYCHOTHERAPY,   020 7435 2873/5512
32 Leighton Road, LONDON, NW5 2QE,
No response received to our enquiries for 2000, entry details as of November 1998

*   **1) Introduction to Analytical Psychotherapy**

**   **2) Qualifying Course in Psychoanalytic Psychotherapy** (inc Analytical Psychology) (UKCP Analytic Psychotherapy Section)

MINSTER CENTRE,   0207 372 4940
1 Drakes Court Yard, 291 Kilburn High Road, LONDON, NW6 7JR,

♿ Groundfloor access; adapted toilet

**   **1) Introduction to Integrative Psychotherapy & Counselling**

Core Model	Integrative Psychotherapy
Duration	1 year, 3x10 week terms; afternoon & eve/week + 2 weekend workshops (approx 159 contact hours)
Entry	1st degree in any subject, equivalent non-degree professional training, or suitable & equivalent life experience

**   **2) Diploma in Integrative Counselling (BAC Acc)/MA in Integrative Counselling** (Univ of Middlesex)

Core Model	Integrative Counselling
Duration	2 years (3x10 week terms/year) part-time (approx 500 contact hrs). MA: 1 additional year (825 hrs in total)
Entry	Successful completion of the Introductory Course or equivalent

**   **3) Diploma in Integrative Counselling (BAC Acc)/MA in Integrative Psychotherapy** (Univ of Middlesex)

Core Model	Integrative Psychotherapy
Duration	4 years, (3x10 week terms/year) part-time, (approx 950 contact hours)
Entry	Successful completion of the Introductory course/equivalent

***   **4) Diploma in Integrative Group Psychotherapy**

Core Model	Integrative Group Psychotherapy
Duration	130 hrs
Entry	Qualifications in counselling or psychotherapy

***   **5) Diploma in Integrative Supervision**

Core Model	Integrative Supervision
Duration	105 hrs (15 evening sessions & 5 weekends)
Entry	Qualification & experience in counselling or psychotherapy

---

*Star System: * Introductory course only • ** 2-3 yr pt-time course to Cert/Dip level •*
*** Professional development for trained counsellors
For added help, see section 'Essential Information for Students', page 1
106

***   **6) Certificate** (1 yr)/Diploma (2 yrs) Courses in Psychosexual Therapy

Duration	130 hrs/year (3x10 week terms & 3 weekends/year)
Entry	Qualifications in counselling or psychotherapy
Apply To:	The Administrator

PERSON-CENTRED ART THERAPY CENTRE,   0181 455 8570

17 Cranbourne Gardens, LONDON, NW11 0HS,

Courses bringing the Person-Centred counselling approach to the therapeutic use of Art in all areas of human development. Workshops and Supervision in Person-Centred Art Therapy

*   **1) Person-Centred Art Therapy**

Duration	30 weeks, 2hrs/week + 1 full-day/term
Entry	ability to apply course learning to work setting
Core Model	Person Centred

**   **2) Post-Certificate Art Therapy Course**

Duration	30 weeks, 2 hrs/week (60hrs)
Entry	Completion of Certificate Course

***   **3) Course for Trainers in Person-Centred Art Therapy**

Duration	30 weeks, 2hrs/week over 3 terms
Entry	Certificate in Person-Centred Art Therapy and Counselling qualification.
Apply To:	Leisle Silverstone, BAC Fellow

PHILADELPHIA ASSOCIATION LTD,   0171 794 2652

4 Marty's Yard, 17 Hampstead High Street, LONDON, NW3 1QW,

No response received to our enquiries for 2000. Entry details as of Nov 1998

*   **1) Introductory Year in Phenomenology & Psychoanalysis**

**   **2) Training in Psychoanalytic Psychotherapy & Community Therapy** (UKCP Recog)

PORTMAN CLINIC,   0171 794 8262

8 Fitzjohns Avenue, LONDON, NW3 5NA,

No response received to our enquiries for 2000. Entry details as of Nov 1999

*   **1) Forensic Casework — A Psychodynamic Approach**

continued...

*Star System: * Introductory course only • ** 2-3 yr pt-time course to Cert/Dip level •
*** Professional development for trained counsellors*
For added help, see section 'Essential Information for Students', page 1

107

*   **2) Workshop for Probation Officers — Forensic Casework — A Psychodynamic Approach**

*   **3) Child Sexual Abuse within the Family**

***   **4) Diploma in Forensic Psychotherapeutic Studies** (Univ Coll London)

PSYCHOTHERAPY SEMINARS,   0171 813 999 FAX 0171 813 0033

Medical Foundation, Star House, 104-108 Grafton Road, LONDON, NW5 4BD,

♿ Access for disabled people

***   **Work Discussion Seminars on Therapeutic Work with Asylum Seekers & Refugees**

Duration	10 Seminars run fortnightly (Oct-March) Wednesdays 4.30pm — 6.00pm
Entry	Psychotherapists, Family Therapists & Counsellors
Apply To:	Sue Michaelides

RE-VISION,   020 8357 8881

(Centre for Integrative, Psychosynthesis), 97 Brondesbury Road, LONDON, NW6 6RY,

No response received to our enquiries for 2000, entry details as of November 1998

*   **1) Introductory/Foundation Course "The Psychology of Transition"**

**   **2) Integrative Psychosynthesis Counselling Diploma Training (BAC Acc)**

***   **3) Advanced Training in Psychosynthesis Psychotherapy**

REGENTS COLLEGE,   020 7487 7406

School of Psychotherapy & Cllg, Inner Circle, Regent's Park, LONDON, NW1 4NS,

No response received to our enquiries for 2000, entry details as of November 1998

*   **1) Certificate in the Fundamentals of Psychotherapy**

**   **2) Diploma in Psychodynamic Counselling & Psychotherapy (BAC Acc)**

**   **3) Diploma in Existential Psychotherapy & Counselling**

**   **4) BA** (Hons) In Counselling & Mental Health (City Univ)

**   **5) Advanced Diploma in Existential Psychotherapy**

Star System: * Introductory course only • ** 2-3 yr pt-time course to Cert/Dip level •
*** Professional development for trained counsellors
For added help, see section 'Essential Information for Students', page 1

108

**   **6) MA in Psychotherapy & Counselling** (City Univ)

***   **7) MPhil/PhD in Psychotherapy & Counselling** (City Univ)

***   **8) Post-MA Group Supervision Programme** (City Univ)

ROYAL FREE HOSPITAL NHS TRUST,   0171 830 2820

AIDS Counselling Prevention &, Social Care Unit, Clinic 8, Pond Street, LONDON, NW3 2QG,

No response received to our enquiries for 2000. Entry details as of Nov 1998

*   **1) Basic Counselling Skills Course** (Systemic Approach)

*   **2) Intensive One Day AIDS Courses/Workshops on Special Topics**

TAVISTOCK CLINIC,   0171 4357111

120 Belsize Lane, Hampstead, LONDON, NW3 5BA,

The Clinic offers a wide range of training to qualified & experienced people from a wide range of professions. These range from brief intro courses to trainings that lead to higher degrees.

♿ Wheelchair access. Specialised toilets

- -

TAVISTOCK MARITAL STUDIES INSTITUTE,   0171 435 7111 X 2484

Tavistock Centre, 120 Belsize Lane, LONDON, NW3 5BA,

♿ Ramp to building and toilet

*   **1) Effective Staff Supervision**

Duration	4 day block course, held annually (usually July)
Entry	For managers and senior staff in public and voluntary health and welfare service, directly responsible for supervising workers' practice.
Apply To:	Felicia Olney

***   **2) Introduction to Marital Interaction**

Duration	10 sessions, 1.5 hours each
Entry	Practitioners working with, or interested in working with, couples
Apply To:	Avi Shmueli

continued...

Star System: ** Introductory course only • ** 2-3 yr pt-time course to Cert/Dip level •*
*** Professional development for trained counsellors
For added help, see section 'Essential Information for Students', page 1

109

*** 3) Psychological Processes in Divorce

Duration	10 evenings in spring term (27 hours)
Entry	Multi-disciplinary course for practitioners whose work involves contact with divorce related difficulties
Apply To:	Christopher Vincent

*** 4) MA/Postgraduate Diploma/Certificate in the Psychoanalytic study of the Couple Relationship (Univ of East London)

Duration	6x10 week terms, afternoon/evening/week
Entry	Basic Professional qualifications and experience of working with couples
Apply To:	Christopher Vincent

*** 5) Programmes of Study in Couple Psychoanalytic Psychotherapy

Duration	At least 2 evenings/week over 1-5 years depending on programme
Entry	Relevant professional qualifications eg: counselling/social work psychiatry/psychotherapy + post-qualifying experience
Apply To:	Joanna Rosenthall

*** 6) Counsellors Working with Couples in Organisational Settings

Duration	2x10 week terms, 2.75 hrs/week
Entry	Counsellors working in organisational settings, who have a qualification in individual psychodynamic counselling or psychotherapy
Apply To:	Felicia Olney

Star System: ** Introductory course only • ** 2-3 yr pt-time course to Cert/Dip level •*
*** Professional development for trained counsellors
For added help, see section 'Essential Information for Students', page 1

110

ASHBOURNE CENTRE FOR GESTALT TRAINING & PSYCHOTHERAPY   0181 693 1512

19 Ashbourne Grove, LONDON, SE22 8RN,

No response received to our enquiries for 2000, entry details as of November 1998

** **Foundation Course in Gestalt Psychotherapy Training for Women**

AFIWE PEARLS,   0181 6702448

30 Gipsy Rd, West Norwood, LONDON, SE27 9TF,

Venue is to be arranged in London. Counselling skills workshops are also offered

♿ There is a policy to accomodate people and their needs wherever possible.

* **1) Introduction to Counselling** (Cert of Basic Counselling Skills and Personal Awareness)

Duration	60 hrs, in various modules of either weekends, weekdays, evenings or mixed
Entry	None stated

** **2) Stepping Stones — Diploma in Cross-Cultural Counselling and Personal Development**

Duration	2 years, part-time, 1 afternoon and eve/week + 3 weekends and 3 day residential each year
Entry	Training in basic counselling skills/introductory course/equivalent experience

*** **3) Reflections — Diploma in Supervision** (Individual or groups)

Duration	22 weeks/sessions part-time, 1 afternoon and eve/week
Entry	Qualified counsellors with experience in the practice of counselling professionally.

*** **4) Opportunities — Counsellor's Further Training & Development** (Advanced Certificate)

Duration	Various modules of either weekends, weekdays or evenings or mixed
Entry	Qualified counsellor with experience in the practice of counselling professionally
Apply To:	Ramona Sterling, Director

Star System: * Introductory course only • ** 2-3 yr pt-time course to Cert/Dip level •
*** Professional development for trained counsellors
For added help, see section 'Essential Information for Students', page 1

111

BETHLEM ROYAL & MAUDSLEY NHS TRUST,　　0171 919 2815

Denmark Hill, LONDON, SE5 8AZ,
No response received to our enquiries for 2000, entry details as of November 1998

*　　**1) Full-time Pastoral Education** (following the philosophy of Clinical Pastoral Education)

***　　**2) Interdisciplinary Supervision & Consultation Course**

***　　**3) Pastoral Supervision & Consultation**

COMMUNITY EDUCATION LEWISHAM,　　0181 691 5959

Mornington Crescent, Stanley Street, LONDON, SE8,
No response received to our enquiries for 2000. Entry details as of Nov 1998

*　　**1) Counselling, an introduction**

*　　**2) Counselling Skills for African-Caribbean People**

*　　**3) Certificate in Counselling Skills** (CPCAB)

GOLDSMITHS COLLEGE,　　0171 919 7171

Art Psychotherapy Unit, 23 St James, New Cross, LONDON, SE14 6NW,
No response received to our enquiries for 2000, entry details as of November 1998

*　　**1) Foundation Art Therapy**

**　　**2) Postgraduate Diploma in Group Psychotherapy**

**　　**3) Postgraduate Diploma in Advanced Training in Ar**

**　　**4) Postgraduate Diploma in Art Therapy**

**　　**5) Certificate in Intercultural Therapy**

***　　**6) MA in Art Psychotherapy**

***　　**7) MA in Group Psychotherapy**

Star System:　* Introductory course only ● ** 2-3 yr pt-time course to Cert/Dip level ●
*** Professional development for trained counsellors
For added help, see section 'Essential Information for Students', page 1

112

GOLDSMITHS COLLEGE, PACE,   0171 919 7171

University of London, New Cross, LONDON, SE14 6NW,

No respnse received to our enquiries for 2000, entry details as of Nov 1998

*   **1) Introduction to Counselling**

*   **2) Certificate in Humanistic & Psychodynamic Counselling**

**   **3) MA in Applied Psychoanalytic Theory**

GOLDSMITHS COLLEGE. DEPT OF PSYCHOLOGY,
0171 919 7171

University of London, New Cross, LONDON, SE14 6NW,

No response received to our enquiries for 2000, entry details as of Nov 1998

**   **1) Diploma in Cognitive Approaches to Counselling & Psychotherapy**

***   **2) MSc in Counselling**

GREENWICH COMMUNITY COLLEGE,   0181 488 4800

Villas Road, Plumstead, LONDON, SE18 7LN,

♿ Lift, wheelchair access

*   **1) Introduction to Counselling Skills** (LOCN)

Duration   10 weeks, 3 hrs/week, day or eve
Entry   Open

*   **2) Counselling Skills in the Development of Learning** (OCR)

Duration   36 weeks, 3 hrs/week, eves + 2 Saturdays
Entry   Completion of Introduction to Counselling Skills

*   **3) Counselling Skills** (CPCAB)

Duration   36 weeks, 3 hrs/week, evening/day + 2 Saturdays
Entry   Completion of Introduction to Counselling Skills

*   **4) Therapeutic Counselling Certificate** (CPCAB)

Duration   36 weeks, 3 hrs/week, eve/day + 2 Saturdays
Entry   Completion of 3) Skills Course

**   **5) Advanced Certificate in Therapeutic Counselling** (CPCAB)

Duration   36 weeks, 6 hrs/week, day + eve
Entry   Completion of 4) Therapeutic Certificate

continued...

Star System: * Introductory course only •   ** 2-3 yr pt-time course to Cert/Dip level •
*** Professional development for trained counsellors
For added help, see section 'Essential Information for Students', page 1

**   6) Diploma in Therapeutic Counselling (CPCAB)

Duration   36 weeks, 6 hrs/week, daytime
Entry   Completion of 5) above

GUY'S, KINGS AND ST. THOMAS' SCHOOL OF MEDICINE

0171 955 4583
0171 955 4919

Bloomfield Centre, Guy's Hospital, St Thomas Street, LONDON, SE1 9RT,

♿ Lectures are at ground floor level

***   **Postgraduate Diploma in Child Art Psychotherapy**

Core Model   Art
Duration   5 hours, academic teaching + clinical placement and supervision
Entry   Professionals such as psychotherapists, psychologists, art therapists,
      psychiatrists, counsellors, social workers, teachers in special
      education
Apply To: Vera Vasarhelyi, Course Leader

INSTITUTE OF PSYCHIATRY,   **0171 919 2371**

Couple Therapy Clinics, Maudsley Hospital, Denmark Hill, LONDON, SE5 8AZ,
Telephone on Monday or Thursday only

♿ Access for disabled people possible, lifts available

***   **1) Diploma in Therapy with Couples** (BASRT)

Duration   2 yrs, 1 day/week (Mondays yr 1, Thursdays yr 2)
Entry   Experienced professionals with counselling or couple work experience,
      selection by interview, applicants must have access to couple therapy
      work

***   **2) MSc in Couple Relationship & Sexual Therapy**

Duration   2 yrs (3 x 10 week terms), 1 day/week
Entry   For graduates in relevant subjects with experience of couple work/
      counselling, commitment to research work essential
Apply To: Dr Mary Griffin/Mary Stuart-Smith, Joint Co-ordinators

---

INSTITUTE OF PSYCHIATRY, LONDON, **0171 919 3242**

Dept of Psychology, De Crespigny Park, LONDON, SE5 8AF,
No response received to our enquiries for 2000. Entry details as of Nov 1998

*   **1) Skills Course in Cognitive Behavioural Therapy**

---

*Star System: * Introductory course only • ** 2-3 yr pt-time course to Cert/Dip level •*
*** Professional development for trained counsellors*
For added help, see section 'Essential Information for Students', page 1

114

** 2) Diploma in Cognitive-Behavioural Therapy

LABAN CENTRE LONDON,   0181 692 4070 FAX 0181 694 8749
Laurie Grove, New Cross, LONDON, SE14 6NH,
In-house, tailor-made training, also 1 week introduction courses, Summer & Easter

** **1) Postgraduate Diploma in Dance Movement Therapy** (City Univ London)

Duration	2 yrs, full-time or 3/4yr part-time
Entry	Degree in appropriate subject or experience & other equivalent qualifications. Movement ability assessed

** **2) MA in Dance/Movement Therapy** (City Univ London)

Duration	3/4 yr part-time or 2 yrs full-time
Entry	Degree in appropriate subject or equivalent qualifications. Movement ability assessed
Apply To:	Mr Laurence Higgens

LEWISHAM COLLEGE,   020 8692 0353
Breakspear's Building, Lewisham Way, LONDON, SE4 1UT,
No response received to our enquiries for 2000, entry details as of November 1998

* **1) Introduction to Counselling Course**

* **2) RSA Course in Counselling Skills** (C&G)

* **3) Certificate in Counselling** (NCFE & C&G)

** **4) Diploma in Person-Centred Counselling (BAC Acc)**

MORLEY COLLEGE,   0171 450 9234
    0171 928 8501
61 Westminster Bridge Road, LONDON, SE1 7HT,
We also run the Certificate & Diploma in Psychoanalytic Psychology (Birkbeck College)

♿ The college offers childcare and disabled access

* **1) Introduction to Counselling** (Certificate of Attendance)

Duration	1 year, part-time, afternoon or evening
Entry	By interview with course tutor

continued...

---

*Star System: * Introductory course only • ** 2-3 yr pt-time course to Cert/Dip level •*
*** Professional development for trained counsellors*
For added help, see section 'Essential Information for Students', page 1

*   **2) Basic Counselling Skills**

Duration   22 weeks, 1 evening/week
Entry   By interview with course tutor

*   **3) Certificate in Counselling Skills in the Development of Learning** (OCR)

Duration   1 year, evening (110 hrs)
Entry   By application

NEW SCHOOL OF PSYCHOTHERAPY & COUNSELLING

020 7928 4344
FAX 020 7401 2231

Royal Waterloo House, 51-55 Waterloo Rd, LONDON, SE1 8TX,

*   **1) Introductory Certificate in Psychotherapy & Counselling**

Duration   1 year, part-time, 1 evening or afternoon/week
Entry   Open

**   **2) Post-graduate Certificate in Existential Psychotherapy & Counselling** (Univ Sheffield)

Core Model   Existential Psychotherapy
Duration   1 year, part-time, daytime or weekend
Entry   Degree/equivalent professional qualification; experience of psychotherapy/counselling or completion of 1) above; personal therapy at least weekly throughout training

**   **3) Post-graduate Diploma in Existential Psychotherapy & Counselling** (Univ Sheffield)

Core Model   Existential Psychotherapy
Duration   1 year, part-time, daytime or weekend
Entry   Completion of 2) above; must attend 2 hours of supervision/week during terms & expected to undertake a minimum of 100 hrs of counselling in approved placement

***   **4) MA in Existential Psychotherapy & Counselling** (Univ Sheffield)

Core Model   Existential psychotherapy
Duration   1 year, part-time, day
Entry   Completion of 3) above; other entry conditions as above; personal therapy throughout the course
Apply To: Claire Penhallow, Course Co-ordinator

Star System: * Introductory course only • ** 2-3 yr pt-time course to Cert/Dip level •
*** Professional development for trained counsellors
For added help, see section 'Essential Information for Students', page 1

PSYCHOSYNTHESIS & EDUCATION TRUST,   020 7403 2100

92/94 Tooley Street, London Bridge, LONDON, SE1 2TH,

No response received to our enquiries for 2000, entry details as of November 1998

*   **1) Essentials of Psychosynthesis**

**   **2) Postgraduate Diploma in Psychosynthesis Counselling (BAC Acc; UEL)**

***   **3) MA/Advanced Diploma in Psychosynthesis Psychotherapy** (UEL)

***   **4) Professional Development Course**

SOUTHWARK ADULT EDUCATION SERVICE,   0171 639 6818

Bradenham Close, LONDON, SE17,

No response was received to our enquiries for 2000. Entry details as of Nov 1998

*   **Introduction to Counselling Skills**

SOUTHWARK COLLEGE,   0171 815 1523

Counselling & Child Care, Surrey Docks Branch, Drummond Road, LONDON, SE16 4EE,

No response received to our enquiries for 2000. Entry details as of Nov 1998

*   **1) Basic Counselling Skills Introduction** (NCFE)

*   **2) RSA Counselling Skills in the Development of Learning**

**   **3) Diploma in Counselling** (NELAF)

UNIVERSITY OF GREENWICH,   0181 3318032

School of Social Sciences, Southwood Site, Avery Hill Road, LONDON, SE9 2HB,

♿ Limited access for disabled people

**   **MSc in Therapeutic Counselling**

Duration	3 years, part-time, afternoon & eve (Sept Start)
Entry	Ability to study at postgraduate level, work experience in a relevant profession Or introductory counselling course, 25 years or over. Selection by interview
Apply To:	John Lees, Pathway Leader

Star System: ** Introductory course only • ** 2-3 yr pt-time course to Cert/Dip level •*
*** Professional development for trained counsellors
For added help, see section 'Essential Information for Students', page 1

117

CAREER COUNSELLING SERVICES,   0181 741 0335

46 Ferry Road, LONDON, SW13 9PW,

No response to our enquiries for 2000, entry details as of Nov 1998

*   **CCS Core Career Counselling Course**

COMMUNITY LEARNING & LEISURE SERVICE,   0181 846 9090

East Fulham Centre, 20 Dawes Road, Fulham, LONDON, SW6 7EN,

No response received to our enquiries for 2000, entry as of Nov 1998

*   **1) Introduction to Counselling**

**   **2) Certificate in Counselling**

KENSINGTON CONSULTATION CENTRE (KCC),   0171 720 7301

2 Wyvil Court, Trenchold Street, LONDON, SW8 2TG,

Short courses & in-house & tailor-made training in counselling skills also available

♿ Full access facilities for disabled, disabled toilets & lifts to all floors

**   **1) Postgraduate Diploma/MSc in Systemic Therapy** (Luton Univ)

Duration	Courses held afternoons/eves + some full days (February & September entry)
Entry	By application form & interview where appropriate

**   **2) MSc/Diploma in Systemic Management & Consultation** (Univ Sunderland)

Duration	Diploma: 2 yrs, part-time (day) MSc: 3 yrs, part-time, day (February & September entry)
Entry	Selection by application form & interview where appropriate

**   **3) Diploma in Conflict Management**

Duration	Proposed course, please contact KCC for further details

**   **4) MSc/Postgraduate Diploma in Systemic Workplace Counselling and Consultation** (Univ of Luton)

Duration	2-3 yrs, part-time
Entry	Intensive Foundation Course available for those without systemic counselling skills

---

Star System: ** Introductory course only* • *** 2-3 yr pt-time course to Cert/Dip level* •
*** Professional development for trained counsellors
For added help, see section 'Essential Information for Students', page 1

118

** 5) MSc/Postgraduate Diploma in Systemic Conflict Management & Consultation
Duration   As 4)
Entry   As 4)

*** 6) Postgraduate Diploma/MA in Systemic Practice — teaching, training, supervision (Univ of Northumbria at Newcastle)
Duration   Afternoons & eves + some full days (February & September entry)
Entry   By application form & interview where appropriate
Apply To: Antony Charles

LAMBETH COLLEGE,   0171 501 5006
School of Social Care, Clapham Centre, 45 Clapham Common Southside, LONDON, SW4 9BL,
No response received to our enquiries for 2000, entry details as of November 1998

* 1) Introduction to Basic Counselling Skills (LOCF)

* 2) Certificate in Counselling Skills Course (CPCAB

* 3) RSA Certificate, Counselling in the Development of Learning

* 4) Certificate in Therapeutic Counselling (CPCAB)

** 5) Advanced Certificate in Therapeutic Counselling

** 6) Diploma in Therapeutic Counselling (CPCAB)

LAMBETH COMMUNITY EDUCATION,   0171 926 6026
Adare Centre, Adare Walk, Mount Earl Gardens, LONDON, SW16 2PW,
No response received to our enquiries for 2000. Entry details as of Nov 1998

* 1) Introduction to Counselling

* 2) Counselling Skills

* 3) Counselling (Birkbeck)

---

*Star System: * Introductory course only • ** 2-3 yr pt-time course to Cert/Dip level •*
*** *Professional development for trained counsellors*
For added help, see section 'Essential Information for Students', page 1

119

LINCOLN CLINIC & CENTRE FOR, PSYCHOTHERAPY
0171 978 1545 FAX: 0171 720 4721

19 Abbeville Mews, 88 Clapham Park Road, Clapham, LONDON, SW4 7BX,
Tailor-made training is also offered

♿ Dependent on venue but the organisation will try to accommodate special needs, one therapist is fluent in BSL

**   1) Observational Studies: application of Psychoanalytical concepts to work with children, young people & families

Duration	Minimum of 2 yrs, part-time (leads to Diploma or MA linked with the Tavixtock Clinic & East London Univ)
Entry	Experience of working with children, young people or families, selection by interview

***   2) Training in Psychoanalytic Psychotherapy (leads to qual. & Associate Membs of the Lincoln Centre

Duration	Approximately 5 yrs, part-time
Entry	Degree + clinical experience in relevant field + personal psychoanalytic psychotherapy, preliminary discussion invited, selection by interview. Open to child psychotherapists

***   3) Training for Qualified Psychoanalytical Adult & Child Psychotherapists (leads to full membership of the Lincoln Centre)

Duration	2 yrs, part-time
Entry	Formal basic training & approved therapy + minimum 2 yrs post-qualification. Child psychotherapists, minimum of 2 yrs experience with adults, preliminary discussion invited, selection by interviews

***   4) Post-qualification course of advanced seminars

Duration	1 yr, 1 eve/week
Entry	For psychoanalytic psychotherapists who wish to deepen their understanding & practice of intensive psychotherapy
Apply To:	Trish Murphy, Centre Administrator

Star System: * Introductory course only • ** 2-3 yr pt-time course to Cert/Dip level •
*** Professional development for trained counsellors
For added help, see section 'Essential Information for Students', page 1

120

MARY PARKER,   0171 274 6531
66 Brixton Water Lane, LONDON, SW2 1QB,
Mary Parker is a BAC Accredited Supervisor; in-house training also offered.

♿ Access for disabled people

***   Diploma in Supervision
Duration   1 year, 1.5 hrs per week
Entry   Counsellors, psychotherapists & health care professionals
Apply To: Mary Parker, Course Administrator

MERTON ADULT COLLEGE,   0181 543 9292
Whatley Avenue, LONDON, SW20,
No response received to our enquiries for 2000. Entry details as of Nov 1998

*   1) Introduction to Counselling Skills

*   2) Advanced Counselling Skills

*   3) Counselling — Psychology Modules

MUNSTER CENTRE, THE,   0171 736 0864
Filmer Road, LONDON, SW6 6AS

♿ Ground floor access on request, loop, signing; personal support arranged by
Brenda Griffiths, Team leader for Special Needs on above telephone number

*   1) Introduction to Counselling
Duration   10 weeks, 2 hrs, 1 eve/week (May start)
Entry   Open

*   2) Introduction to Counselling
Duration   20 weeks, 2 hrs, 1 eve/week, (September start)
Entry   Open
Apply To: Valerie Jacques, Team Leader Personal Development

PROMIS COUNSELLING CENTRE,   0171 584 6511
2a Cromwell Place, LONDON, SW7 2JE,
No response received to our enquiries for 2000, entry details as of Nov 1998

**   Advanced Diploma in Counselling in Addictive Behaviour

Star System: * Introductory course only • ** 2-3 yr pt-time course to Cert/Dip level •
*** Professional development for trained counsellors
For added help, see section 'Essential Information for Students', page 1

121

ROEHAMPTON INSTITUTE LONDON,   0181 392 3000

Senate House, Roehampton Lane, LONDON, SW15 5PU,
No response received to our enquiries for 2000. Entry details as of Nov 1998

*   **1) Certificate in Dramatherapy** (Roehampton Instit)

**   **2) Diploma in Humanistic Counselling and Psychotherapy**

**   **3) Diploma in Psychological Counselling**

**   **4) BSc Psychology & Counselling**

**   **5) Certificate in Play Therapy** (Roehampton Instit)

**   **6) Diploma in Fundamentals of Dance Movement Therapy** (Roehampton Instit)

**   **7) Graduate Diploma in Music Therapy**

**   **8) MA/ Graduate Diploma in Dance Movement Therapy** (Surrey Univ)

**   **9) Certificate in Art & Play in Therapeutic Work with Children**

**   **10) Diploma in Play Therapy** (Roehampton Instit)

**   **11) MA/Graduate Diploma in Dramatherapy**

**   **12) Diploma in Art & Therapeutic Work with Children**

**   **13) MA/Graduate Diploma in Play Therapy** (Univ of Surrey)

***   **14) MSc in Psychological Counselling & Psychotherapy**

***   **15) MSc in Counselling Psychology**

SOUTH THAMES COLLEGE,   0181 918 7000

Wandsworth High Street, LONDON, SW18,
No response received to our enquiries for 2000. Entry details as of Nov 1998

*   **1) Certificate in Counselling Skills** (AEB)

*   **2) Certificate in Counselling Theory** (AEB)

**   **3) Diploma in Counselling** (AEB)

---

*Star System: * Introductory course only • ** 2-3 yr pt-time course to Cert/Dip level •*
*** Professional development for trained counsellors*
For added help, see section 'Essential Information for Students', page 1

SOUTH WEST LONDON & ST GEORGE'S MENTAL HEALTH NHS TRUST   **0181 682 6195**

Prudence Skynner Family Therapy Clinic, Springfield Hsp, 61 Glenburnie Road, LONDON, SW17 7DJ,

Workshops offered in Family Therapy skill and theory. In-house training may be available please contact the organiser

♿ Groundfloor based, Wheelchair access and toilet facilities for the disabled in adjacent building. Blind and deaf people should discuss their needs with course director

*   1) **Foundations of Systemic Practice Applications and skills** (Assoc Family Therapy)

Duration	66 hrs, 1 full day + 20 x 3hr sessions
Entry	Professional qualification or equivalent

*   2) **Creating Possibilities for Change — Solution Focused Brief Therapy**

Duration	15 hours
Entry	None Stated

**   3) **Postgraduate Clinical Diploma in Family Therapy** (Qualification Level accredited by Assoc for Family Therapy) 120 Credits-Level H

Duration	2 years, part-time (420 hrs clinical experience 280 hrs taught theory)
Entry	Professional qualification/equivalent; completion of a foundation course in family therapy or equivalent

***   4) **Clinical Practicum**

Duration	120 hrs, supervised clinical practice (30x0.5 days per annum)
Entry	Trained Family Therapists
Apply To:	Ms Barbara Warner, Course Director

WANDSWORTH ADULT COLLEGE/,SOUTH THAMES COLLEGE   **0181 918 7555**

Gatton Road, Tooting, LONDON, SW17 0DS,

No response received to our enquiries for 2000. Entry details as of Nov 1998

*   1) **Counselling Introduction**

*   2) **Certificate in Counselling Skills**

*   3) **Certificate in Counselling Theory**

**   4) **Diploma in Counselling** (CSCT)

---

*Star System: * Introductory course only • ** 2-3 yr pt-time course to Cert/Dip level •*
*** Professional development for trained counsellors
For added help, see section 'Essential Information for Students', page 1   *123*

ADLERIAN SOCIETY OF THE UK & INSTITUTE OF INDIVIDUAL PSYCHOLOGY 0181 567 8360

73, South Ealing Road, LONDON, W5 4QR,

In-house/tailor-made training offered

♿ For facilities for the disabled, please enquire

* **1) Certificate in Theory of Individual Psychology**

Duration 2 years, week-end, days

Entry None stated

** **2) Diploma in Adlerian Counselling**

Duration 2 years, week-end days

Entry Completion of 1) above

*** **3) Programme for Professional Development of Counsellors & Therapists**

Duration Weekends over 2 yrs

Entry Certificate, Diploma or equivalent

BIRKBECK COLLEGE, 020 7631 6626

FAX: 020 7631 6679

Faculty Of Continuing Education, 26 Russell Square, LONDON, WC1B 5DQ,

A number of short courses are also offered by Women's Studies tel: 0171 6316674 and Psychology Section tel: 6316669

♿ No wheelchair access, other disabilities welcomed and accommodated

* **1) Introduction to Counselling** (Cert of Attendance; 20 CATS points)

Duration 20 weeks, 2 hrs/week, evenings

Entry None specified (first come — first served)

Apply To: Sally Pearson tel: 0171 631 6669

* **2) Certificate in Counselling**

Duration 3 hrs/week, day or evening, run to June + 4 Saturdays (120 CATS points) mixed or women only

Entry For anyone who has basic experience of guidance or counselling and who wants a course to enhance their skills and knowledge or prepare for professional training.

Apply To: Application forms from Amanda Beattie tel: 0171 631 6653

Star System: ** Introductory course only* • *** 2-3 yr pt-time course to Cert/Dip level* •
*** Professional development for trained counsellors

For added help, see section 'Essential Information for Students', page 1

124

*   3) Personal Tutoring & Student Support (joint Westminster University)

Duration	2 terms, part-time, afternoons
Entry	For those engaged in a tutorial, counselling or advisory capacity in educational centres.
Apply To:	Ellen Noonan tel: 0171 631 6626

*   4) Certificate and Diploma in Psychodynamic Counselling in Primary Care

Duration	4 terms, 1 day/wk
Entry	Anyone working in Primary Care

**   5) Certificate in Psychodynamic Counselling

Duration	1 year, part-time. morning/week
Entry	Must have a counselling component in their work with children, adolescents or adults; an intermediate level course; selection by interview.

**   6) MSc in Psychodynamic Counselling (BAC Acc)

Duration	3 years, part-time, 1 day/week
Entry	Degree or equivalent + relevant current work in counselling in any setting.,

**   7)Certificate and Diploma in Work with the Mentally Ill in Hospital and the Community

Duration	4 terms, aprt-time, 1 day/week
Entry	Must be working in a hospital or community setting with the mentally ill; other professional qualification eg: Nursing, OT, Psychology etc desirable
Apply To:	Ms E Noonan, Head of Section

BRIEF THERAPY PRACTICE,   **0181 968 0070**
FAX: 0181 964 4192
BRIEF3@AOL.COM

4d Shirland Mews, LONDON, W9 3DY,
Courses and Conferences throughout Britain

*   Solution Focused Brief Therapy with Individuals & Families

Duration	1, 2 and 4 day course or 8 week evening course
Entry	Those working in counselling/mental health/welfare/caring professions
Apply To:	Brief Therapy Practice

Star System: * Introductory course only • ** 2-3 yr pt-time course to Cert/Dip level •
*** Professional development for trained counsellors
For added help, see section 'Essential Information for Students', page 1

CENTRE FOR COUNSELLING & PSYCHOTHERAPY EDUCATION   0171 266 3006

Beauchamp Lodge, 2 Warwick Crescent, LONDON, W2 6NE,

Courses based on a holistic model, using analytical, humanistic, transpersonal approach. Also offers workshops.

*   1) Foundation Course (Certificate Level)

Duration	1 year, part-time, 1 evening/week + 4 weekend workshops. January start.
Entry	Selection by interview.

**   2) MA/Diploma in Counselling and Psychotherapy (BAC Acc, UKCP Recog) (acc by De Montfort Uni)

Duration	4 years, part-time, 1 evening/week + 6 weekend workshops/year. (Starts January)
Entry	Relevant degree, or equivalent experience in the field; foundation course in counselling ; 75 hrs therapy prior to the course; aged over 26 years

***   3) Supervisor Training

Duration	1 year, part-time, 30 meetings of 1 morning/week (2.5 hrs/week) + 4 weekends.
Entry	Qualifications in counselling and psychotherapy + 1 year post qualification professional experience

***   4) Advanced Psychotherapy Training

Duration	a) 2 years, part-time + 4 weekends + 2 retreats (group & indiv) or as a) + 1 extra year total: b) 3 years, part-time, including 1 year Dream Interpretation course
Entry	Completion of CCPE Supervisor Training Course or equivalent experience
Apply To:	Course Administrator

***   5) MA in Child, Adolescent and Family Therapy (acc by De Montfort Uni)

Duration	2 years, part-time + 7 weekends & 1x6 day intensive (September start)
Entry	Professional qualification in counselling & psychotherapy; relevant degree; at least 3 years, post qualification professional experience
Apply To:	The Administrator

---

*Star System: * Introductory course only • ** 2-3 yr pt-time course to Cert/Dip level •
*** Professional development for trained counsellors*
For added help, see section 'Essential Information for Students', page 1

126

CHIRON CENTRE FOR BODY PSYCHOTHERAPY,   0181 997 5219
26 Eaton Rise, Ealing, LONDON, W5 2ER,
No response received to our enquiries for 2000. Entry details as of Nov 1998

*   1) Introduction to Psycho-motor Development

**   2) Somatic Trauma Therapy

**   3) Certificate & Diploma in Body Psychotherapy (UKCP)

**   4) Groupleading Training Course

***   5) Understanding Borderline Patients

***   6) Intake Assessment of Clients

***   7) Introduction to Object Relations Therapy

***   8) Transference & Counter Transference

***   9) Towards Integrative Practice

***   10) Thematic Body Psychotherapy Training Workshops

***   11) Experiential Body Psychotherapy Group

***   12) When Cultures Clash — Working with Diversity

***   13) The Body in Counselling

***   14) Cycles of Transformation (transpersonal approach)

***   15) Supervision Training Course

HAMMERSMITH & W LONDON COLLEGE,COUNSELLING & ADVICE SERVICE   020 8741 1688
Gliddon Road, LONDON, W14 9BL,
No response received to our enquiries for 2000, entry details as of November 1998

*   1) Introduction to Counselling

*   2) RSA Counselling Skills in the Development of Learning

Star System: * Introductory course only • ** 2-3 yr pt-time course to Cert/Dip level •
*** Professional development for trained counsellors
For added help, see section 'Essential Information for Students', page 1

127

KENSINGTON & CHELSEA COLLEGE,   0171 573 5333

Wornington Centre, Wornington Road, LONDON, W10 5QQ,
No response received to our enquiries for 2000. Entry details as of Nov 1998

*   **1) Introduction to Counselling Skills**

*   **2) Co-counselling**

*   **3) Introduction to Transactional Analysis**

*   **4) Certificate in Counselling Skills** (AEB)

**   **5) Certificate in Counselling** (LOCF)

LONDON SCHOOL OF COUNSELLING,& PSYCHOTHERAPY
0207 328 9054 FAX 0207 372 9855
E-MAIL ISCPY@HOTMAIL.COM

City Of Westminster College, 25 Paddington Green, LONDON, W2 1NB,
Professional training in counselling, groupwork, in-house; also workshops. Intake Sep/Nov/Jan/Feb/April/May/June

♿ Wheelchair access, blind and deaf people should discuss their needs with the school

*   **1) Introduction to Counselling,** (LOCN Validated + Certificate)

Duration	Two Terms, Intake: Sept — Jan — April, Term 1- Basic Counselling Skills and Theory — 12 weeks, 2.45 hrs/week evening + 2 Saturdays (40 hrs), Term 2: Intermediate Counselling Skills and Theory — 12 weeks, 2.45 hrs/week + 1 Saturday (35 hrs)
Entry	Term 1: Open for those new to counselling; Term 2: Completion of Term 1, and/or selection by interview

**   **2) Certificate/1st Year Diploma in Counselling,** (LOCN Validated + Certificate)

Duration	30 wks, 3.00 hrs/week + 3 weekend workshops (135 hrs), evenings, Sept — Jan — April start
Entry	Introduction to Counselling, or equivalent. Selection by interview

**   **3) Diploma in Integrative Counselling, 2nd & 3rd year**

Duration	2 yrs, 3.00 hrs/week + wknd workshop/term (300 hrs), evenings, September start
Entry	Completion of 1) and 2) or equivalent (min 200 hrs). Selection by interview
Core Model	Integrative

Star System: * Introductory course only • ** 2-3 yr pt-time course to Cert/Dip level •
*** Professional development for trained counsellors
For added help, see section 'Essential Information for Students', page 1
128

**   4) **Advance Diploma in Psychodynamic Counselling**

Duration	2 yrs, 3.00 hrs/week + wknd workshop/term (300 hrs), evenings, Sept start
Entry	Completion of 1) and 2) or equivalent (min 200 hrs). Selection by interview
Core Model	Psychodynamic

**   5) **Diploma in Person Centred Counselling, 2nd & 3rd year**

Duration	2 yrs, 3.00 hrs/week + 1 wknd workshop/term (300 hrs), evenings, Sept start
Entry	Completion of 1) and 2) or equivalent (min 200 hrs). Selection by interview
Core Model	Person Centred

*   6) **Introduction to Psychology of C G Jung,** (LOCN Validated + Certificate)

Duration	10 wks, 2hrs/week (20 hrs) evenings
Entry	Open. No previous knowledge is required
Core Model	Jungian Psychology

*   7) **Introduction to Group Counselling**

Duration	10 wks, 2hrs/week (20 hrs) Sept-Jan start
Entry	Open to members of caring professions and other professionals interested in Existential/Humanistic groupwork. No previous knowledge is required.
Apply To:	Jane Kirwan, Administrator
Core Model	Existential/Humanistic groupwork

METANOIA INSTITUTE,   020 8579 2505
FAX 020 8566 4349

13 North Common Road, Ealing, LONDON, W5 2QB,

Offers courses in psychotherapy, supervision, counselling & personal development

♿ Needs of blind & deaf students can usually be met. Disabled access and facilities are available

**   1) **Diploma in Person-Centred Counselling (BAC Acc) Option for additional BA** (Hons) in Counselling (Middx University)

Duration	Minimum of 3 years, part-time, 8x3 modules/year
Entry	Application form + 2 references + 3 day Introductory Module
Core Model	Person Centred

continued...

---

*Star System: * Introductory course only • ** 2-3 yr pt-time course to Cert/Dip level •*
*** *Professional development for trained counsellors*
For added help, see section 'Essential Information for Students', page 1

129

**   2) Diploma in Transactional Analysis Counselling. Option for BA (Hons) in Counselling (Middx University)

Duration	Minimum of 3 years, part-time, 10 weekend modules/year + clinical practice & supervision
Entry	Application form + 2 references; assessment session; 2 day Introductory Workshop (TA101)
Core Model	Transactional Analysis

**   3) MSc/Diploma in Gestalt Psychotherapy (MSc: Middx University)

Duration	Minimum 4 academic years, 10 weekends/yr/equivalent Gestalt workshops + supervision + clinical practice
Entry	Relevant degree equivalent in one of the helping professions or entry via APEL; CV + 2 references; assessment interview; 2 day Introductory Workshop (Gestalt Fundamentals)
Apply To:	Cathy Simeon, Course Administrator
Core Model	Gestalt

**   4) MSc/Diploma in Integrative Psychotherapy (MSc:Middx University Diploma:Metanoia) Diploma/MSC leads to UKCP registration

Duration	Minimum 4 years, 10 weekends/year + supervision + clinical practice
Entry	Relevant degree/equivalent qual. in one of the helping professions or via APEL; CV + 2 references; assessment interview; 2 day Introduction Workshop. Dip/MSc leads to UKCP registration
Core Model	Integrative Psychotherapy

**   5) MSc/Diploma in Transactional Analysis Psychotherapy (MSc: Middx Univ; Dip Metanoia: Certification: ITAA/EATA)

Duration	Minimum 4 years, 10 weekends/year + supervision + clinical practice
Entry	Relevant degree/equivalent qualification in the helping professions or entry via APEL; CV + 2 references; assessment interview; 2 day Introductory Workshop (TA 101); Dip/MSc offers eligibility for UKCP registration
Core Model	Transactional Analysis

***   6) Diploma in Principles of the Theory & Practice of Supervision

Duration	Yr 1: 10x2 day modules; Yr 2: Dissertation & submission of audio tapes with commentary
Entry	Psychotherapists, Counsellors or those with relevant qualifications in one of the helping professions; context for practising supervisors; 2 day Introductory Workshop, CV + 2 references
Apply To:	Cathy Simeon, Course Administrator

*Star System: * Introductory course only • ** 2-3 yr pt-time course to Cert/Dip level • *** Professional development for trained counsellors*

For added help, see section 'Essential Information for Students', page 1

130

***   7) Masters/Doctorate in Psychotherapy by Professional Studies

Duration	3-7 yrs, part-time.
Entry	BAC Accreditation/UKCP Registration. Substantial experience as a practitioner. Academic competence, e.g. degree
Apply To:	Kate Fromant
Core Model	Psychotherapy

PCP EDUCATION & TRAINING LTD,   0181 994 7959

20 Cleveland Avenue, LONDON, W4 1SN,

No response received to our enquiries for 2000. Entry details as of Nov 1998

*   1) Foundation Course

**   2) Advanced/Diploma

***   3) Continuing Professional Development Courses

PHYSIS,   0181 567 0388

12 North Common Road, LONDON, W5 2QB,

No response received to our enquiries for 2000. Entry details as of Nov 1998

***   1) Learning by Enquiry: Counselling Psychology, Advanced Psychotherapy Theory & Supervision Course

***   2) Advanced Supervision & Consultation Course for Psychologists & Psychotherapists

POSITIVE HEALTH EDUCATION & TRAINING SERVICE
0181 752 0412
PHEATS@COMPUSERVE.COM

71 The Drive, LONDON, W3 6AG,

*   **Substance Abuse Counselling**

Duration	24 weeks; 2hrs per week
Entry	None Stated. Candidates must attend all seminars as a condition of passing the course.
Apply To:	Peter Albrecht

Star System: ** Introductory course only • ** 2-3 yr pt-time course to Cert/Dip level •*
*** Professional development for trained counsellors
For added help, see section 'Essential Information for Students', page 1
131

PSYCHOTHERAPY & HYPNOSIS TRAINING ASSOCIATION
0181 994 3580

137 Fielding Road, LONDON, W4 1DA,

Enquiries can be made to the Director of Training (PHTA)

♿ Parking facilities for disabled people

* 1) Counselling Skills

Duration	6 day workshops, 8.5 hrs tuition/day
Entry	All applications taken on merit

** 2) Diploma in Psychotherapy & Hypnotherapy

Duration	1 day/month (180 hrs face to face teaching), Saturday + 4-5 hrs/month groupwork (Homestudy 6-8hrs/week)
Entry	Graduate ot equivalent qualification in caring profession or experience in the field; or personal growth work. Also personal development; selection by interview.

** 3) Diploma in Clinical Hypnosis (National Council for Hypnotherapy)

Duration	16 day workshop, 8.5 hrs/day
Entry	Every applicationis treated on its merit

*** 4) Advanced Diploma in Psychotherapy & Hypnotherapy (Practitioner)

Duration	1 day/month, 4 hrs (48 hrs, face to face teaching) Saturday + homestudy
Entry	Practitioners in the field with experience of hypnosis

RICHMOND FELLOWSHIP TRAINING & CONSULTANCY SERVICES
0171 603 6373

8 Addison Road, Kensington, LONDON, W14 8DL,

No response received to our enquiries for 2000, entry details as of November 1998

* 1) Basic Counselling Skills

*** 2) RSA Diploma in Post-Traumatic Stress Counselling

Star System: * Introductory course only • ** 2-3 yr pt-time course to Cert/Dip level •
*** Professional development for trained counsellors

For added help, see section 'Essential Information for Students', page 1

132

THAMES VALLEY UNIVERSITY,   0181 579 5000
Wolfsen Institute Of Health Sciences, 32-36 Uxbridge Road, Ealing, LONDON, W5 2BS,

♿ Wheelchair access, lifts and learning support

*   1) Basic Counselling Skills (TRAC Certificate)

Duration	10 weeks, 30 hours, evening
Entry	No formal entry qualifications

**   2) Certificate in Counselling; Pre-Practitioner Training

Duration	One year part-time, evening and weekends (200 hours)
Core Model	Person Centred
Entry	No formal entry qualifications. minimum of 30 hrs skills training eg: as above

***   3) Postgraduate Diploma in Counselling (TVU) (BAC Acc Course)

Duration	2 years, part-time, 6 hrs/week + 4x2-day worlskops + 2 residentials, 480 hrs minimum.
Core Model	Person Centred + Existential
Entry	Completion of 2) or equivalent; degree/professional qualification or evidence of academic ability
Apply To:	Learning Advice Centre 0181 231 8001

UK COLLEGE FOR COMPLEMENTARY HEALTH,CARE STUDIES   0181 964 1206
St Charles Hospital, Exmoor Street, LONDON, W10 6DZ,
No response received to our enquiries for 2000. Entry details as of Nov 1998

*   1) BTEC Professional Development Certificate in Complementary Health Care (partnership with de Montfort Univ)

*   2) Certificate in Counselling & Hypnotherapy (Skills)

Star System: * Introductory course only • ** 2-3 yr pt-time course to Cert/Dip level •
*** Professional development for trained counsellors
For added help, see section 'Essential Information for Students', page 1

133

WESTMINSTER ADULT EDUCATION SERVICE,   0171 641 8143

Amberley Centre, Amberley Road, LONDON, W9 2JJ,

In-house, tailor-made training. Also one-day sessions on different aspects of counselling.

♿ Ramps, adapted toilet, minicom, loop

*   1) Introduction to Counselling Skills (Credits from LOC)

Duration	20 weeks, part-time, 1 evening/week or daytime
Entry	Open to all

*   2) Introduction to Co-counselling (LOCN)

Duration	10 weeks, part-time, 1 day/week
Entry	None stated

*   3) Certificate in Counselling Skills & Theory (CPCAB)

Duration	36 weeks, part-time, daytime or evening
Entry	Evidence of 60 hrs counselling skills training , selection by interview

**   4) Diploma in Therapeutic Counselling (CPCAB)

Duration	2 years, part-time, daytime
Entry	Evidence of 210 hrs counselling training, selection by interview
Apply To:	Courses Administrator

WESTMINSTER PASTORAL FOUNDATION(WPF),   020 7937 6956
FAX: 020 7937 1767

23 Kensington Square, LONDON, W8 5HN,

Runs a variety of short courses eg: 'Is counsellor training for you?'

♿ 1 building wheelchair accessible, lift available for those with mobility difficulties, BSL interpreters available for some courses, text to speech machine available.

*   1) Certificate in Counselling Skills & Attitudes

Duration	Cert: 30 weeks, part-time or 2 week intensive summer course + 4 weekends between Sept and July
Entry	Those who use counselling skills in their work or considering counselling as a career
Apply To:	Send SAE or tel: 0171 937 4523

*   2) Diplomas in Counselling Skills. Specialisms- Groupwork, couns in organisations/access to psychodynamic couns training

Duration	30 weeks, part-time, morning or evening option
Entry	Those who use counselling skills in their work or are considering counselling as a career

---

Star System: * Introductory course only • ** 2-3 yr pt-time course to Cert/Dip level •
*** Professional development for trained counsellors

For added help, see section 'Essential Information for Students', page 1

134

**   3) Advanced Diploma in Psychodynamic Counselling (BAC Acc) (MSc option)

Duration	1 year full-time + 1 year, part-time, or 3-4 years, part-time
Entry	Relevant experience; basic counselling skills training; self-development work and appropriate life experience

**   4) Qualification in Individual Psychoanalytic Psychotherapy (UKCP Recog)

Duration	At least 2 years
Entry	Completion of 4)/equivalent

**   5) Qualification in Group-Analytic Psychotherapy (Leads to UKCP Registration)

Duration	3 years, part-time
Entry	Diploma in Applied Group-Analytic Skills or basic counselling skills; experience of group-work

***   6) Diploma in Supervision

Duration	1 taught year, (30 seminars + supervision) — additional year of supervised supervision may be necessary for some people
Entry	Experienced counsellors and psychotherapists

***   7) Post-qualifying Course in Time-Limited Therapy/Counselling

Duration	At least 2 years, (Seminars + Supervision)
Entry	Qualified counsellors or psychotherapists only
Apply To:	Send SAE or tel: 0171 376 9340

**   8) Applied Psychodynamic Theory in Professional Development (Diploma Level)

Duration	Part-time, modules which can be taken over a 1 or 2 year period
Entry	Completion of Certificate level counselling skills course , or other professional training

*   9) Certificate in Counselling Skills and Pastoral Care

Duration	2x10 week terms + 3 w/end modules part-time
Entry	For those who use counselling skills in the course of their pastoral work
Apply To:	Jennifer Jones

Star System: * Introductory course only • ** 2-3 yr pt-time course to Cert/Dip level •
*** Professional development for trained counsellors
For added help, see section 'Essential Information for Students', page 1

135

CAMBRIDGESHIRE CONSULTANCY IN COUNSELLING
01223 290416

14 Old Station Court, Blunham, BEDFORD, MK44 3PN,

No respone received to our enquiries for 2000, entry details as of November 1998

*   **1) Towards Becoming A Counsellor — Foundation Course**

**   **2) Becoming a Counsellor**

CAMBRIDGE UNIVERSITY,   01954 280226 FAX: 01954 280200

Board of Continuing Education, Madingley Hall, Madingley, CAMBRIDGE, CB3 8AQ,

Please see Cambridgeshire entry for further details

COUNSELLING TRAINING INITIATIVES LTD,(CTI) 0115 944 7849

Galtee House, 1 Heanor Road, ILKESTON, Derbyshire, DE7 8DY,

Please see the National Section for Fuller details of courses offered

 ♿ No response received to our enquiries for 2000, entry details as of Nov 1998

---

*Star System: * Introductory course only • ** 2-3 yr pt-time course to Cert/Dip level •*
*** Professional development for trained counsellors*

For added help, see section 'Essential Information for Students', page 1

136

FOCUS (FEDERATION OF CHRISTIAN CARING & COUNSELLING)   0118 957 5120

32 Western Elms Avenue, READING, RG30 2AN,

Also in Bucks & Oxon. One day courses available e.g. Focused Time Limited Counselling, Trauma Counselling, Suicide and self harm, Supervision

 ♿ Where possible training is held in accessible buildings

*** **A range of affordable workshops are run regularly for professional counsellors and carers who are practising Christians — non members welcome**

Apply To: Sheila Stephen, Chairman

NO 5 YOUNG PEOPLES COUNSELLING ADVICE & INFORMATION CENTRE   01189 585 304

2/4 Sackville Street, READING, RG1 1NT,

Also offers in-house/tailor-made training & short courses in counselling skills

 ♿ Lower floor wheelchair access & hearing loop

*   **1) Initial Counselling** (Oxford Univ/WJEC)

Duration   60 contact hours + 60 hours study

Entry   No formal requirement but a commitment to learn

*   **2) Counselling Diploma Training Course**

Duration   10 days (Sept-Nov)

Entry   Certificate course above and experience in using counselling skills in a work situation

Apply To: Pete Francis

READING COLLEGE & SCHOOL OF ARTS & DESIGN
0118 967 5000

Faculty Of Education & Care, Kings Road, READING, RG1 5RQ

 ♿ Access Via Lift. Equal Opportunities Policy applies

     1) Preliminary Counselling Skills (CENTRA)

Duration   8 weeks evening or day attendance. Course starts October, January, & April

Entry   None

continued...

Star System: * Introductory course only • ** 2-3 yr pt-time course to Cert/Dip level •
*** Professional development for trained counsellors
For added help, see section 'Essential Information for Students', page 1

137

2) Certificate of Counselling Theory (CSCT/AEB)

Duration	75 hrs evening attendance
Entry	Open entry, but preferably completion of a preliminary counselling course

3) Certificate in Counselling Skills (CSCT/AEB)

Duration	75hrs evening attendance & Saturday workshops
Entry	Open entry, but preferably completion of a preliminary counselling course

4) Advanced Certificate in Counselling Skills Theory (CSCT/AEB)

Duration	150 hrs evening attendance & Saturday workshop
Entry	Completion of CSCT/AEB Certificates in Counselling Skills & Counselling Theory
Apply To:	Carol Spillett 0118 967 5425

UNIVERSITY OF READING,   0118 931 8848

Dept of Community Studies, Bulmershe Court, Woodlands Avenue, READING, RG6 1HY,

No response received to our enquiries for 2000, entry details as of November 1998

**   **1) Part I — Postgraduate Diploma in Counselling (BAC Acc)**

***   **2) Part II — MA in Counselling** (Univ of Reading)

EAST BERKSHIRE COLLEGE,   01753 793 169

Claremont Road, WINDSOR, Berkshire, SL4 3AZ,

♿ Suitable for some disabled people; wheelchair access, appropriate toilet facilities & learning support as required

*   **1) Introduction to Counselling Skills**

Duration	10 weeks, part-time, eves
Entry	For anyone with an interest in counselling

*   **2) Working with Loss & Bereavement**

Duration	8 weeks, part-time, eves

*   **3) Foundation in Counselling Skills**

Duration	1 yr, part-time, day or eve
Entry	For anyone with an interest in counselling

Star System: ** Introductory course only • ** 2-3 yr pt-time course to Cert/Dip level •*
*** Professional development for trained counsellors
For added help, see section 'Essential Information for Students', page 1

138

**   **4) Certificate in Counselling Skills**

Duration   2 yrs, part-time, eve or day
Entry   Anyone working in the caring professions

**   **5) Diploma in Counselling**

Duration   2 yrs, part-time, afternoon
Entry   Completion of a certificate course of 200 hrs minimum, placement in a counselling agency approved by course team; weekly personal counselling

***   **6) Counselling in Primary Care**

Duration   8 weeks, part-time, eve
Entry   Minimum of 120 hrs of initial training & counselling/counselling skills
Apply To: Secretary for Counselling Courses

Star System: *Introductory course only • ** 2-3 yr pt-time course to Cert/Dip level •*
*** Professional development for trained counsellors*
For added help, see section 'Essential Information for Students', page 1

139

BRISTOL UNIVERSITY, GRADUATE SCHOOL OF EDUCATION
0117 928 7166

8-10 Berkeley Square, Clifton, BRISTOL, BS8 1HH,

No response received to our enquiries for 2000, entry details as of November 1998

*   1) Communication & Counselling Skills

*   2) Further Counselling Skills

*   3) Loss & Bereavement Counselling Skills

*   4) Basic Groupwork Skills

**   5) Certificate in Counselling Skills

**   6) Diploma/MSc in Counselling (BAC Acc)

**   7) Diploma/MSc in Counselling at Work (BAC Acc)

**   8) Diploma/MSc in Counselling in Primary Care/Health Settings (BAC Acc)

**   9) Diploma in Adult Guidance & Counselling Skills

*** 10) MSc in Counselling (Supervision & Training)

*** 11) MSc in Counselling Studies (Modular)

FILTON COLLEGE,   0117 931 2121

Filton Avenue, Filton, BRISTOL, BS12 7AT,

Counselling/counselling skills workshops

♿ Access & toilets for disabled students, disability officer

*   1) Intermediate Level Certificate in Counselling Skills

Duration   2 yrs, 1 full day/week (HNC) + 1 yr, as above (HND) + placement + self study

Entry   Selection by interview

Star System: *Introductory course only* • *** 2-3 yr pt-time course to Cert/Dip level* •
*** Professional development for trained counsellors

For added help, see section 'Essential Information for Students', page 1

140

**   2) HNC/HND in Counselling (Edexcel [BTEC])

Duration	1 full day/week over 2 yrs HNC, 1 yr HND (3 in total) + placement + self study
Entry	Selection by interview
Core Model	Egan (HNC), Gestalt (HND)
Apply To:	Pam Prentice

SEVERNSIDE INSTITUTE FOR PSYCHOTHERAPY, 01275 333 266

11 Orchard Street, BRISTOL, BS1 5EH,

No response received to our enquiries for 2000, entry detials as of Nov 1998

**   Training in Psychoanalytic Psychotherapy

SYNTHESIS,   0117 968 7748

12 Avon Vale, Stoke Bishop, BRISTOL, BS9 1TB,

The next intake will be February 2000 for the 15 month professional development course.

*   1) Foundation course in Psychosynthesis

Duration	3 weekends of 15 hours each
Entry	Open

**   2) Diploma in Psychosynthesis Counselling

Duration	3 years and 4 months, part-time, evenings and weekends
Entry	At least 28 years of age, have had prior experience of counselling or psychotherapy, and completion of introductory course in Psychosynthesis

***   3) Professional Development Course in Psychosynthesis, Counselling and Therapy

Duration	15 months, 14x3 day weekends + 26 Fridays
Entry	For counsellors who have already a diploma
Core Model	Psychosynthesis
Apply To:	Kunderke Kevlin, Course Director

*Star System: * Introductory course only • ** 2-3 yr pt-time course to Cert/Dip level •*
*** Professional development for trained counsellors
For added help, see section 'Essential Information for Students', page 1

141

UNIVERSITY OF THE WEST OF ENGLAND,   0117 965 5384

Dept of Psychology, Oldbury Court Road, Fishponds, BRISTOL, BS16 2JP,
In-house & tailor made training also offered. Short courses & workshops in
counselling/counselling skills available

♿ Support via Learning Assistance Resource Centre

*   **1) Certificate in Counselling Skills**

Duration	1 year, part-time, 3 hrs, 1 eve/week + 2 weekends
Entry	Paid of voluntary role using counselling skills; willingness to engage in self-exploration; some evidence of ability to study
Apply To:	Katharine Downey, Course Administrator X4406

**   **2) Diploma in Professional Studies in Counselling (BAC Acc)**

Duration	2 years, part-time, 1 day/week + 1 week long block toward the beginning of the second year
Entry	Certificate in Counselling Skills; evidence of the ability to study; current involvement in counselling in a paid or voluntary setting; personal counselling/therapy for the period of the course
Apply To:	Katharine Downey, Course Administrator X4406

**   **3) MSc Counselling Psychology/Post MSc Diploma in Counselling Psychology**

Duration	MSc: part-time, day for 2 years. Post MSc Diploma: part-time day (proposed course contact college for details)
Entry	Graduate basis for registration with BPS; certificate in counselling skills; minimum age of 25
Apply To:	Katharine Downey, Course Administrator X4406

COUNSELLING TRAINING INITIATIVES LTD,(CTI)   0115 944 7849

Galtee House, 1 Heanor Road, ILKESTON, Derbyshire, DE7 8DY,
Please see National Section for fuller details of courses offered

♿ No response received to our enquiries for 2000, entry details as of Nov 1998

CENTRAL SCHOOL OF COUNSELLING & THERAPY,
0800 243463

80 Paul Street, LONDON, EC2A 4UD,
See National Section entry for full details.

Star System: * Introductory course only • ** 2-3 yr pt-time course to Cert/Dip level •
*** Professional development for trained counsellors
For added help, see section 'Essential Information for Students', page 1

142

PRACTICE & TRAINING CENTRE,   **01934 613 040**

25 Boulevard, WESTON-SUPER-MARE, Avon, BS23 1NX,
No response received to our enquiries for 2000. Entry details as of Nov 1998

*   **1) Foundation Programme:Skills, Theory**

**   **2) Diploma in Counselling** (CTI/Open Univ)

Star System: * Introductory course only ● ** 2-3 yr pt-time course to Cert/Dip level ●
*** Professional development for trained counsellors
For added help, see section 'Essential Information for Students', page 1

143

AMERSHAM & WYCOMBE COLLEGE,   01494 735557 X340

Stanley Hill, AMERSHAM, Buckinghamshire, HP7 9HN,

In house/tailor-made training in counselling and counselling skills.

 Access

*   1) Introduction to Counselling (CENTRA)

Duration   30 hours day or evening (3 intakes per year)
Entry   None

**   2) Intermediate Certificate (CENTRA)

Duration   130 hours day or evening + 2 weekends
Entry   Centra 1 or equivalent
Core Model   Person centred

**   3) Advanced Diploma in Counselling (CENTRA)

Core Model   Person Centred
Duration   450 hours day or evening + two weekends
Entry   Centra 2 or CSCT Certificate Theory/Skills or equivalent foundation
                certificates

**   4) Counselling (Bucks Chilterns University) (HNC/HND)

Duration   2 years part time HNC, 2 years full time HND
Entry   Foundation course in Counselling
Apply To: Gill Garratt

ADLERIAN WORKSHOPS & PUBLICATIONS,   01296 482148

216 Tring Road, AYLESBURY, Buckinghamshire, HP20 1JS,

Some courses are run at Coniston House, 36 Dobbins Lane, Wendover, Bucks,
HP22 6DH

*   1) The Fundamentals of Individual Psychology

Duration   3x10 week terms
Entry   None stated

*   2) Creative Approaches to Counselling

Duration   1 year, 3 hrs/week + 1 residential weekend (Spring Term)
Entry   Open to those who wish to learn about the principles & practice of
                Individual psychology
Core Model   Individual Psychology

Star System: * Introductory course only ● ** 2-3 yr pt-time course to Cert/Dip level ●
*** Professional development for trained counsellors
For added help, see section 'Essential Information for Students', page 1

144

**   **3) Training Programme**

Duration   3 yrs, part-time, 1 eve/week + 2 weekends. An optional 4th year, concerned with creative approaches is available
Entry   Interview required prior to final acceptance.
Apply To: Dr L Beattie/Neil Ajmal

MARLOW PASTORAL FOUNDATION,   01494 440199

89 Easton Street, HIGH WYCOMBE, Buckinghamshire, HP11 1LT,
WPF Affiliate. Also in-house training available

 ♿   Unfortunately the premises are not friendly to disabled people

**   **Training in Psychodynamic Counselling** (WPF)

Duration   3 years, part-time, evenings & occasional weekends
Entry   Applicants should be members of the Christian Church
Apply To: Mrs J. Harbour, Training Co-ordinator

CENTRAL SCHOOL OF COUNSELLING & THERAPY,
0800 243463

80 Paul Street, LONDON, EC2A 4UD,
See National Section entry for full details.

MILTON KEYNES COLLEGE,   01908 684 444

Community Studies, Wolverton Cntre,Stratford Road, Wolverton, MILTON KEYNES, MK12 5NU,
No response received to our enquiries for 2000, entry details as of Nov 1998

**   **Professional Development Certificate in Counselling Skills** (BTEC)

MILTON KEYNES COUNSELLING FOUNDATION,   01908 230644

c/o Church of Christ, Cornerstone, 300 Saxon Gate West, MILTON KEYNES, MK9 2ES,

*   **1) Certificate in Counselling Skills** (WPF)

Duration   30 weeks, 3 hrs/week
Entry   Open entry; selection by interview

**   **2) Diploma in Psychodynamic Counselling** (WPF)

Duration   30 weeks, 3hrs/week + workshops
Entry   Completion of above or similar
Apply To: Christine Franks, Co-ordinator

---

*Star System: * Introductory course only • ** 2-3 yr pt-time course to Cert/Dip level •*
*** *Professional development for trained counsellors*
For added help, see section 'Essential Information for Students', page 1

145

ADLERIAN SOCIETY (CAMBRIDGE), 01223 314827

Bottisham Village College, Bottisham, CAMBRIDGE, CB5 9DL,

1-3 day workshops tailor-made to organisations. eg Adlerian approaches; conflict resolution; creative approaches etc

♿ Those with hearing or visual impairment/other disabilities should discuss their needs to ensure appropriate facilities are available.

** 1) Certificate in Adlerian Counselling Theory & Practice (ASIIP)

Duration	2 years, 250 hrs, part-time, 1 eve/week + 5 days/year, next entry Sept 2000
Entry	Pre-requisite — minimum 20 hrs basic counselling skills training; selection by interview in May/June 2000
Apply To:	Prospectus/application forms from the Community Education Manager, Bottisham Village College, Bottisham, Cambridge, CB5 9DL Tel: 01223 811372
Core Model	Adlerian

** 2) Diploma in Adlerian Counselling (ASIIP)

Duration	Minmum 1 yr counselling practice under supervision + minimum 200 hrs skills/theory training over 2 years
Entry	Satisfactory completion of 1)
Apply To:	Bottisham Village College, Tel: 01223 811372 for prospectus. For general discussion re: course contact Anthea Millar Tel: 01223 314827
Core Model	Adlerian

CAMBRIDGE GROUP WORK, 01223 364543

4 George Street, CAMBRIDGE, CB4 1AJ,

Once weekly Therapy Groups are available

* 1) General Course in Groupwork (IGA recog)

Duration	1 year, part-time, 30 weeks, 3.5 hrs/week
Entry	None specified

** 2) The Advanced Programme

Duration	3-5 yrs, in 5 modules
Entry	Completion fo 1) or equivalent

---

*Star System: * Introductory course only • ** 2-3 yr pt-time course to Cert/Dip level •*
*** Professional development for trained counsellors
__For added help, see section 'Essential Information for Students', page 1__
146

CAMBRIDGE REGIONAL COLLEGE,   01223 532218
    01223 418200

New Market Road, CAMBRIDGE, CB5 8EG,

*   **1) Level 1 Counselling Skills & Theory**(CSCT/AEB)

Duration	75 hrs each for theory and skills
Entry	10 week introduction to counselling course

**   **2) Level 2 Advanced Certificate, Counselling Skills & Theory** (CSCT/AEB)

Duration	150 hrs
Entry	Level 1 Certificate or equivalent

**   **3) Diploma in Therapeutic Counselling** (CSCT/AEB)

Duration	200 hrs
Entry	Level 2 Certificate or equivalent
Apply To:	Sally Lane, Course Manager/Alison Still, Coordinating Tutor

---

CAMBRIDGE REGIONAL COLLEGE,   01223 532218/418200
Newmarket Road, CAMBRIDGE, CB5 8EG,

♿ Those with disabilities should contact the college

*   **1) Level 1 Counselling Skills** (AEB)

*   **2) Level 2 Counselling Theory** (AEB)

**   **3) Advanced Certificate in Counselling Skills & Theory**

**   **4) Diploma in Therapeutic Counselling**

CAMBRIDGE UNIVERSITY,   01954 280226 FAX: 01954 280200
Board of Continuing Education, Madingley Hall, Madingley, CAMBRIDGE, CB3 8AQ,
Course 1) is also offered in Bedford & Peterborough

**   **1) Certificate of Higher Education** (Counselling)

Duration	2 yrs, part-time
Entry	Open entry subject to interview

**   **2) Advanced Diploma in Counselling**

Duration	2 yrs, part-time
Entry	Certificate of Higher Education (Counselling), application & interview
Apply To:	Dr Liz Morfoot

continued...

Star System: * Introductory course only • ** 2-3 yr pt-time course to Cert/Dip level •
*** Professional development for trained counsellors
For added help, see section 'Essential Information for Students', page 1

147

CAMBRIDGE UNIVERSITY,　　　　　01954 210 636

Couns Serv Training In Couns, 14 Trumpington Street, CAMBRIDGE, CB2 1QA,
No response received to our enquiries for 2000, entry details as of Nov 1998

** 　1) **Certificate in Counselling**

** 　2) **The Three year Training in Counselling (BAC Acc)**

CAMBS UNIVERSITY DEVELOPMENTAL PSYCHIATRY
01223 336 098

Douglas House, 18b Trumpington Road, CAMBRIDGE, CB2 2AH,
No response received to our enquiries for 2000, entry details as of Nov 1998

*** 　**Lowenfeld Projective Psychotherapy with Children and Adolescents**
　　 (Certificate)

UNIVERSITY OF CAMBRIDGE SCHOOL OF EDUCATION
01223 369631

Courses Office, Shaftsbury Road, Courses Office, Shaftsbury Rd, CAMBRIDGE,
CB2 2BX,
Short courses & in-house training in counselling also available

♿ Access to main elements of the building, ramps , toilet facilities

* 　1) **Introduction to Counselling & Guidance**
Duration　　　1 term, 1 day/week
Entry　　　　 Open to all

** 　2) **Diploma in Counselling & Guidance**
Duration　　　1 year, part-time, 3 terms, 1 day/week, September start
Entry　　　　 Selection by interview. Aimed primarily at those working with young
　　　　　　 people and children
Apply To:　　 Colleen McLaughlin

CENTRAL SCHOOL OF COUNSELLING & THERAPY,
0800 243643

80 Paul Street, LONDON, EC2A 4UD,
See National Section entry for full details.

---

*Star System:　* Introductory course only • ** 2-3 yr pt-time course to Cert/Dip level •*
*　　　　　　*** Professional development for trained counsellors*
For added help, see section 'Essential Information for Students', page 1

148

PETERBOROUGH REGIONAL COLLEGE,   01733 762181
Park Crescent, PETERBOROUGH, PE1 4DZ,
Workshops in Handling Agression, Youth Work/ Communication Skills

♿ All courses are housed on the ground floor of a Centre for Adult Learning and offer access for students with disabilities

*   **1) A) Introduction to Dramatherapy** (OCNSEM level 3, 2 credits)
Duration   10 weeks paert-time (40hrs)
Entry   Mature Student (21yrs)

*   **2) B) Dramatherapy with Adolescents & Young People** (OCNSEM level 3, 2 credits)
Duration   10 weeks part-time (40hrs)
Entry   Mature students aged 21yrs
Apply To: Ann Wilson, Counselling Co-ordinator

*   **3) Counselling Skills: Modules** (Leics OCN, Levels 1 or 2, 1 credit)
Duration   6 modules, each 30hrs.
Entry   Open, module 1 is a pre-requisite to further training
Core Model   Person Centred

*   **4) Introduction to Person-Centred Counselling** (Foundation Certificate RSA, LOCN level2)
Duration   1 yr part-time (105hrs) + 60hrs private study
Entry   Selection by interview and preferably with counselling skills experience equivalent to module 1; those with or intending to have a counselling role within their lives/profession
Core Model   Person Centred

**   **5) Developing Person-Centred Counselling** (Advanced Cert RSA, LOCN level 3, 12 credits
Duration   2 years, part-time (210hrs) + privte study
Entry   Successful completion of Foundation Certificate or equivalent; personal therapy during the course
Apply To: Ann Wilson, Counselling Co-ordinator
Core Model   Person Centred

*Star System: * Introductory course only • ** 2-3 yr pt-time course to Cert/Dip level •*
*** Professional development for trained counsellors
For added help, see section 'Essential Information for Students', page 1
149

ELAN INSTITUTE,　　　　　　　　　　　　　　0161 928 9997
Hilltop Centre, 217 Ashley Road, Hale, ALTRINCHAM, Cheshire, WA15 9SZ,
Also offers in-house/tailor-made and counselling skills courses

♿ Handrails; full access for partially mobile but no wheelchair access

* 　1) Fundamentals Skills in Transactional Analysis (UKCP, ITA)
Duration　　　8 months, 2 days/month (96 hrs)
Entry　　　　　Degree, Diploma or life experience /equivalent, assessment interview,
　　　　　　　　 introductory course in Transactional Analysis

** 　2) Advanced Transactional Analysis (UKCP,ITA)
Duration　　　8 months, 2 days/month (96 hrs)
Entry　　　　　Degree, Diploma, life experience/equivalent, 2 years Transactional
　　　　　　　　 Analysis training, assessment interview

** 　3) Skills Development in Transactional Analysis (UKCP, ITA)
Duration　　　8 months, 2 days/month (96 hrs)
Entry　　　　　Degree, Diploma, or life experience equivalent, one yr Transactional
　　　　　　　　 Analysis training, assessment interview
Apply To:　　　Robin Hobbes, Director of Training

SOUTH TRAFFORD COLLEGE,　　　　　　　　0161 952 4600
Manchester Road, West Timperley, ALTRINCHAM, Cheshire, WA14 5PQ,
No response received to our enquiries for 2000. Entry details as of Nov 1986

* 　1) Introduction to Counselling Level 1 (CENTRA)

** 　2) Certificate in Counselling Level II (CENTRA)

** 　3) Loss & Bereavement (CENTRA)

*** 　4) Person-Centred Studies Course (CENTRA)

KEN LEWIS — COUNSELLING & OCCUPATIONAL
PSYCHOLOGY CONSULTANT　　　　　　　　01244 336744
7 Brown Heath Road, Waverton, CHESTER, CH3 7PP,
No response received to our enquiries for 2000, entry details as of Nov 1998

* 　Cognitive Behavioural Counselling & Therapy Skills

Star System:　* Introductory course only • ** 2-3 yr pt-time course to Cert/Dip level •
*** Professional development for trained counsellors
For added help, see section 'Essential Information for Students', page 1
150

UNIVERSITY COLLEGE, CHESTER,   01244 375444

Parkgate Road, CHESTER, CH1 4BJ,
No response received to our enquiries for 2000, entry details as of November 1998

*   1) Introduction to Counselling Training

**   2) Diploma in Counselling (Liverpool Univ)

**   3) Diploma in Advanced Studies in Counselling Skills

**   4) MEd Human Resource Development

**   5) Post-Graduate/Advanced Diploma in Counselling (BAC Acc)

***   6) MA in Counselling Studies

SOUTH CHESHIRE COLLEGE,   01270 654654 X 206

Social and Community Care, Dane Bank Avenue, CREWE, CW2 8AB,
No response received to our enquiries for 2000. Entry details as of Nov 1998

*   1) Foundation Course in Counselling Skills (OCN/Staffs Univ)

*   1) Foundation course in Counselling Skills (OCN/Staffs Univ)
Duration   15 sessions, 2 hrs/week, morning or evening (30 hrs)
Entry   Open access

*   2) Intermediate Course in Counselling Skills (0CN/Staffs Univ)

*   2) Intermediate course in Counselling Skills(OCN/Staffs Univ)
Duration   15 sessions, 3 hrs/week, evenings (45hrs)
Entry   completion of Foundation Course

**   3) Certificate/Diploma in Counselling (Manchester Uni)
Duration   3 years, part-time, 7 hrs/week (540 hrs)
Entry   Normally aged 25 yrs or over; have appropriate experience in relevant
        area; have 5 GCSE A_C passes or equivalent; formal application;
        interview; willingness to engage in personal therapy
Apply To: Peter Gubi/Christina James-Gardiner

**   3) Certificate/Diploma in Counselling (Manchester Univ)

Star System: * Introductory course only • ** 2-3 yr pt-time course to Cert/Dip level •
*** Professional development for trained counsellors
For added help, see section 'Essential Information for Students', page 1

151

COUNSELLOR TRAINING, MACCLESFIELD,   01625 426178

13 Westbrook Drive, MACCLESFIELD, Cheshire, SK10 3AQ,

Offers ongoing personal development groups for those who have completed a certificate level course

♿ Wheelchair access, other needs considered

*   1) Introduction to Counselling & Counselling Skills (CENTRA)

Duration	10 weeks, 3 hours/week, day and evening groups
Entry	No formal requirement

**   2) Certificate in Counselling (CENTRA)

Core Model	Person Centred Approach
Duration	140 hours, (total), day + evening groups
Entry	Completion of Introductory course/similar; selection by interview
Apply To:	Sylvia James/ Mary-Rose Woodburn

THE GRANGE CENTRE, WEST CHESHIRE COLLEGE,
01244 670 313
FAX 01244 670380

Regent Street, Ellesmere Port, SOUTH WIRRAL, L65 8EJ,

♿ Access for wheelchairs

*   1) Introduction to Counselling Skills (MOCN)

Duration	10 weeks, 3 hrs/week
Entry	Interest in counselling

*   2) Counselling Skills & Theory (MOCN)

Duration	20 weeks, 3 hrs/week or 10 weeks, 6 hrs/week
Entry	Introduction to counselling skills or Basic Skills in Counselling course

**   3) Certificate of Higher Education in Counselling (Univ of Manchester) (120 CATS points)

Duration	1 year + 1 term, 1 day/week
Entry	Completion of 90 hours of guided learning in counselling skills & theory

**   4) Diploma of Higher Education in Counselling (Univ of Manchester) (120 CATS points)

Duration	2 years, 1 day/week
Entry	Certificate of Higher Education in Counselling
Apply To:	Kate Keogh, BAC AccC, Course Leader

Star System: * Introductory course only • ** 2-3 yr pt-time course to Cert/Dip level •
*** Professional development for trained counsellors
For added help, see section 'Essential Information for Students', page 1

152

NORTHERN SCHOOL OF PSYCHODRAMA,   0161 427 3307
Glebe Cottage, Church Road, Mellor, STOCKPORT, Cheshire, SK6 5LX,
No response received to our enquiries for 2000. Entry details as of Nov 1998

Advanced Diploma (Manchester Victoria Univ, BPA)

STOCKPORT COLLEGE OF F&H EDUCATION
0161 958 3101/3549
Faculty of Appli Soc Science, Highfield Close, Davenport, STOCKPORT, Cheshire,
SK3 8UA,
In-house/tailor-made training also offered

♿ Access for people with disability, support services available

*   **1) Basic Counselling Skills**
Duration   10 weeks (several courses per term)
Entry   None
Apply To: Gina Tezcan, Basic Counselling Course Co-ordinator

*   **2) Certificate in Counselling** (Univ of Manchester)
Duration   1 year, part-time, day or eve + 2 weekend residentials
Entry   Over 21, 5 GCSEs or equivalent & completion of 1) or similar, access
         to practice needed, September & January start
Apply To: Fred Wolstenholme

*   **3) Introduction to Counselling** (CENTRA)
Duration   20 hs, day or eve
Entry   Open
Apply To: Gina Tezcan, Course Secretary

*   **4) Certificate in Counselling Skill — Level 2** (CENTRA) Learning
Duration   1 yr, part-time, eve + 3 day workshop (residential)
Entry   No formal requirements
Apply To: Sue Copeland, Course Tutor

*   **5) Introduction to Personal Development** (G Man Open Coll Fed)
Duration   15 hrs, 10 weekly sessions, afternoons
Entry   Open
Apply To: Gina Tezcan, Course Secretary
Core Model   Person-centred

continued...

Star System: ** Introduction course only • ** 2-3 yr pt-time course to Cert/Dip level •*
*** Professional development for trained counsellors
For added help, see section 'Essential Information for Students', page 1

153

*   6) Introduction to Transactional Analysis (G Man Open Coll Fed)

Duration   20 hrs, eves
Entry   Open
Apply To: Gina Tezcan, Course Secretary
Core Model   TA

*   7) Introduction to Counselling Children & Adolescents (CSCT/AEB)

Duration   30 hrs, eves and workshop
Entry   Completion of Introduction to Counselling or relevant professional/ voluntary experience
Apply To: Gina Tezcan, Course Secretary

*   8) Introduction to Bereavement Counselling (CENTRA)

Duration   20 hrs, eves
Entry   Open, suitable for students completing basic counselling or professionals with interest in bereavement
Apply To: Gina Tezcan

*   9) Advanced Certificate in Counselling Skills (National Open Coll Network)

Duration   120 hrs, day or eve, + day workshops
Entry   Basic counselling course/5 GCSEs (or equivalent)
Apply To: Fred Wolstenholme, Programme Manager
Core Model   Rogers & Egan

**   10) Diploma in Counselling (Univ of Manchester)

Duration   15 months, part-time, day + 2 weekend residentials or 2 yrs part-time, 1 eve/week + 2 residentials
Entry   Over 21, 5 GCSEs or equivalent, completion of 2) above or equivalent, APL available
Apply To: Peter Jenkins, Course Tutor

**   11) Advanced Diploma in Counselling (NOCR)

Duration   300 hrs, daytime Sept 2000 — Dec 2001, eve Sept 1999 — July 2001
Entry   Cert. in Couns Skills or APL, ability to study at HE level, access to 100 hrs practice
Apply To: Gina Tezcan, Course Secretary
Core Model   Rogers & Egan

***   12) Diploma in Casework Supervision

Duration   1 yr (Sept — June)
Entry   Counsellors, therapists, social & youth workers
Apply To: Sue Copeland, Course Tutor

Star System: * Introductory course only • ** 2-3 yr pt-time course to Cert/Dip level •
*** Professional development for trained counsellors
For added help, see section 'Essential Information for Students', page 1
154

WARRINGTON COLLEGIATE INSTITUTE, 01925 494 494

Professional & Education, Studies, University College, Crab Lane, WARRINGTON, WA2 0DB,

No response received to our enquiries for 1998. Entry details as of Nov 1998

*　　1) Introduction to Counselling (CENTRA)

*　　2) Certificate in Counselling Skills (CENTRA)

**　3) Diploma in Counselling (CENTRA)

HALTON COLLEGE, 0151 423 1391

Kingsway, WIDNES, Cheshire, WA8 7QQ,

No response received to our enquiries for 2000, entry details as of November 1998

*　　1) Introduction to Counselling

**　2) Certificate in Counselling Skills (Manchester Univ)

**　3) Diploma in Counselling (Manchester Univ)

MID-CHESHIRE COLLEGE OF FE, 01606 558278

The Verdin Centre, High Street, WINSFORD, Cheshire, CW7 2AY,

No response received to our enquiries for 2000, entry details as of November 1998

*　　1) Introduction to Counselling (NWRAEA)

*　　2) Certificate in Counselling Skills (NWRAEA)

*　　3) Introduction to Bereavement Counselling (NWRAEA)

**　4) Diploma in Counselling (NWRAEA) (Proposed Course)

---

*Star System:　* Introductory course only　•　** 2-3 yr pt-time course to Cert/Dip level　•*
*** Professional development for trained counsellors
For added help, see section 'Essential Information for Students', page 1

155

CENTRE FOR THERAPEUTIC CHANGE,   01503 262171

Vine Cottage, Princess Street, LOOE, Cornwall, PL13 2ER,
In-house and tailor-made training also available; also workshops eg: anger, grief,
working with young adults etc.

♿ None at present

*   1) Certificate in Counselling Skills (CPCAB)

Duration	120 hrs, evenings + 3 whole days during the course
Entry	Open access

*   2) Certificate in Counselling Theory (CPCAB)

Duration	120 hrs, 1 evening/week + 3 whole days
Entry	Open access

*   3) Certificate in NLP (Centre for Therapeutic Change)

Duration	30 weeks, 1 evening/week (78 hours) + assessment day — West Looe
Entry	No formal requirements

**   4) Advanced Certificate in Therapeutic Counselling (CPCAB)

Duration	32 Sundays, 190 hours
Entry	Certificate in Counselling or APL route

**   5) Practitioners Diploma in NLP Therapy

Duration	36 weeks, evenings (126 hours) fortnightly
Entry	Certificate in NLP
Apply To:	Jean Saunders/Veronica Eatough

**   6) Diploma in Therapeutic Counselling (CPCAB)

Duration	30 weeks, Saturdays (180 hours) in West Looe
Entry	Advanced Certificate in Counselling or APL route

***   7) Advanced Diploma in Therapeutic Counselling (CPCAB)

Duration	30 whole days, (180 hours)
Entry	Recognised Diploma in Counselling or APL route
Apply To:	Jeannie Saunders, Principal

***   8) Post Diploma Professional Development

Duration	3 day modules (45 hours) in: Small Group Facilitation, Cognitive Therapy (Aaron Beck), Counselling Supervision
Entry	Diploma in Counselling

Star System: ** Introductory course only* • *** 2-3 yr pt-time course to Cert/Dip level* •
*** Professional development for trained counsellors

For added help, see section 'Essential Information for Students', page 1

156

PENWITH COLLEGE,   01736 335000

St. Clare Street, PENZANCE, TR18 2SA,

Certificate in Counselling Skills in the Development of Learning

Duration	Day time, 26 x 4hr sessions = 104hrs
Entry	No formal requirement
Apply To:	Mr Jonathan Jones

*   Counselling Skills basic Certificate

Duration	60hrs evenings
Entry	None stated

CORNWALL INSTITUTE OF PROFESSIONAL STUDIES
01209 616263

Penhaligon Building, Trevenson Lane, Pool, REDRUTH, Cornwall, TR15 3RD,
Courses also held in Dartington, Plymouth and Barnstable. In-house and workshops available in counselling/skills.

♿ Ground floor access; toilets for disabled people; lifts; support with learning ＼ difficulties are available at the Cornwall venue.

**   1) Certificate in Advanced Counselling Studies (Univ of Plymouth)

Duration	1 year, part-time, (130 hrs) September start
Entry	Completion of an introductory counselling course or experience in helping professions/voluntary sector

**   2) Diploma in Professional Studies in Counselling (Univ of Plymouth)

Duration	2 years, part-time, 1 day/week (460 hours) September start
Entry	Completion of 1) or equivalent; over 24; experience in caring professions or voluntary sector
Apply To:	Maureen Mason/Kate Roskilly

ST AUSTELL COLLEGE,   01726 67911 EXT 3140

Trevarthian Road, ST. AUSTELL, Cornwall, PL25 4BU,
Reductions for those on means tested benefits, help with childcare costs

♿ Lifts, toilets, slopes, parking for those with disabilities

*   1) Introduction to Counselling (CSCT/AEB) Foundation Level

Duration	15 weeks, part-time, 2 hrs/week, daytime/eve (Autumn & Spring)
Entry	Open access

continued...

Star System: * *Introductory course only* • ** *2-3 yr pt-time course to Cert/Dip level* •
*** *Professional development for trained counsellors*
For added help, see section 'Essential Information for Students', page 1

157

*   **2) Combined Certificate Skills & Theory** (CSCT/AEB) Level 1

Duration   1 yr, 32 weeks, 1 day, afternoon or eve/week. Includes personal development sessions

Entry   Introductory certificate or those wanting counselling skills within their work role, selection by interview

**   **3) Advanced Certificate Skills & Theory** (CSCT/AEB) Level 2

Duration   1 yr, 36 weeks, 1 day/week + 7 awareness day workshops

Entry   Satisfactory completion of Combined Certificate, selection interview, supervised counselling placement in the last term or APL

    4) Diploma in Therapeutic Counselling (CSCT/AEB) — Humanistic Route Level 3

Duration   1 yr, 36 weeks, 2 days a week + 10 awareness day workshops

Entry   Satisfactory completion of Advanced Certificate and selection interview or APL

Apply To: Helen Manning, Counselling Courses Manager

IRON MILL INSTITUTE,   01392 219200

Pentraze, TRURO,

No response received to our enquiries for 2000. Entry details as of Nov 1998. For full list of courses, refer to entry in Devon

**   Advanced Diploma in Counselling — Integrative (BAC Acc)

TRURO COLLEGE,   01872 264251

College Road, TRURO, Cornwall, TR1 3XX,

♿ Ramps, lifts, disabled access to all classrooms/toilets

*   **1) RSA Counselling Skills in the Development of Learning**

Duration   90 hrs, 3 hrs/week, evening

Entry   None

*   **2) Basic Counselling Skills** (NCFE)

Duration   36 hrs, 3 hrs/week, evening

Entry   None

Apply To: Nanette Wherry

Star System: ** Introductory course only • ** 2-3 yr pt-time course to Cert/Dip level •*
*** Professional development for trained counsellors
For added help, see section 'Essential Information for Students', page 1

158

CARLISLE COLLEGE, 01228 819 000

Health & Social Care, Victoria Place, CARLISLE, CA1 1HS,
No response received to our enquiries for 2000. Entry details as of Nov 98

*   1) Counselling Level 1 (CENTRA)

*   2) Counselling Level 2 (CENTRA)

**   3) Diploma in Counselling (CENTRA)

KENDAL COLLEGE, 01539 724 313

Milathorpe Road, KENDAL, Cumbria, LA9 5AY,
No response received to our enquiries for 2000. Entry details as of Nov 1998

*   1) Introduction to Counselling Skills (CENTRA)

*   2) Intermediate Counselling Skills (CENTRA)

**   3) Advanced Counselling Diploma (CENTRA)

ADLERIAN SOCIETY FOR INDIVIDUAL PSYCHOLOGY
01539 620 952

Underknotts, Fir Bank, SEDBERGH, Cumbria, LA10,
No response to our enquiries for 2000, entry details asof Nov 1998

*   Introductory Course in Adlerian Counselling

Star System: * Introductory course only • ** 2-3 yr pt-time course to Cert/Dip level •
*** Professional development for trained counsellors
For added help, see section 'Essential Information for Students', page 1
159

NATURAL THERAPY TRAINING COLLEGE,   01773 603880

44/45 High Street, Swanwick, ALFRETON, Derbyshire, DE55 1AA,
Workshops in counselling/counselling skills

 ♿ Full wheelchair access. Access to support in learning

*   **1) Certificate in Counselling** (CPCAB)

Duration   1 yr part-time — 1 day per week (150 hrs)
Entry   By interview

**   **2) Diploma in Counselling** (CPCAB)

Duration   2 yrs, part-time (300 hrs)
Entry   By interview

***   **3) Certificate in Counselling Supervision** (CPCAB)

Duration   1 yr, part-time (120 hrs)
Entry   By interview

*   **4) Counselling in a Health/GP Setting** (CPCAB)

Duration   120 hrs
Entry   By application form and interview

***   **5) Training the Trainer** (Pilot Scheme)

Duration   120 hrs in 3 modules
Entry   By application form and interview
Apply To: Julia Shaw

CHESTERFIELD COLLEGE OF TECHNOLOGY AND ART
01246 500 535

Infirmary Road, CHESTERFIELD, Derbyshire, S41 7NG,
No response received to our enquiries for 2000, entry details as of November 1998

*   **Basic Counselling Skills** (College Certificate & Accred by South Yorks
       Open Federation)

Star System: * Introductory course only • ** 2-3 yr pt-time course to Cert/Dip level •
*** Professional development for trained counsellors
For added help, see section 'Essential Information for Students', page 1

160

BERNE INSTITUTE, THE,

**TEL/FAX: 01509 673649
TA@THEBERNE.U-NET.COM**

Berne House, 29 Derby Road, Kegworth, DERBY, DE74 2EN,

**   1) Professional Training in Transactional Analysis Psychotherapy
(UKCP, ITAA, EATA, recog)

Duration   4 years, 20 days in each academic year
Entry   A professional qualification at degree level or equivalent in training and
experience; interview

**   2) MSc in Transactional Analysis Psychotherapy (Middlesex University).

Duration   4 years, 20 days in each academic year
Entry   A professional qualification at degree level or equivalent in training and
experience ; interview.

**   3) Foundation Certificate in Transactional Analysis

Duration   1 year, 20 days
Entry   By interview

**   4) Diploma in Transactional Analysis Counselling

Duration   3 years, 20 days in each academic year
Entry   By interview

**   5) Postgraduate Diploma in Transactional Analysis (Middlesex
University).

Duration   3 years, 20 days in each academic year
Entry   A professional qualification at degree level or equivalent in training and
experience; interview

*****   6) Post-qualification Training in Transactional Analysis Supervision and
Training** (ITAA and EATA recog)

Duration   5-7 years, 10 days in each academic year
Entry   Accreditation in Transactional Analysis Psychotherapy
Apply To: The Course Registrar

*Star System: * Introductory course only • ** 2-3 yr pt-time course to Cert/Dip level •
*** Professional development for trained counsellors*
For added help, see section 'Essential Information for Students', page 1
161

DERBY TERTIARY COLLEGE — WILMORTON STUDENT SERVICES　　　　01332 757570 X 237

London Road, DERBY, DE24 8UG,

Offers in-house/tailor-made and counselling/skills workshops

♿ Wheelchair access; key learning skills; signers/sight impaired assistance; large print out of learning material

*　　**1) Introduction to Counselling Skills** (NEMAP)

Duration	10 weeks, 3 hrs/week day or evening
Entry	Those with an interest in counselling

*　　**2) Certificate in Counselling Skills** (CPCAB)

Duration	30 weeks, 3 hrs/week day or evening + 4 full Saturdays
Entry	No previous training or experience is required although completion of the Introduction to Counselling Course is advantageous

**　　**3) Certificate in Therapeutic Counselling** (CPCAB)

Duration	30 weeks, 3 hrs/week, evenings + 4 full Saturdays
Entry	Successful completion of a Certificate in Counselling Skills (CPCAB, CSCT/equivalent)

**　　**4) Advanced Certificate in Therapeutic Counselling** (CPCAB)

Core Model	Humanistic
Duration	220 hours, 1 afternoon + 1 evening /week + 1 weekend
Entry	CPCAB Certificate in Counselling Skills, CPCAB Certificate in Therapeutic Counselling or equivalent
Apply To:	Liz Kent

UNIVERSITY OF DERBY,　　　　　　　　　01332 622222 X 2014

Unit for Counselling Practice, & Research, Mickleover Campus, Western Avenue, DERBY, DE22 5GX,

In-house training & short courses in counselling offered eg: Counselling Dilemmas, Anger Management, Problem Assessment

♿ Access for those with disabilities

*　　**1) Certificate in Psychotherapeutics**

Duration	100 hrs, weekend & evenings, 4 modules
Entry	None stated, successful students may go on to post-graduate courses

---

Star System:　* Introductory course only • ** 2-3 yr pt-time course to Cert/Dip level •
*** Professional development for trained counsellors

For added help, see section 'Essential Information for Students', page 1

**   2) Post-graduate Certificate in Counselling Practice

Duration   1 year, 1day/week

Entry   Particularly relevant for those who wish to work in General Practice, medical/statutory settings, successful completion of 1)

**   3) Post-graduate Diploma in Counselling Practice

Duration   2 years, 1 day/week

Entry   As above

**   4) MA in Counselling Practice

Duration   3 years, 1 day/week

Entry   As above

**   5) Post-graduate Certificate in Counselling Studies

Duration   1 year, 1 day/week

Entry   Professionals whose work involves the use of counselling skills, successful completion of 1)

**   6) Post-graduate Diploma in Counselling Studies

Duration   2 years, 1 day/week

Entry   As above

***   9) PhD

Duration   5 years, part-time

Entry   Good undergraduate degree/equivalent

**   10) Post-graduate Certificate in Cognitive Behavioural Therapy

Duration   1 year, 1 day/week

Entry   Professionals wishing to develop the theory and practice of Cognitive Behavioural Therapy

**   11) Post-graduate Diploma in Cognitive Behavioural Therapy

Duration   2 years, 1 day/week

Entry   Professionals wishing to develop the theory & practice of Cognitive Behavioural Therapy

**   12) MSc in Cognitive Behavioural Psychotherapy

Duration   3 years, 1 day/week

Entry   As above

***   13) Post-graduate Certificate in Clinical Supervision

Duration   Open & distance learning + weekends

Entry   Counsellors, psychotherapists/other holistic practitioners

continued...

Star System: * Introductory course only • ** 2-3 yr pt-time course to Cert/Dip level •
*** Professional development for trained counsellors
For added help, see section 'Essential Information for Students', page 1

163

*** **14) Post-graduate Diploma in Clinical Supervision**
Duration   Open & distance learning + weekends
Entry   As above

*** **15) MSc in Clinical Supervision**
Duration   Open & distance learning + weekends
Entry   As above

**   **16) MA in Counselling Studies**
Duration   3 years, 1 day/week
Entry   As above

**   **17) MPhil Counselling**
Duration   3 years, full time
Entry   Good undergraduate degree/equivalent
Apply To: Kim Hunt, Unit Administrator

SOUTH EAST DERBYSHIRE COLLEGE,   0115 932 4212 X 418

Mundy Street, HEANOR, Derbyshire, DE75 7DZ,

In-house and Tailor-made training is available for organisations. Workshops in counselling/counselling skills available on request.

♿ There is access for disabled people. Blind & deaf people should discuss their needs with the college.

*   **1) Certificate in Counselling**
Duration   30 weeks, 3hrs/week, evening and some weekends
Entry   Successful completion of introductory/foundatioon course in
                counselling/counselling skills. Selection by interview

**   **2) Advanced Certificate in Counselling** (OCN)
Duration   30 weeks, 3hrs/week, evenings and some weekends
Entry   Successful completion of Certificate in Counselling. Selection by
                interview

**   **3) Diploma in Counselling** (OCN)
Duration   30 weeks, 3 hrs/week, evenings and some weekends
Entry   successful completion of Advanced Certificate in Counselling or
                equivalent. Selection by unterview
Apply To: Roger Campbell
Core Model   Integrative

---

*Star System: * Introductory course only • ** 2-3 yr pt-time course to Cert/Dip level •*
*** Professional development for trained counsellors
For added help, see section 'Essential Information for Students', page 1
164

COUNSELLING TRAINING INITIATIVES LTD,(CTI)   0115 944 7849

Galtee House, 1 Heanor Road, ILKESTON, Derbyshire, DE7 8DY,

Please see the National Section for fuller details of the courses offered

♿ No response received to our enquiries for 2000, entry details as of Nov 1998

Star System: ** Introductory course only • ** 2-3 yr pt-time course to Cert/Dip level •*
*** Professional development for trained counsellors
For added help, see section 'Essential Information for Students', page 1

165

CENTRE FOR HUMANISTIC PSYCHOLOGY & COUNSELLING
01395 446 307

Warren Croft, 56 East Budleigh Road, BUDLEIGH SALTERTON, Devon, EX9 6EJ,
Also offer in-house and tailor-made courses and counselling workshops. Courses
certifcated by Exeter College

♿ Ground floor access to group room can be arranged

*   1) Personal Growth Weekends (Gestalt)

Duration	2 or 3 weekends throughout the year
Entry	Open to all; by application form and optional interview

*   2) Gestalt Basics

Duration	One weekend, held 3x/year
Entry	Introductory course prior to psychotherapy traininf and also a basic introduction to Gestalt

*   3) Foundation in Counselling Skills

Duration	9 weeks, 1 day/week (run 3 times/year) also available as a weekend course
Entry	By interview. Anyone wishing to learn basic counselling skills who os considering going on to a professional training in counselling or psychotherapy

**   4) Diploma in Humanistic Counselling

Duration	2 years, 1 day/week for six terms
Entry	By interview; foundation or equivalent course

**   5) Diploma in Gestalt Psychotherapy/Gestalt Counselling

Duration	Modular, (10 weekends + 1x5 day residential/year)
Entry	By interview; Basics, foundation or equivalent course. Prior experience of Gestalt training will be taken into account in determining appropriate entry level.
Apply To:	Course Director

FEEDBACK COMMUNICATIONS,   0113 266 4481

Queensgate House, 48 Queen Street, EXETER, EX4 3SR,
No response received to our enquiries for 2000, entry details as of November 1998

*   1) RSA Certificate Counselling Skills

*   2) RSA Certificate in Bereavement & Loss

**   3) RSA Advanced Diploma in Counselling & Groupwork

---

*Star System: * Introducory course only • ** 2-3 yr pt-time course to Cert/Dip level •
*** Professional development for trained counsellors*
For added help, see section 'Essential Information for Students', page 1

166

IRON MILL INSTITUTE,(FORMERLY IRON MILL CENTRE)
01392 219200

Hems Studio, Longbrook Street, EXETER, EX4 9AP,
No response received to our enquiries for 2000. Entry details as of Nov 1998

*   **1) Certificate in Counselling**

**   **2) Advanced Diploma in Counselling — Integrative (BAC Acc)**

**   **3) Masters Degree/Postgraduate Diploma in Professional Studies** (Assoc with Bath Coll of HE/Strode College)

**   **4) MA in Advanced Professional Studies** (Transactional Analysis Couns or Psychotherapy)

***   **5) MA in Advanced Professional Studies** (Integrative Psychotherapy Training)

***   **6) Transpersonal Training Workshops**

***   **7) Supervisor's Diploma**

***   **8) Modules in Primary Care & Cancer Counselling** (linked with Bath Coll of HE)

***   **9) Certificate in Counselling for Children**

UNIVERSITY OF EXETER,   01392 411 907

Dept of Continuing & Adult Ed, Cotley, Streatham Rise, EXETER, EX4 4PE,
No response received to our enquiries for 2000, entry details as of Nov 1998

*   **1) An Introduction to Counselling**

**   **3) Certificate in Counselling** (120 credits at Level 1, Univ Exeter)

COUNSELLING TRAINING INITIATIVES LTD,(CTI)   0115 944 7849

Galtee House, 1 Heanor Road, ILKESTON, Derbyshire, DE7 8DY,
Please see National Section for fuller details of the courses offered

♿ No response received to our enquiries for 2000, entry details as of Nov 1998

Star System: * Introductory course only • ** 2-3 yr pt-time course to Cert/Dip level •
*** Professional development for trained counsellors
For added help, see section 'Essential Information for Students', page 1

167

CENTRAL SCHOOL OF COUNSELLING & THERAPY,
0800243463

80 Paul Street, LONDON, EC2A 4UD,
See National Section entry for full details.

KARUNA INSTITUTE,   01647 221457

Natsworthy Manor, Widecombe-in-the-Moor, NEWTON ABBOT, Devon, TQ13 7TR,
Offers professional trainings in Core Process Psychotherapy (a Buddhist informed training, UKCP recognised)

**   1) Foundation Course in Core Process Psychotherapy

Duration	1 weekend/month for 6 months + 5 day residentials (130 hrs)
Entry	Interview, biography
Core Model	Core Process Psychotherapy

**   2) Professional Training in Core Process Psychotherapy

Duration	4 yrs, par-time, weekends + 5 day residentials
Entry	Completion of 1) and assessment, interview, CV & application, degree or equivalent, life-experience, background in field, counselling training & 2 references

***   3) Post Graduate Trainings for Professionals contemplating Supervision

Duration	i) 2 x 5 day modules ii) 4 x 5 day modules
Entry	i) 1 yr training in Core Process Psychotherapy ii) for accredited practitioners
Core Model	Core Process Psychotherapy

INTERNATIONAL INST FOR COUNSELLING & PROFESSIONAL DEVELOPMENT   01752 250056

45a New Street, The Barbican, PLYMOUTH, PL1 2ND,
No response received to our enquiries for 2000, entry details as of November 1998

*   1) Working with Anger

*   2) Stage 1 Counselling Skills (Introductory) (Certificate of Attendance)

*   3) Groups & Group Processes

**   4) Diploma in School Counselling (IICPD)

**   5) Diploma in Professional Counselling

**   6) Advanced Diploma in Professional Counselling

Star System: ** Introductory course only • ** 2-3 yr pt-time course to Cert/Dip level •*
*** Professional development for trained counsellors

For added help, see section 'Essential Information for Students', page 1

***   7) Certificate in Supervision

***   8) Diploma in Supervision/Diploma in Training (incorporating City & Guilds 7307)

EAST DEVON COLLEGE, 01884 235295
Bolham Road, TIVERTON, Devon, EX16 6SH,
No response received to our enquiries for 2000, entry details as of November 1998

*   1) An Introduction to Counselling Skills (OCNSW)

*   2) RSA Certificate, Counselling Skills in the Development of Learning

*   3) Certificate in Counselling Theory

**   4) Diploma in Counselling (CENTRA)

DEVON PASTORAL COUNSELLORS, 01803 864444
43 Fore Street, TOTNES, Devon, TQ9 5HN,

*   1) Foundation Course in Psychodynamic Counselling Skills (WPD Cert in Couns Skills)

Duration   1 year, part-time, 1x5 hrs session/week for 3x10-12 week terms + 1 weekend during the year + 1-2 one-day workshops (Sat)

Entry   For those whose work involves care of others, whether in helping professions or business, or those intending to have or already with a counselling role in their lives, or as a requirement towards application to Advanced Course. Application + Interview

**   2) Advanced Training in Psychodynamic Counselling (WPF Cert in Psychodynamic Couns)

Duration   2 years, part-time, 1x5 hrs session/week for 3x10-12 week terms + 1 weekend/year + 2-3 one-day workshops/year (Sat) + 1-3 hrs/week for clients and supervision

Entry   Please enquire

continued...

*Star System: * Introducing course only • ** 2-3 yr pt-time course to Cert/Dip level •*
*** Professional development for trained counsellors
For added help, see section 'Essential Information for Students', page 1
169

**   **3) Further Qualifications in Counselling — Certificate of Internal Accreditation**

Duration	1-3 years, supervised counselling, working with clients as part of DPC's service
Entry	Those wishing to become professional counsellors; those holding the WPF Certificate in Psychodynamic counselling and those wishing to upgrade their qualifications
Apply To:	Training Co-ordinator

PLYMOUTH COLLEGE OF FURTHER EDUCATION,
01752 305073

Goschen Centre, Saltash Road, Keyham, PLYMOUTH, PL2 2BD,

In-house and Tailor-made training and short courses are also available

♿ Access for disabled people; blind & deaf people should discuss their needs with the college

*   **1) Certificate in Counselling Skills** (CPCAB)

Duration	6 months day or evening
Entry	None — all applicants are interviewed

**   **2) Certificate in Therapeutic Counselling** (CPCAB)

Duration	6 months day or evening
Entry	RSA Certificate or equivalent

**   **3) Advanced Certificate in Therapeutic Counselling** (CPCAB)

Duration	1 year, day or evening
Entry	Certificate in Therapeutic Counselling or equivalent

**   **4) Diploma in Therapeutic Counselling** (CPCAB)

Duration	1 year, 1 evening/week + Saturday Workshops
Entry	Advanced Certificate in Therapeutic Counselling; University Level 1 Certificate in Counselling (120 CAT points)
Apply To:	Rik Haws

Star System: *Introductory course only • ** 2-3 yr pt-time course to Cert/Dip level • *** Professional development for trained counsellors*

For added help, see section 'Essential Information for Students', page 1

170

BOURNEMOUTH & POOLE COLLEGE OF FE,   01202 465526

Centre For Counselling, Training And Development, BOURNEMOUTH,
In-house/tailor-made training available and short courses. Stress Management, Art
Therapy, Bereavement and Loss, Children and Adolescents

 ♧ Ramps, toilets, special tuition/support with writing etc.

*   1) Personal Development

Duration   30 hrs, day
Entry   Personal interview

*   2) CPCAB Introduction to Communication and Human Relationship Skills

Duration   39 hrs, day and evening, to include personal development programme
Entry   Independant character reference, Interview, Essay

*   3) CPCAB Certificate in Group Facilitation

Duration   120 hrs
Entry   Must be working with groups ie: counsellors, psychotherapists, social
                 workers etc.
Apply To: Mrs L Baker

*   4) Health Counselling (CPCAB)

Duration   120 hrs, day/evening
Entry   Personal interview, reference, working within the field of possible

*   5) Certificate in Counselling Skills (CPCAB)

Duration   120 hrs, day/evening
Entry   Personal statement; personal interview; reference
Apply To: Mrs L Baker/Mrs Ruth Collins

*   6) Certificate in Therapeutic Counselling (CPCAB)

Duration   120 hrs, day/evening
Entry   Personal statement; personal interview; reference

**   7) Combined Certificate in Counselling Skills & Therapeutic Counselling (CPCAB)

Duration   210 hrs, day/evening
Entry   Basic counselling skills course; existing work in the field; personal
                 interview/reference; 1000 word essay
Apply To: Mrs L Baker

continued...

---

*Star System: * Introductory course only • ** 2-3 yr pt-time course to Cert/Dip level •*
*** Professional development for trained counsellors*
For added help, see section 'Essential Information for Students', page 1

**   **8) Advanced Certificate in Therapeutic Counselling** (CPCAB)

Duration	210 hrs, day/evening
Entry	Certificate in Skills and Therapeutic Counselling; APL 1/2 day interview

**   **9) Diploma in Therapeutic Counselling** (CPCAB)

Duration	210 hrs, day/evening
Entry	CPCAB Skills/Theory or Combined CPCAB Advanced Certificate; interview; reference; 1000 word essay if APL
Apply To:	Mrs L Baker

***   **10) Certificate in Supervision** (CPCAB)

Duration	120 hrs, day
Entry	Must be practising counsellor of at least 3 years including 1 year post qualifying, ability to be able to supervise at least 2 supervisees (not novice trainees) over a period of 6 months.
Apply To:	Mrs J Gower

***   **11) Diploma in Supervision** (CPCAB)

Duration	120 hrs day
Entry	Certificate in Supervision; at least 2 years post qualifying; able to supervise at least 2 supervisees over a period of 6 months
Apply To:	Mrs J Gower

BOURNEMOUTH ADULT EDUCATION,   01202 557131

West Howe Community Centre, More Avenue, West Howe, BOURNEMOUTH,
In-house/tailor-made training and workshops in counselling and counselling skills

**   **1) CPCAB Advanced Certificate in Therapeutic Counselling**

Duration	240 hrs over 40 wks (3hrs/wk) + residentials (Day and evening courses available)
Entry	Acceptance subject to attendance of an advice and guidance session and by prior interview

**   **2) CPCAB Combined Certificate in Counselling Skills and Therapeutic Counselling**

Duration	240 hrs over 40 wks (3hrs/wk) + 3 residentials (Day and evening courses available)
Entry	Acceptance subject to attendance of an advice and guidance session and by prior interview.
Core Model	Person centred/Humanistic

---

*Star System: * Introductory course only • ** 2-3 yr pt-time course to Cert/Dip level •*
*   *** Professional development for trained counsellors*
For added help, see section 'Essential Information for Students', page 1

172

**   3) CPCAB Diploma Certificate in Therapeutic Counselling

Duration	240 hrs over 40 wks (3hrs/wk) + 3 residentials (day and evening courses available)
Entry	Acceptance subject to attendance at an advice and guidance session and by prior interview
Apply To:	Derek Parker

CENTRAL SCHOOL OF COUNSELLING & THERAPY,
0800 243463

80 Paul Street, LONDON, EC2A 4UD,
See National Section entry for full details.

Star System: ** Introductory course only • ** 2-3 yr pt-time course to Cert/Dip level •*
*** Professional development for trained counsellors
For added help, see section 'Essential Information for Students', page 1

173

BISHOP AUCKLAND COLLEGE,   01388 443000
Woodhouse Lane, BISHOP AUCKLAND, Co Durham, DL14 6JZ,
In-house/tailor-made courses. Workshops in counselling and counselling skills.

♿ Designated parking and mobility assistance. Lap top computers loan evaluation/
emergency equipment and alert system

*   **Basic Counselling Skills**
Duration   30 hrs (10 weeks 3hrs/week) day or evening
Entry   All applicants meet the course tutor to discuss the nature and content
                of the scheme.
Core Model   Person centred

*   **Certificate in Counselling** (NCFE)
Duration   90 hrs (30 weeks 3hrs/week) day or evening
Entry   Completion of the Basic Skills course (NCFE or equivalent). All
                applicants meet with the course tutor to discuss the nature and
                content of the course.
Core Model   Eclectic/Structured around Egan's Model

***   **Higher National Certificate in Counselling**
Duration   360 hrs (30 weeks 6 hrs/week x 2 years). Day time
Entry   Appropriate level 3 qualification and/or NCFE Certificate or equivalent.
                All applicants are interviewed and must have planned contact with
                clients
Apply To: Vince Purcell
Core Model   Largely Person Centred

DARLINGTON COLLEGE OF TECHNOLOGY,   01325 503 033
Cleveland Avenue, DARLINGTON, Co Durham, DL3 7BB,
No respopnse received to our enquiries for 2000, entry details as of Nov 1998

*   **1) Certificate in Basic Counselling Skills** (NCFE)

*   **2) Certificate in Counselling** (NCFE)

---

*Star System: * Introductory course only • ** 2-3 yr pt-time course to Cert/Dip level •*
*** Professional development for trained counsellors
For added help, see section 'Essential Information for Students', page 1
174

DURHAM UNIVERSITY,   0191 3743485

Centre for Studies in Counselling, School of Ed., Leazes Road, DURHAM, DH1 1TA,

Counselling workshops also available eg Assertiveness, Stress, Relaxation, Bereavement, Working with Metaphor

♿ Adapted toilets, hand rails & ramps, but this site is on a hill & may be difficult for those with certain disabilities

**   1) Advanced Certificate in Counselling Skills

Duration	1 year, part-tiime, eves + 1 weekend or 1 day/week
Entry	No formal qualifications but preference given to those with short course training. Selection by interview & reference

**   2) Advanced Courses in Counselling:Post Graduate Certificate/Post Graduate Diploma (BAC Acc) /MA

Duration	3 yrs, part-time, eves + weekends or 1 day/week
Entry	Preference given to applicants holding a Durham Advanced Certificate in Counselling Skills/ university supervised experience & degree or professional qualification. Selection by reference & interiview

**   3) Post Grad Diploma/MA Counselling Studies

Duration	1 year, full-time,
Entry	Normally have a good Honours degree/equivalent and be able to study at postgraduate level. Selection by reference & interview

***   4) Post Grad Certificate in Counselling Supervision

Duration	1 year, part-time, eves
Entry	Experienced practitioners with 450 hrs of supervised counselling practice + 450 hrs of training. Selection by reference & form

***   5) MA, MPhil, PhD by thesis

Duration	Varies with level of qualification
Entry	Normally good honours degree/equivalent qualification & be abel to study at postgraduate level. Selection by interview and/or submission of written work
Apply To:	Rachael Hastie

EAST DURHAM COMMUNITY COLLEGE,   0191 518 2000

Burnhope Way Centre, PETERLEE, Co Durham, SR8 1NU,

No response received to our enquiries for 2000, entry details as of November 1998

*   1) Certificate in Basic Counselling Skills (City & Guilds)

continued...

Star System: * Introductory course only • ** 2-3 yr pt-time course to Cert/Dip level •
*** Professional development for trained counsellors
For added help, see section 'Essential Information for Students', page 1

**   **2) Certificate in Counselling** (City & Guilds/NCFE)

**   **3) Further Certificate in Counselling** (NCFE)

**   **4) Diploma in Counselling** (NCFE)

STOCKTON CENTRE FOR PSYCHOTHERAPY & COUNSELLING   **01642 649004**

77 Acklam Road, Thornaby-on-Tees, STOCKTON-ON-TEES, Cleveland, TS17 7BD,
No response received to our enquiries for 2000, entry details as of Nov 1998

**   **1) Diploma in Psychotherapy**

**   **2) Diploma in Humanistic Counselling (BAC Acc)**

**   **3) Training in Transactional Analysis** (HIPS section of UKCP)

***   **4) MSc in Integrative Psychotherapy/MA/Post Graduate Diploma in Integrative Psychotherapy** (Univ of Wales)

***   **5) MSc/MA/Post Graduate Diploma in Therapeutic Counselling** (Uni of Wales)

***   **6) Certificate in the Practice of Supervision**

*Star System: * Introductory course only • ** 2-3 yr pt-time course to Cert/Dip level •*
*** *Professional development for trained counsellors*
For added help, see section 'Essential Information for Students', page 1

176

BRAINTREE COLLEGE, 01376 321711

Church Lane, BRAINTREE, Essex, CM7 5SN,

No response received to our enquiries for 2000, entry details as of November 1998

** 1) BTEC Professional Development Certificate in Counselling Skills

** 2) BTEC Professional Development Diploma in Counselling

ANGLIA POLYTECHNIC UNIVERSITY 01245 493131

Ashby House, Brook Street, CHELMSFORD, CM1 1UH,

In-house & tailor-made/short courses in counselling also available

 ♿ Those with sight or hearing difficulties should discuss needs with the University

* 1) Initial Post Professional Award in Counselling Skills

Duration	24 weeks, 4 hrs/week
Entry	Open access, selection by interview
Apply To:	Roy Widgery

** 2) Certificate in Professional Studies (Counselling)

Duration	24 weeks, 4 hrs/week
Entry	Initial Post Professional Award in Counselling Skills/equivalent 1 year foundation course
Apply To:	Sue Ward-Booth

** 3) Diploma in Professional Studies (Counselling)

Duration	36 wks, 4 hrs/week + weekly supervision for 16 months. Personal counselling for 40 sessions; counselling caseload
Entry	Initial Post Professional Award in Counselling Studies + Certificate in Professional Studies (Couns)/equivalent 2 yr study
Apply To:	Steve Decker

---

*Star System: * Introductory course only • ** 2-3 yr pt-time course to Cert/Dip level •*
*** Professional development for trained counsellors*
For added help, see section 'Essential Information for Students', page 1

177

CHELMSFORD COUNSELLING FOUNDATION,   01245 284890
FAX: 01245 359905

42 Cedar Avenue, CHELMSFORD, CM1 2QH,

A counselling agency which operates a large counsellor training dept. Also offers workshops eg: listening/responding

♿ Those with disabilities are welcome but should discuss their needs with the Foundation

*   **1) Foundation Certificate in Counselling Skills**

Duration   1 year, part-time, morning or evening

Entry   By selection interview but no formal academic requirements

**   **2) Diploma in Counselling Skills**

Duration   1 year, part-time, evening (access course to clinical training, the Diploma in Psychodynamic Counselling)

Entry   By selection interview after an approved Foundation course

***   **3) Diploma in Psychodynamic Counselling — Clinical Training (BAC Acc)**

Duration   2 years, part-time

Entry   By selection interview and assessment after completion of a Foundation course; all applicants must be in therapy

Apply To: Margarete Briggs, Training Co-ordinator

SYCAMORE,   01245 359353

Friars House, 6-10 Parkway, CHELMSFORD, CM2 0NF,

Short courses in effective listening, reflective practice in supervision, working with children

♿ First floor with lift (Toilets require a few steps)

*   **1) Sycamore Certificate in Counselling Studies** (Children)

Duration   1 year, 1 eve/week + 3 Sats + 4 day residential

Entry   Applicants selected by interview

**   **2) Sycamore Advanced Certificate in Counselling Studies** (Children)

Duration   2 years, 1 eve/week + 3 Sats + 4 day residential

Entry   Sycamore Certificate or equivalent prior learning; Interview

**   **3) Sycamore Diploma in Psychodynamic Counselling** (Children)

Duration   3/4 years, 1 eve/week + Sats + 4 day residential + 150 hours clinical work and supervision

Entry   Sycamore Advanced Certificate or equivalent prior learning; Interview

---

Star System: ** Introductory course only • ** 2-3 yr pt-time course to Cert/Dip level •*
*** Professional development for trained counsellors
For added help, see section 'Essential Information for Students', page 1

178

*   **4) Sycamore Certificate in Counselling Studies — Level 1**

Duration   1 year, 1 eve/week + 3 Sats + 4 day residential
Entry   By interview

**   **5) Sycamore Advanced Certificate in Counselling Studies** (Leicester Univ validated)

Duration   2 years, 1 eve/week + 6 Sats + 2x4 day residential
Entry   Sycamore Certificate or equivalent prior learning; Interview

***   **6) Sycamore Diploma in Psychodynamic Counselling Studies** (Leicester Univ vaildated)

Duration   3/4 years, 1 eve/week + 3 Sats/year + 3x4 day residential, 150 hours clinical work + supervision
Entry   Sycamore Advanced Certificate or equivalent prioe learning; Interview
Apply To: Linda Hopper, Director

COLCHESTER INSTITUTE — SCHOOL OF HEALTH,   01206 718618

Sheepen Road, COLCHESTER, CO3 3LL,
No response received to our enquiries for 2000. Entry details as of Nov 1998 The Courses below lead to the Diploma in Professional Studies (Humanistic, Person-Centred Counselling) 3 stages

*   **1) Introductory Stage — Certificate of Assessed Satisfactory Completion** (Stage 1)

**   **2) Certificate in Counselling** (Skills) (Stage 2)

**   **3) Diploma** (Stage 3) (BAC Acc)

LIFE-FORCE SCHOOL OF COUNSELLING,   01206 572 642

21 Oxford Road, COLCHESTER, CO3 3HT,

♿ No disabled access unfortunately

*   **1) Certificate in Person-Centred Art Therapy** (Person-Centred Art Therapy Centre)

Duration   32 weeks, part-time, 1 eve/week (7-9.30p.m.) + 1 full day/term (100 hrs)
Entry   Anyone able to use art both therapeutically & creatively in a work setting

continued...

Star System: * Introductory course only • ** 2-3 yr pt-time course to Cert/Dip level •
*** Professional development for trained counsellors
For added help, see section 'Essential Information for Students', page 1

179

**   2) Therapeutic Diploma in Integrative Counselling (CSCT/AEB)

Duration   3 yrs, part-time, mostly week-ends (450 hrs total)
Entry   Anyone who can read and write and is interested in acquiring
                Counselling Skills. (Introduction is 10 weeks [30 hr] only)
Apply To: Nicole Joyce, Director

UNIVERSITY OF ESSEX,   01206 873745

Centre for Psychoanalytic, Studies, Wivenhoe Park, COLCHESTER, CO4 3SQ,
Programmes relevant to clinical practice, workshops on psychodynamic understanding
eg Transference & Counter-transference, Post-Natal Depression, Psychosis also
available

♿ University has a policy of accommodating disabled students. Individual applicants
should enquire

*   1) An Introduction in Psychoanalytic Thinking & Methods

Duration   1 year, half day/week
Entry   Members of the caring professions, and those who are interested in
                psychoanalytically oriented psychotherapy

****   2) MA Programmes on the Application of Psychoanalytic Thinking &
Method to Specialist Skills**

Duration   2 years, part-time, 1 day/week OR 1 year full-time options available
Entry   Members of the caring professions wishing to deepen their
                psychoanalytic understanding & approach to their work, non-clinicians
                with an interest in psychoanalytic theory or in psychoanalytic
                understanding of contemporary issues
Core Model   Psychoanalytic

*****   3) Various Courses on Psychoanalytic Theory, Method, Application to
Clinical /Cultural Issues**

Duration   Normally 1 term (20 hrs) or 2 terms (40 hrs)
Entry   Good first degree/equivalent professional experience in a relevant field
Core Model   Psychoanalytic
Apply To: Mrs Marilyn Ward, Centre Administrator

HARLOW COLLEGE,   01279 868000

College Square, The High, HARLOW, Essex, CM20 1LT,
No response received to our enquiries for 2000, entry details as of November 1998

*   1) Taster Programme

*   2) Foundation Certificate in Counselling Skills — Modular Programme

---

Star System: * Introductory course only • ** 2-3 yr pt-time course to Cert/Dip level •
*** Professional development for trained counsellors
For added help, see section 'Essential Information for Students', page 1
180

*   3) RSA Certificate in Counselling Skills in the Development of Learning

**   4) Diploma in Psychodynamic Counselling (Univ Middlesex)

INSTITUTE FOR PERSON-CENTRED LEARNING,   0181 220 6961
220 Ashurst Drive, Barkingside, ILFORD, Essex, IG6 1EW,
No response received to our enquiries for 2000, entry details as for Nov 1998

**   1) Diploma in Client Centred Psychotherapy/Counselling & PCA (BAC Acc): not currently in-taking

***   2) Supervising Person-Centred Practice

***   3) Advanced Learning in Client-Centred Therapy

CENTRAL SCHOOL OF COUNSELLING & THERAPY,
                                                0800 243463

80 Paul Street, LONDON, EC2A 4UD,
See National Section entry for full details.

EPPING FOREST COLLEGE,   0181 508 8311
                        DBERGER@EPPING.FOREST.AC.UK
Counselling, Health & Student Affairs, Borders Lane, LOUGHTON, Essex, IG10 3SA,
Also offer in-house/tailor-made training and short courses

♿ All rooms are wheelchair accessible, staff have experience in working with sight & hearing impairment.

*   1) Introduction to Counselling Skills (Accreditation Consortium of South Anglia [ACSA])

Duration	11 sessions of 3hrs/week including 1 individual tutorial
Entry	Commitment to the whole duration and an interest in the subject
Apply To:	Lyn Emberson: 0181 508 8311 x 807

*   2) Foundation in Counselling (ACSA)

Duration	1 full day (6 hrs) + 35x3 hrs/week + 3 hrs tutorials (114 hrs)
Entry	Completion of Introductory course, commitment to complete the course, interest in self development, concern to help others, preferably some experience in a helping capacity
Apply To:	Jan Collins tel: 0181 508 8311 x 826

continued...

*Star System: * Introductory course only • ** 2-3 yr pt-time course to Cert/Dip level •
*** Professional development for trained counsellors*
For added help, see section 'Essential Information for Students', page 1
181

** 3) Intermediate Certificate in Counselling (ACSA)

Duration	1 full day (6 hrs) + 30x4.25 hrs/week + 3 hrs tutorials (136.5 hrs)
Entry	Foundation course or equivalent, commitment to experiential learning and development of self-knowledge, evidence of experience in helping others, ability to conceptualise & express abstract ideas

** 4) Diploma in Psychodynamic Counselling (CENTRA Level III)

Duration	2 years, 3 residential weekends + 2x32 weeks, 6 hrs/week (400 hrs)
Entry	Foundation and/or completion of Intermediate certificate course to a high standard, high level of commitment to experiential learning, strong evidence of ability to conceptualise/express abstract ideas, counselling placement
Apply To:	David Berger tel: 0181 508 8311 x 730

HAVERING COLLEGE OF FE & HE,   01708 462763
Dept of Social Services, Quarles Campus, Tring Gdns, Harold Hill, ROMFORD, RM3 9ES,

* 1) Introduction to Counselling (CENTRA)

Duration	10 weeks, 3hrs/week, day or evening or Saturday (run each term)
Entry	Open

* 2) Certificate in Counselling Skills (CENTRA)

Duration	3 terms, part-time, day or evening + 1 residential weekend
Entry	Progression from Level 1 or direct entry with appropriate alternative

* 3) Certificate in Person Centred Art Therapy

Core Model	Person Centred
Duration	90 hrs. 30 weeks x 2.5 hrs + 3 full days
Entry	Open, but with placement opportunity for client work

** 4) Advanced Diploma in Counselling (BAC Acc, CENTRA)

Duration	2 years, part-time, afternoon to evening + residential weekend each year, or full day
Entry	Progression from Level II or direct entry with appropriate alternative

** 5) BTEC Higher National Certificate in Counselling Skills

Duration	2 years/(6 hrs x 36 wks x 2 yrs), afternoon to evening
Entry	Progression from CENTRA II or III, A levels (Social Sciences), GNVQ Health & Social Care
Apply To:	Teresa Cosgrove

Star System: ** Introductory course only • ** 2-3 yr pt-time course to Cert/Dip level •*
*** Professional development for trained counsellors
For added help, see section 'Essential Information for Students', page 1

VICTORIA COUNSELLING & TRAINING SERVICE,
01702 354118

135-137 Victoria Avenue, SOUTHEND-ON-SEA, Essex,
No response was received to our enquiries for 2000. Entry details as of Nov 1998

*   **1) Introduction to Transactional Analysis**

*   **2) Transactionals Analysis — 2**

*   **3) Introduction to Cognitive Behavioural Therapy**

*   **4) Cognitive Behavioural Therapy — 2**

*   **5) Certificate in Counselling Skills** (AEB)

*   **6) Certificate in Counselling Theory** (AEB)

**   **7) Advanced Certificate in Counselling** (AEB)

**   **7) Diploma in Counselling** (AEB)

***   **8) Diploma in Counselling Supervision** (AEB)

*Star System: * Introductory course only • ** 2-3 yr pt-time course to Cert/Dip level •*
*** Professional development for trained counsellors*
For added help, see section 'Essential Information for Students', page 1

183

GLOUCESTERSHIRE COLLEGE OF ARTS,& TECHNOLOGY
01242 532 045

GLOSCAT Campus, 73 The Park, CHELTENHAM, Gloucestershire, GL50 2RR,
No response received to our enquiries for 2000. Entry details as of Nov 1998

*　　　1) **Introduction to Counselling Skills — Level 1** (OCN)

*　　　2) **RSA Counselling Skills in the Development of Learning**

**　　3) **Advanced Diploma in Counselling & Group Work Skills**

SCENARIO,　　　　　　　　　　　　　　01242 580 080

Flat 2, 3 Queens Road, CHELTENHAM, Gloucestershire, GL50 2LR,
No response received to our enquiries for 2000, entry details as of Nov 1998

*　　　**Certificate in Dramatherapy** (Worcester Col of HE)

ROYAL FOREST OF DEAN COLLEGE,　　　01594 833 416

Five Acres Campus, Berry Hill, COLEFORD, GL16 7JT,

*　　　1) **Introduction to Counselling** (OCN) Level II
Duration　　　10 weeks, evenings, 20 hrs
Entry　　　　　Discussion with tutor

*　　　2) **Certifcate in Counselling Skills** (CPCAB)
Duration　　　121 hrs over 1 year, daytime & evening groups
Entry　　　　　For those using or intending to use counselling skills as part of their
　　　　　　　　work; selection by application & interview

**　　3) **Certificate in Therapeutic Counselling** (CPCAB)
Duration　　　1 year, 121 hrs, evenings
Entry　　　　　Certificate in Counselling Skills or equivalent; selection by application
　　　　　　　　& interview

**　　4) **Combined Certificate in Counselling Skills & Therapeutic
Counselling** (CPCAB)
Duration　　　1 year. day/evening (212 hrs)
Entry　　　　　For those with some experience of using counselling skills at work;
　　　　　　　　selection by application and interview

---

*Star System:　* Introductory course only ● ** 2-3 yr pt-time course to Cert/Dip level ●*
*** Professional development for trained counsellors*
For added help, see section 'Essential Information for Students', page 1

184

**   **5) Advanced Certificate in Therapeutic Counselling** (CPCAB)

Duration	1 year, part-time, 212 hrs, afternoon/evening
Entry	2) & 3) above or equivalent training experience; selection by application & interview

**   **6) Diploma in Therapeutic Counselling** (CPCAB)

Duration	1 year, part-time, 212 hrs, day/evening
Entry	4 & 5 above or equivalent training & experience; selection by interview
Apply To:	John Anderson, Curriculum C0-ordinator

GLOUCESTERSHIRE COUNSELLING SERVICE,   01453 766310
FAX 01453 767322
GCS@TESCO.NET

50 Lansdown, STROUD, Gloucestershire, GL5 1BN,
A variety of counselling skills workshops available

♿ Some facilities for disabled people; equal opportunities

*   **1) Introduction to Counselling**

Duration	10 weeks, part-time, evenings or mornings
Entry	Available to anyone wishing to explore some basic counselling skills & approaches

*   **2) Certificate in Counselling Skills** (WPF, GCS)

Duration	1 year, part-time, either morning, afternoon or evening + 1 full day/ term, totalling 105 hrs
Entry	Minimum age 30 with some existing counselling function in work or voluntary capacity; selection by interview

**   **3) Diploma in Psychodynamic Counselling** (Agency) (GCS)

Duration	2 years, part-time, 1 day/week (520 hrs in total), including supervised clinical work
Entry	Completion of 2) and those over 30; selection by interview
Apply To:	The Head of Training

SOUTH COTSWOLD CENTRE FOR PSYCHOTHERAPY & COUNS TRAINING   01453 750 716

Red House Farm, Foxmoor Lane, Westrip, STROUD, Gloucestershire, GL5 4PL,
No response received to our enquiries for 2000. Entry details as of Nov 1998

**   **Transactional Analysis Counselling Diploma**

Star System: * *Introductory course only* • ** *2-3 yr pt-time course to Cert/Dip level* •
*** *Professional development for trained counsellors*
For added help, see section 'Essential Information for Students', page 1

185

RIDGE DANYERS COLLEGE,   **0161 485 4372**

Cheadle Road, Cheadle Hulme, CHEADLE, SK8 5HA,

Courses also held on Marple Campus 0161 427 7733. Workshops in counselling skills offered in eating disorders, bereavement, communicating with young people

♿ Access for disabled people. Applications are welcomed from disabled people

1) Counselling Skills Level One (CENTRA)

Duration	25 hrs over 10 weeks, day and evening and also week-end as appropriate.
Entry	Open access for mature students (19+)
Core Model	Egan
Apply To:	Annique Seddon (Senior Counsellor) or Janet Phillips (Counselling Course Co-ordinator)

2) Coounselling Skills Level Two (CENTRA)

Duration	120 hrs 2.5 hrs per week evenings, 1 Saturday Workshop + 2 days residential weekend
Entry	Level One Certificate or equivalent also interview.
Core Model	Person Centred
Apply To:	Annique Seddon ((Senior Counsellor) Janet Phillips (Counselling Course Co-ordinator

---

CITY COLLEGE MANCHESTER,   **0161 957 1763**

Learning Resources Centre, Arden Centre, Sale Road, Northenden, West Didsbury, MANCHESTER, M23 0DD,

No response received to our enquiries for 2000, entry details as of November 1998

*   **1) Introduction to Counselling** (CENTRA Level 1)

*   **2) Introduction to Counselling for Deaf People** (CENTRA Level 1)

*   **3) Certificate in Counselling Skills** (CENTRA Level 2)

**   **4) Advanced Diploma in Therapeutic Counselling** (CENTRA Level 3)

**   **5) Advanced Diploma in Therapeutic Counselling for Deaf People**

**   **6) Advanced Diploma in Therapeutic Counselling (BAC Acc, Centra Level 3)**

Star System: ** Introductory course only • ** 2-3 yr pt-time course to Cert/Dip level •*
*** Professional development for trained counsellors

For added help, see section 'Essential Information for Students', page 1

186

HESTER ADRIAN RESEARCH CENTRE,   **0161 275 3540**

The University, Oxford Road, MANCHESTER, M13 9PL,
No response received to our enquiries for 2000, entry details as of November 1998

** **Diploma in Behavioural Approaches**

MANCHESTER AREA BEREAVEMENT FORUM,   **0161 371 8860**

362 Manchester Road, Droylsden, MANCHESTER, M43 6QX,
We can tailor make a course to fit your requirements. Please contact the office

♿ Wheelchair Access

* **1) Bereavement Skills Training — Level 1/Level 2** (CENTRA)

Duration Please enquire
Entry   Open to organisations and individuals working with situations of loss
          and bereavement. Courses can be tailor made to fit requirements

* **2) Counselling Skills — Level 1** (CENTRA)

Duration Please enquire
Entry   Open to organisations and individuals working with situations of loss
          and bereavement

* **3) Post Traumatic Stress — Level 1** (CENTRA)

Duration Please enquire
Entry   Open to organisations and individuals working with situations of loss
          and bereavement

* **4) Child Grief — Level 1** (CENTRA)

Duration Please enquire
Entry   Open to organisations and individuals working with situations or loss
          and bereavement.
Apply To: Manchester Area Bereavement Forum, 362 Manchester Road,
          Droylsden, Manchester, M43 6QX

MANCHESTER GESTALT CENTRE,   **0161 257 2202**

7 Norman Road, Rusholme, MANCHESTER, M14 5LF,
No response received to our enquiries for 2000, entry details as of November 1998

* **1) Working with Gestalt**

** **2) Training in Gestalt** (GPTI acc)

*** **3) Diploma in Supervision**

continued...

*Star System: * Introductory course only • ** 2-3 yr pt-time course to Cert/Dip level •*
*** *Professional development for trained counsellors*
For added help, see section 'Essential Information for Students', page 1
187

MANCHESTER INSTITUTE FOR PSYCHOTHERAPY,
0161 862 9456

Lifestream House, 454 Barlow Moor Road, Chorlton, MANCHESTER, M21 1BQ,
No response received to our enquiries for 2000. Entry details as of Nov 1998

*   **1) '101' Introduction to Transactional Analysis Training**

**   **2) Psychotherapy Training in Transactional Analysis** (EATA)

MANCHESTER UNIVERSITY,   **0161 275 3307**

Centre for Educational Needs, Faculty of Education, MANCHESTER, M13 9PL,
Offers a wide variety of short courses for professional counsellors

♿ Suitable for those with impaired sight, hearing or mobility

*   **1) Counselling Skills**
Duration   10 weeks, part-time
Entry   None specified

*   **2) Certificate in Counselling Skills** (Level II) — 30 Faculty Certificate
Duration   1 year, part-time, 4 hours/week, evenings (Monday) 5-9 pm
Entry   People using counselling in their work; selection by interview

**   **3) Advanced Diploma in Counselling (BAC Acc)**
Duration   2 years, part-time, (Weds or Thurs) + 3 residentials
Entry   Those who use counselling skills as part of their working role; first degree in relevant area, and/or professional qualifications & relevant experience required; selection by interview

***   **4) MA in Counselling Studies**
Duration   1-2 years, part-time, evenings
Entry   either, Manchester University Advanced Diploma OR substantial qualificiation in counselling from another institution

***   **5) Post Graduate Certificate in the Supervision of Counselling & the Helping Professions — 60 Credit University Award**
Duration   1 year, part-time, 4 hrs/week, Monday afternoons
Entry   Completion of recognised counsellor training; be experienced counsellors & be acting as supervisor

***   **6) MPhil/PhD in Counselling Studies**
Duration   2-3 years, full-time, 4-6 years part-time
Entry   Advanced Diploma in Counselling/equivalent; University requirements
Apply To: Shelley Darlington, 0161 275 3510

Star System: * Introductory course only • ** 2-3 yr pt-time course to Cert/Dip level •
*** Professional development for trained counsellors
For added help, see section 'Essential Information for Students', page 1

NORTH TRAFFORD COLLEGE,   0161 886 7070

Social & Community Care Sect., Talbot Road, Stretford, MANCHESTER, M32 0XH,
In-house & tailor-made training offered, various professional development workshops,
ranging from 1-5 days. Entry requirements include level 3 diploma in counselling.

♿ Specialist equipment for visually & hearing impaired students, ramps & lifts for
those with mobility difficulties

*   **1) Basic Counselling Skills** (CENTRA Level 1)

Duration	8 weeks, 2.5 hours/week, evening or part-time day
Entry	No formal qualifications

*   **2) Certificate in Counselling Skills** (CENTRA Level 2)

Duration	36 weeks, 3.5 hours/week, evening. Additional 1 day workshop & residential weekend
Entry	Over 21 years of age; successful completion of Level 1 or equivalent; use of counselling skills in a work or voluntary capacity is highly recommended

**   **3) Diploma in Counselling** (CENTRA Level 3)

Duration	40 weeks, 7 hrs/week (1 full day/week) + additional res. weekend + 3 non-res weekends; 2 day placement and supervision pre-course
Entry	Over 21 years of age, successful completion of Level 2 or equivalent; access to a minimum of 100 hrs counselling practice
Apply To:	Denise Samuels

NORTH WEST INSTITUTE OF DYNAMIC PSYCHOTH,
0161 273 2762

Gaskell House, Swinton Grove, MANCHESTER, M13 0EU,
No response received to our enquiries for 2000, entry details as of Nov 1998

***   **North West Regional Diploma in Dynamic Psychothe**

NORTH WEST TRAINING,   0161 4341448

Didsbury Therapy Centre, 42a Barlow Moor Road, Didsbury, MANCHESTER,
M20 8GJ,
No response received to our enquiries for 2000. Entry details as of Nov 1998

*   **1) '101' Introduction to Transactional Analysis** (EATA)

**   **2) Psychotherapy Training in Transactional Analysis**

Star System: * Introductory course only • ** 2-3 yr pt-time course to Cert/Dip level •
*** Professional development for trained counsellors
For added help, see section 'Essential Information for Students', page 1
189

NORTHERN SCHOOL OF PSYCHODRAMA,   0161 957 1763
City College Manchester, Arden Centre, Sale Road, MANCHESTER, M23 0DD,
No response received to our equiries for 2000. Entry details as for Nov 1998

**   Diploma in Psychodrama

NORTHERN SCHOOL OF PSYCHODRAMA,   0161 4341448
2 Palatine Road, Withington, MANCHESTER, M20 3JA,
No response received to our enquiries for 2000. Entry details as of Nov 1998

**   Advanced Diploma in Psychodrama (British Psychodrama Association)

PERSON CENTRED COUNSELLING SERVICES,   0161 877 9877
Paragon House, 48 Seymour Grove, Old Trafford, MANCHESTER, M16 0LN,
No response received to our enquiries for 2000, entry details as of Nov 1998

*   1) Introduction to Counselling (CENTRA)

*   2) Foundation Year: Certificate in Counselling Skills (CENTRA)

**   3) Diploma in Person-Centred Counselling (BAC Acc)

***   4) Post-Diploma Programme — Selection of Bolt-on Training Courses

***   5) Certificate in Supervision in Counselling & the Helping Peofessions

REDWOOD WOMEN'S TRAINING ASSOCIATION,   0161 643 1986
20 North Street, Middleton, MANCHESTER, M24 6BD,
No response was received to our enquiries for 2000. Entry details as for Nov 1998

***   1) Training for Assertiveness Trainers, Leading to Redwood Diploma

***   2) Training for Trainers in Sexuality

SALFORD COLLEGE,   0161 886 5556
Wardley Campus Mardale Ave, Swinton, MANCHESTER, M27 3QP,
No response received to our enquiries for 2000, entry details as of November 1998

***   1) Advanced Certificate in Stress and Anxiety Management (CENTRA)

***   2) Advanced Certificate in Therapeutic Groupwork (CENTRA)

Star System: ** Introductory course only* • *** 2-3 yr pt-time course to Cert/Dip level* •
*** Professional development for trained counsellors
For added help, see section 'Essential Information for Students', page 1
190

***   **3) Joint Diploma/Certificate in Psycho-Hypnotherapy** (CENTRA/ National College)

OLDHAM COLLEGE, THE,   **0161 958 3101**
Rochdale Road, OLDHAM, OL9 6AA,
No response received to our enquiries for 2000. Entry details as of Nov 1998

*   **1) Introductory Counselling Certificate** (CENTRA Level 1)

**   **2) Counselling Skills** (CENTRA Level II)

**   **3) Diploma in Counselling** (CENTRA Level III)

UNIVERSITY OF SALFORD,   **0161 295 5000/2373**
                                             FAX 0161 295 2378
Allerton Building, Frederick Road, SALFORD, M6 6PU,

*   **1) Introduction to Counselling** (CENTRA)

Duration	10 weeks, 2 hrs/week, afternoon or evening (October start)
Entry	None stated

**   **2) Certificate in Counselling** (Salford Univ, 120 CATS)

Duration	30 weeks, part-time, 3.5 hrs/week, morning, or evening + residential
Entry	Professional qualifications & completion of introductory course; for those using counselling skills in their work; selection by interview
Apply To:	Andy Hill, Course Leader

**   **3) Diploma in Counselling (BAC Acc, Salford Univ)** (240 CATS points + Dip in Higher Education

Duration	2 years, 31 weeks/year, 6.5 hrs/week, afternoon & evening + 2 residentials with additional practice & supervision
Entry	Degree &/or professional qualification; completion of 2) + counselling experience

***   **4) MSc Counselling Studies — 3 Routes** (i) Counselling Supervision; (ii) Counselling in Primary Care; (iii) Workplace Counselling

Duration	3 hrs/week + directed study & practice. Proposed course for Sept 1999
Entry	Professional counselling qualification plus experience + degree or other professional qualification
Apply To:	Valerie J Monk, Counselling Course Tutor

continued...

*Star System: * Introductory course only • ** 2-3 yr pt-time course to Cert/Dip level •*
*** Professional development for trained counsellors
For added help, see section 'Essential Information for Students', page 1

191

**   **5) BSc** (Joint Hons) — choice of 3 courses — (i) Counselling Studies & Complementary Medicine; (ii) Counselling Studies & Health Sciences; (iii) Counselling Studies & Social Policy

Duration	3 year, modular programme. Full time
Entry	Please enquire
Apply To:	UCAS direct, contact Liz Coldridge on 0161 295 2223/2484 for information.

MANCHESTER COLLEGE OF ARTS & TECHNOLOGY
0161 953 5995
Moston Campus, Ashley Lane M9 4WU

*   **Diploma in Counselling (BAC Acc)**

Star System: ** Introductory course only* • *** 2-3 yr pt-time course to Cert/Dip level* •
*** Professional development for trained counsellors
For added help, see section 'Essential Information for Students', page 1

192

ALTON COLLEGE,   01420 88118
Old Odiham Road, ALTON, Hampshire, GU34 2LX,
No response received to our enquiries for 2000, entry details as of November 1998

*   RSA Certificate in Counselling Skills in the Development of Learning

---

BASINGSTOKE & DISTRICT COUNSELLING SERVICE
01256 843125
Goldings, London Road, BASINGSTOKE, Hampshire, RG21 4AN,
No response received to our enquiries for 2000, entry details as of November 1998

**   1) WPF Certificate in Counselling Skills & Attitudes

**   2) WPF Certificate in Psychodynamic Counselling

COUNSELLING & PSYCHOTHERAPY SERVICES,   01256 381 787
Coudray House, Herriard, BASINGSTOKE, Hampshire, RG25 2PN,
No response received to our enquiries for 2000. Entry details as of Nov 1998

*   1) Foundation course in Personal Construct Psychology (Centre for Personal Construct Psychology, London)

*   2) Certificate in Counselling Skills (CPCAB)

**   3) Certificate in Therapeutic Counselling (CPCAB)

**   4) Advanced Certificate in Therapeutic Counselling (CPCAB)

**   5) Diploma in Therapeutic Counselling (CPCAB)

***   6) Advanced Diploma in Therapeutic Counselling (CPCAB)

***   7) Certificate in Counselling Supervision

Star System: * Introductory course only • ** 2-3 yr pt-time course to Cert/Dip level •
*** Professional development for trained counsellors
For added help, see section 'Essential Information for Students', page 1

193

EASTLEIGH COLLEGE,   01703 326326 EXT 1077
01703 322140

Cranbury Road, EASTLEIGH, Hampshire, SO5O 5HT,

Saturday workshops on a range of related topics, contact Kim Miller for details

♿ Access for disabled people, ground floor, disabled toilets, relatively easy access — please contact college to discuss needs & for information pack

*   **1) Certificate in the Basics of Counselling** (Open College)

Duration	4 days/7 weeks/9weeks, 22.5 hours: day/evening/weekends
Entry	For those in the caring professions, or anyone interested in counselling; no entry qualifications

*   **2) RSA Counselling Skills in the Development of Learning**

Duration	30 weeks, part-time, 1 evening or morning + 3 weekends (120 hrs)
Entry	Some previous short training in counselling skills essential, selection by interview
Apply To:	Tony Cook, Centre Manager

FAREHAM COLLEGE,SCHOOL OF SCIENCE & COMMUNITY STUDIES   01329 815200

Bishopsfield Road, FAREHAM, Hants, PO14 1NH,

Myers-Briggs Workshops

♿ Wheelchair access, suitable for visually impaired people. Tandem scheme, learning support services

*   **1) Gestalt Concepts** (SRCET Accredited)

Duration	6 weeks, part-time, Wednesday evenings, November & May start
Entry	For those who have previously completed a counselling skills course
Apply To:	Richard MacKrory

*   **2) First Steps in Counselling Skills** (SRCET Accredited)

Duration	7 weeks, part-time, Thursday eves & 1 Saturday (run in all 3 terms)
Entry	None specified
Apply To:	Richard Mackrory

**   **3) OCR** (RSA) Certificate, Counselling Skills in the Development of Learning

Duration	1 year, part-time, mornings, afternoons or eves + 3 Saturdays (120 hrs class contact in total)
Entry	For those helping others
Apply To:	Richard Mackrory

Star System: * Introductory course only • ** 2-3 yr pt-time course to Cert/Dip level •
*** Professional development for trained counsellors
For added help, see section 'Essential Information for Students', page 1

194

** 4) Diploma in GESTALT Counselling (BAC Acc) (Gestalt Approaches)

Duration	2 yrs, part-time
Entry	Applicants should be suitable for training, have relevant life experience and academic qualifications, have access to clients and be willing to undergo supervision, minimum 100 hrs training in counselling skills necessary
Apply To:	Andrew Kitching

FARNBOROUGH COLLEGE OF TECHNOLOGY,   01252 405 555

Boundary Road, FARNBOROUGH, Hampshire, GU14 6SB,

No response received to our enquiries for 2000. Entry details as of Nov 1998

* 1) Certificate in Basic Counselling Skills

* 2) Cerificate in Counselling Theory (CSCT/AEB)

* 3) Certificate in Counselling Skills (CSCT/AEB)

** 4) Advanced Certificate in Counselling Skills/Theory (CSCT/AEB)

** 5) Diploma in Therapeutic Counselling (CSCT/AEB)

COUNSELLING TRAINING INITIATIVES LTD,(CTI) 0115 944 7849

Galtee House, 1 Heanor Road, ILKESTON, Derbyshire, DE7 8DY,

Please see the National Section for fuller details of the courses offered

♿ No response received to our enquiries for 2000, entry details as of Nov 1998

CENTRAL SCHOOL OF COUNSELLING & THERAPY,
0800 243463

80 Paul Street, LONDON, EC2A 4UD,

See National Section entry for full details.

Star System: *Introductory course only • ** 2-3 yr pt-time course to Cert/Dip level •
*** Professional development for trained counsellors*
For added help, see section 'Essential Information for Students', page 1

195

HIGHBURY COLLEGE PORTSMOUTH,   02392 313361

Dovercourt Road, Cosham, PORTSMOUTH, PO6 2SA,

Workshops in counselling/counselling skills, in-house and tailor-made training offered

♿ Considerable resources for people with disabilities but priority is given to students on courses with substantial hours — we do try our best to meet individual needs

*   **1) Certificate in Basic Counselling Skills** (NCFE)

Duration   2 terms, 2.5 hrs/week, day or evening (50 hrs) repeated in Jan term

Entry   Open

*   **2) Certificate in Counselling** (NCFE)

Duration   1 academic year, 3 hrs/week, evenings + tutorials (102 hrs)

Entry   1) above/equivalent alternative/comparable course (eg CRUSE, Samaritans)

Apply To: Jo Reid, College Counselling Co-ordinator

UNIVERSITY OF PORTSMOUTH,   01705 894 392

Counselling Service, Gun House, Ravelin Park Hampshire Terrace, PORTSMOUTH, Hants, PO1 2QX,

No response received to our enquiries for 2000. Entry details as of Nov 1998

**   **Diploma of Higher Education in Counselling** (120 credits Level 2)

SOUTHAMPTON CITY COLLEGE,   01703 577 382

St Mary Street, SOUTHAMPTON, SO14 1AR,

No response received to our enquiries for 2000, entry details as of Nov 1998

*   **1) Introduction to Counselling Skills** (CENTRA Level 1)

*   **2) Certificate in Counselling Skills** (CENTRA Level II)

*   **3) Applying The Arts in A Counselling Skills Context** (CENTRA Level II)

**   **4) Advanced Diploma in Person Centred Counselling (BAC Acc CENTRA Level III)**

***   **5) Diploma in Casework Supervision** (CENTRA)

Star System: ** Introductory course only • ** 2-3 yr pt-time course to Cert/Dip level •*
*** Professional development for trained counsellors
For added help, see section 'Essential Information for Students', page 1

196

SOUTHAMPTON PASTORAL COUNSELLING,   **01703 639966**
Union Road, Northam, SOUTHAMPTON, SO14 0PT,
Also offers short courses — send SAE to the Administrator
♿ Disabled people should discuss suitability when considering the course

**   **1) National Certificate in Counselling Skills & Attitudes** (WPF)

Duration	2 yrs part-time, 2 full days + 1 eve weekly for 30 wks/academic yr
Entry	Those wishing to explore counselling skills & associated topics to help their paid or voluntary work, their personal development or as preparation for the Westminster Pastoral Foundation National Diploma in Psychodynamic Counselling

**   **2) National Diploma in Psychodynamic Counselling** (WPF)

Duration	2 yrs, 0.5 day/week through academic year + 2-3 hrs counselling clients at SPCS
Entry	Those wishing to qualify as counsellors in an agency, WPF National Certificate in Counselling Skills & Attitudes/equivalent, selection by interview + in-depth personal assessment

***   **3) Certificate in Supervision** (WPF)

Duration	10 Saturdays at monthly intervals over 1 academic year
Entry	Previous training to at least certificate level, previous therapy, considerable experience of client work, availability of supervisees
Apply To:	Josephine Mulvey, Head of Training

TOTTON COLLEGE,   **01703 261439**
Water Lane, Totton, SOUTHAMPTON, SO40 32X,
♿ The college is wheelchair accessible

*   **1) Level 1 Counselling Skills** (CENTRA)

Duration	20 hours
Entry	None
Core Model	Person Centred

**   **2) Level 2 Counselling Skills** (CENTRA)

Duration	122 hours, Thurs eve+ 2 non-residential weekends
Entry	A basic introduction to counselling skills course and/or experience in a work setting. Students are expected to attend an interview
Apply To:	Julia Russell
Core Model	Psychodynamic

Star System: ** Introductory course only • ** 2-3 yr pt-time course to Cert/Dip level •*
*** Professional development for trained counsellors
For added help, see section 'Essential Information for Students', page 1

197

UNIVERSITY OF SOUTHAMPTON,   01703 597261
New College, The Avenue, SOUTHAMPTON, SO17 1BG,
No response was received to our enquiries for 2000. Entry details as of Nov 1998

** 1) **Certificate of Higher Education + Counselling Skills, Theory & Practice**

** 2) **Certificate in Advanced Educational Studies: Psychosexual Counselling & Therapy**

** 3) **Diploma of Higher Education: Counselling** (Univ of Southampton)

GROUPWORK CONSULTATION & TRAINING,   020 8858 6627
Groupwork Consultation & Train, SOUTHSEA, Hampshire, PO4 0YP,
No response received to our enquiries for 2000, entry details as of November 1998

* 1) **Foundation Group Skills Course**

* 2) **Intermediate Groupwork**

** 3) **Advanced Groupwork Certificate** (60 CATS points)

** 4) **Diploma in Groupwork**

HADIQA CENTRE,   01705 863266
16 Victoria Grove, SOUTHSEA, PO5 1NE,

♿ Wheelchair access is possible if required. Allowances made for Guide Dogs

** **Diploma in Counselling the Body, Gestalt & the Spiritual**

Core Model	Gestalt, Spiritual
Duration	450 hrs, 1 weekday/weekends
Entry	RSA Certificate in Counselling or equivalent
Apply To:	Brian Attridge

SOUTH DOWNS COLLEGE,   01705 797979
College Road, WATERLOOVILLE, Hampshire, PO7 8AA,
Short courses and workshops also offered

* 1) **Certificate in Basic Counselling Skills — A Counselling Approach to Working with People** (NCFE/C&G)

Duration	12 weeks, 3hrs/week, day or eve, Sept, Jan, March start
Entry	By application form

---

*Star System: * Introductory course only • ** 2-3 yr pt-time course to Cert/Dip level •*
*** Professional development for trained counsellors*

For added help, see section 'Essential Information for Students', page 1

198

*   **2) Certificate in Further Counselling Skills** (NCFE/C&G)

Duration	22 weeks, 3 hrs/week, day or eve, Sept, Jan start
Entry	Minimum of 36 hrs of counselling skills experience, selection by application and interview

**   **3) Humanistic Diploma in Counselling**

Duration	2 yrs, 6 hrs/week, 32 weeks/yr + day workshops, October start
Entry	Minimum 120 hrs counselling theory & skills training or considerable experience working as counsellor in counselling setting, selection by application & interview
Apply To:	Wendy Young, Course Manager

KING ALFRED'S UNIVERSITY COLLEGE, WINCHESTER
01962 824315

School of Health & Community, Studies, WINCHESTER, Hampshire, SO22 4NR,
In-house training and workshops in counselling skills, bereavement, assertiveness, group skills

♿ Ground floor access to most buildings and a lift in the Students' Union

*   **1) Introduction to Counselling**

Duration	10 weeks, 1 eve/day/week
Entry	Open

*   **2) RSA Certificate in Counselling Skills in Learning**

Duration	1 morning or eve/week, + 2 Saturday workshops (90 hrs)
Entry	21+ with an interest in counselling skills, application
Apply To:	Alma Jones, Course Administrator

PETER SYMONDS' COLLEGE,   01926 886 166

Adult Cont. Education Centre, Stoney Lane, Weeke, WINCHESTER, Hampshire, SO22 6DR,
No response received to our enquiries for 2000, entry details as of Nov 1998

*   **1) Introductory Certificate in Counselling** (CENTRA

*   **2) RSA Counselling Skills in the Development of Le**

**   **3) Diploma in Humanistic Counselling** (based on TA)

***   **4) Counselling Supervision Certificate**

Star System: * *Introductory course only* • ** *2-3 yr pt-time course to Cert/Dip level* •
     *** *Professional development for trained counsellors*
For added help, see section 'Essential Information for Students', page 1

199

UNIVERSITY OF BIRMINGHAM,   0121 4145602
School of Continuing Studies, Edgbaston, BIRMINGHAM, B15 2TT,
Course is run in Birmingham, Shrewsbury, Worcester

*   Certificate in Counselling Skills
Duration   1 year, 1 eve/week + 6 Saturdays/Sundays
Entry   Over 21 yrs of age and committed to developing self-awareness
Apply To: Angela Webb

NORTH EAST WORCESTERSHIRE COLLEGE,   01527 572701
Faculty of Community Services, Blackwood Road, BROMSGROVE, Worcestershire,
B60 1PQ,

♿ Every effort will be made to include students with disabilities

*   1) Introduction to Counselling (CSCT/AEB)
Duration   30 hours
Entry   No qualifications required

*   2) Certificate in Counselling Theory (CSCT/AEB)
Duration   75 hrs
Entry   No qualifications required

3) Certificate in Counselling Skills (CSCT/AEB)
Duration   75 hrs
Entry   No qualifications required

**   4) Higher National Certificate in Counselling Skills
Duration   Please contact college for further details
Entry   Please contact college for further details
Apply To: Zen Kyle or Allie Fellows

Star System: * Introductory course only • ** 2-3 yr pt-time course to Cert/Dip level •
*** Professional development for trained counsellors
For added help, see section 'Essential Information for Students', page 1
200

HEREFORDSHIRE COLLEGE OF TECHNOLOGY,
01432 352235 X 369
FAX 01432 353449

Folly Lane, HEREFORD, HR1 1LS,

Workshops in counselling/counselling skills offered for helath care professionals and disability issues

♿ Equal Opportunities/Access

*   1) **Professional Development Certificate in Counselling Skills** (BTEC)

Duration	3 hrs per week, day or evening, 1 yr
Entry	Basic Counselling Skills training or relevant experience/knowledge
Apply To:	Suzanne Salmon
Core Model	Person Centred

**   2) **Professional Development Diploma in Counselling** (BTEC)

Duration	4 hrs per week, 2 x Saturday (12 hrs), 1 residential 14 hrs per year. Total 310 hrs. 2 year course
Entry	BTEC Cert Counselling Skills or equivalent
Apply To:	Mike Booth
Core Model	Integrative

UNIVERSITY OF BIRMINGHAM,   0121 414 5593

Hereford Sixth Form College, Folly Lane, HEREFORD,

No response to our enquiries for 2000, entry details as of Nov 1998

**   **Post Experience Certificate in Counselling**

WEST MERCIA INSTITUTE OF COUNSELLING,   01432 353 539

Mortimer House, Holmer Road, HEREFORD, HR4 9SP,

Short courses and in-house training offered. Courses 2) & 3) venues in Hereford/ Shrewsbury

♿ Access for disabled people. Blind and deaf people should discuss suitability with tutor.

*   1) **Introduction to Counselling**

Duration	10 weeks
Entry	Open

*   2) **Foundation Course** (BTEC)

Duration	1 year
Entry	Introductory course/equivalent

continued...

*Star System: * Introductory course only • ** 2-3 yr pt-time course to Cert/Dip level •*
*** Professional development for trained counsellors
For added help, see section 'Essential Information for Students', page 1

201

**   3) Diploma Course (BTEC)

Duration   1 year
Entry   Foundation course/equivalent

**   4) Advanced Diploma in Counselling (BTEC)

Duration   Contact Institute for further details
Entry   Diploma course/equivalent

***   5) Diploma in Counselling Supervision (BTEC)

Duration   120 hours (also available via distance learning)
Entry   For practising counsellors with supervision prospects
Apply To: Mr C Tatton, Co-Principal

GESTALT EDUCATION MIDLANDS CENTRE,   01905 841 512

2 Bowbrook Close, Peopleton, PERSHORE, Worcestershire, WR10 2EZ,
No response received to our enquiries for 2000, entry details as of Nov 1998

*   1) Weekend Gestalt Groups

**   2) Gestalt Psychotherapy Diploma Course

***   3) Supervision Groups

WORCESTER COLLEGE OF TECHNOLOGY,   01905 716 002

Dept of Adult Education, The Learning Shop, 28 The Cross, WORCESTER, WR1 3PZ,
No response received to our enquiries for 2000. Entry details as of Nov 1998

*   1) Counselling Skills

*   2) Personal Development

*   3) Working with Young People

*   4) Counselling Skills Stage 1 (AEB)

*   5) Counselling Skills Stage 2

*   6) Professional Development Certificate in Counselling Skills

---

Star System: * Introductory course only • ** 2-3 yr pt-time course to Cert/Dip level •
*** Professional development for trained counsellors

For added help, see section 'Essential Information for Students', page 1

202

UNIVERSITY OF HERTFORDSHIRE,   01707 285812
Meridian House, 32-36 The Common, HATFIELD, AL10 0NZ,

♿ Access, those with hearing or sight impairment should discuss their needs with the University

**   1) Certificate in Counselling
Duration   2 years, part-time, morning, afternoon or eve
Entry   Yr 1: None but aimed at workers in the helping professions. Yr 2: Either successful completion of Yr 1 Or experience in the caring professions, selection by interview

**   2) Postgraduate Diploma in Counselling (BAC Acc)
Duration   2 years, part-time, 1 full day/week
Entry   Completion of 1)/equivalent & demonstrate ability to study at postgraduate level by possession of a degreee or professional equivalent

***   3) MA in Counselling Enquiry
Duration   2 years, minimum, part-time up to 5 years
Entry   Completion of Postgraduate Diploma in Counselling/equivalent + BAC Accreditation

***   4) MA in Psychoanalytic Psychotherapy
Duration   1 year, part-time
Entry   Membership of an appropriate UKCP professional body. Course is run by Guild of Psychotherapists
Apply To: Dr Julia Buckroyd

***   5) Postgrad Cert in Counselling Supervision
Duration   30 x ½ days
Entry   Diploma level counselling + experience

SUPPORT GROUP & COUNSELLING SERVICE,   01707 659 996
PO BOX 30, POTTERS BAR, Hertfordshire, EN6 3JD,
No response to our enquiries for 2000, entry details as of Nov 1998

*   Counselling in GP Practices

---

*Star System: * Introductory course only • ** 2-3 yr pt-time course to Cert/Dip level •
*** Professional development for trained counsellors*
For added help, see section 'Essential Information for Students', page 1
203

HERTS AND BEDS PASTORAL FOUNDATION,   01727 868585

1 College Yard, Lower Dagnall Street, ST. ALBANS, Hertfordshire, AL3 4PA,
Affiliated to WPF. Courses also available from Bates House, Fosterhill Road, Bedford,
M40 2EN, Tel 01234 346077

*   1) Discovering Counselling

Duration	10 weeks. 1.5 hrs/week
Entry	Interest in counselling , personal development

*   2) Certificate in Counselling Skills (WPF)

Duration	1 year, 30 weeks, 3 hrs/day/evening
Entry	The ability to relate counselling theory to personal experience; experience of formal or informal caring role is an advantage

**   3) Advanced Certificate in Counselling Skills (WPF

Duration	2 years, 30 weeks, 3 hrs, day/evening
Entry	Completion of 1)

**   4) Diploma in Agency Counselling

Duration	2 years, 30 weeks, 4.5 hrs/day/evening. 30 weeks. (seminars & supervision)
Entry	Completion of 1); ongoing experience of using informed counselling in voluntary or professional setting

**   5) Diploma in Professional Studies in Psychodynamic Counselling (Univ of Herts)

Core Model	Psychodynamic
Duration	2 yrs, 30 weeks, 4.5 hrs/day-evening, (seminars & supervision — 15 wks, 1.5 hrs p.a. (supervision) + counselling practice
Entry	Completion of 1); assessment to work within HBPF Counselling Service; on-going personal therapy

***   6) Advanced Diploma in Psychodynamic Counselling (WPF)
(Membership of Institute of Psychotherapy and Counselling)

Core Model	Psychodynamic
Duration	2 years, 30 weeks x 4.5 hrs + 15 weeks x 1.5 p.a. (seminars & supervision) + counselling practice
Entry	Completion of 5); continuing assessment to work within HBPF counselling service; on-going personal therapy
Apply To:	Sue Freeman (St. Albans), Michael Philps (Bedford)

*Star System: * Introductory course only • ** 2-3 yr pt-time course to Cert/Dip level •*
*** Professional development for trained counsellors*
For added help, see section 'Essential Information for Students', page 1
204

KENNETH CHITTY,   01727 874 567

Silver Birches, 2a Burston Drive, ST. ALBANS, Hertfordshire, AL2 2HR,
Workshops in counselling/counselling skills, weekend and residential holiday courses
in London, Midlands, Spain

* **Healing Dialogues for the Inner Child — Structures of the Unconscious — subpersonalities — & creative therapies**

Duration	Seminar and workshop teaching as 1 day, weekend, weekend + residential holiday courses
Entry	For those in healthcare professions, relevant experience/previous counselling experience an advantage. Telephone interviews for selection
Apply To:	Course Secretary or Kenneth Chitty

OAKLANDS COLLEGE,   01727 737000 FAX 01727 737010

St Albans City Campus, St Peters Road, ST. ALBANS, Hertfordshire, AL1 3RX,
Training also available in Welwyn Garden City and Boreham Wood

♿ Limited access depending on degree of disability. Please enquire at the above number

* **1) Foundation Year in Counselling** (Cert. of Attendance, credits with OCN)

Entry	Anyone with an interest in counselling at first level. No previous experience necessary, but commitment to experiential learning & personal development is essential

** **2) Intermediate Year in Counselling** (Certificate, credits with OCN)

Duration	30 weeks, part-time, 4.25 hrs, afternoon/evening
Entry	Foundation year or equivalent. This course is intended to build on the experience of the Foundation Year, particularly developing experiential learning & integrating some theory

** **3) Diploma in Counselling** (Hertfordshire Univ)

Duration	2 years, part-time, 1.15pm — 830pm each Monday + 2 residential weekends/year
Entry	Foundation Year; course aims to provide counselling training reflecting both psychodynamic & client-centred theory (450 hrs theory and skills training); Interview and personal therapy strongly recommended
Apply To:	Counselling Course Scheme Tutor

---

*Star System: * Introductory course only • ** 2-3 yr pt-time course to Cert/Dip level •*
*** *Professional development for trained counsellors*
For added help, see section 'Essential Information for Students', page 1

205

NORTH HERTFORDSHIRE COLLEGE,   **01462 424242**

Monkswood Way, STEVENAGE, Hertfordshire, SG1 1LA,

♿ Access and facilities for additional learning support

---

*   **1) Introduction to Counselling** (OCN — 2 credits — Level 2)

Duration	40 hours, 12 weeks, 1 eve/week + 2 Saturdays
Entry	Those with an interest in counselling and who may wish to gauge their suitability for further training.

*   **2) Certificate in Counselling Skills** (CPCAB — CS01)

Core Model	Person Centred
Duration	120 hours, 34 weeks, 1 x am or eve/week + 3 Saturdays
Entry	Anyone who has or intends to have a counselling role in their lives. Selection is by interview.

*   **3) Certificate in Therapeutic Counselling** (CPCAB — TC01)

Core Model	Person Centred
Duration	120 hours, 34 weeks, 1 x am or eve/week + 3 Saturdays
Entry	Those who have completed CS01 or it's equivalent

**   **4) Diploma in Counselling** (CPCAB — TC02 + TC03)

Apply To:	Pat Bailey
Core Model	Person Centred
Duration	2 years, 464 hours, part-time 1 day/week — 1pm — 7pm + 4 Saturdays and 2 x 2-day residentials
Entry	Those who have complted CS01 and TC01 or their equivalent

---

*Star System: * Introductory course only • ** 2-3 yr pt-time course to Cert/Dip level •*
*** Professional development for trained counsellors*
For added help, see section 'Essential Information for Students', page 1
206

BEXLEY COLLEGE,   **01322 404000**
Tower Road, BELVEDERE, Kent, DA17 6JA,

♿ Access for disabled people, lift and car park provision.

* **1) Basic Counselling Skills** (NCFE)

Duration	18 weeks, 2.5 hrs/week, day or evening
Entry	Interest in counselling and self-development

* **2) RSA Certificate: Counselling Skills in the Development of Learning**

Duration	30 weeks, 3 hrs/week + 1 weekend
Entry	Those in the caring professions/relevant voluntary organisations or wishing to train for a career in counselling.

** **3) Integrative Diploma in Counselling** (NCFE)

Duration	2 yrs part-time, 1 day/week (7 hrs)
Entry	At least 120 hrs tuition in counselling & theory, with relevant certificate, or considerable experience, working in a counselling setting.
Apply To:	Elizabeth Holborn, Counselling Co-ordinator

CLIFTONVILLE CENTRE FOR THE ADVANCEMENT, OF COUNSELLING   **01843 864 116**
1 Westover Gardens, St Peter's, BROADSTAIRS, Kent, CT10 3EY,
No response received to our enquiries for 2000. Entry details as of Nov 1998

* **1) NCPE Bereavement Course**

* **2) Basic Counselling Skills** (NCFE)

* **3) Certificate in Counselling** (NCFE)

* **4) Certificate in Counselling Theory** (AEB)

* **5) Certificate in Counselling Skills** (AEB)

** **6) Advanced Certificate in Counselling** (AEB)

** **7) Advanced Diploma in Counselling** (CTI)

---

*Star System: * Introductory course only • ** 2-3 yr pt-time course to Cert/Dip level •*
*** Professional development for trained counsellors*
For added help, see section 'Essential Information for Students', page 1

BROMLEY ADULT EDUCATION COLLEGE, 0181 460 0020

Widmore Centre, Nightingale Lane, Church Lane, BROMLEY, BR1 2SQ,

Workshops also available eg: Effective Listening, Basic Counselling Skills etc

♿ These vary from centre to centre, please contact the organisation for further details

* 1) Basic Counselling Skills

Duration	12 weeks, 2 hrs/week, day
Entry	Open
Apply To:	Janet Austin

* 2) Creative Listening and Basic Counselling

Duration	7 wks, 2hrs/week, day or evening
Entry	Open
Apply To:	Mandy Ffrench

BROMLEY COLLEGE OF FURTHER & HIGHER,EDUCATION
0181 295 7075
FAX: 0181 295 7082

Old Town Hall, Tweedy Road, BROMLEY, Kent, BR1 3PP,

In-house and tailor-made training also available. Also workshops eg: Assessment, Crisis intervention, PTSD

♿ Wheel chair access 'talking' computer

** 1) Certificate in Integrative Counselling

Duration	1 year, 3x10 week terms, 5 hrs/week afternoon and evening
Entry	Anyone who has, or intends to have, a counselling role in thier lives; selection by interview

** 2) Diploma in Integrative Counselling (BAC Acc)

Duration	2 years, each 3x10 week terms, 5hrs/week afternoon and evening. Supervised counselling placements available
Entry	Successful completion of the certificate in Therapeutic Counselling/ equivalent; selection by interview

*** 3) Diploma in Supervision (Integrative)

Duration	1 year, 3hrs/fortnightly, morning
Entry	Counsellors with at least 2 years post-qualifying experience
Apply To:	Sue Telling, Counselling Course Director

---

*Star System: * Introductory course only • ** 2-3 yr pt-time course to Cert/Dip level •*
*** *Professional development for trained counsellors*

For added help, see section 'Essential Information for Students', page 1

CANTERBURY COLLEGE,   01227 811111

New Dover Road, CANTERBURY, Kent, CT1 3AJ,

In-house/tailor-made courses

♿ Approx 80% access for wheelchair users

*** 1) Diploma in Supervision of Counsellors and Therapists

Duration	4 hrs/week + 3 Saturdays over 1 year
Entry	Intended for qualified counsellors with minimum 2 years experience (post qualifying) Students will need to be working with 2 supervisees

*** 2) Diploma in Therapeutic Counselling

Duration	7.25 hrs/week + 4 Saturdays over 1 year
Entry	Students need to have completed the Advanced Certificate in Counselling Skills and Theory or equivalent. Students will need to have placements offering 100 hrs of supervised counselling

** 3) Advanced Certificate in Counselling Skills and Theory

Duration	4 hrs/week + 2 Staurdays per term over 30 weeks
Entry	Students will need to have completed both the Certificates in Skills and Theory or other appropriate courses. Develops students for the diploma

** 4) Certificate in Specialist Counselling Skills (cancer)

Duration	3 hrs/week for 1 year
Entry	For students who have already undertaken some training/education in counselling and who are interested in working with patients/clients who have cancer.

** 5) Certificate in Specialist Counselling (disability)

Duration	3 hrs/week for 1 year
Entry	This course is intended for people who are interested in working with people with physical disabilities (who have some counselling training/ education)

* 6) Certificate in Counselling Skills

Duration	2.5 hrs/week for 1 year
Entry	For students who have already undertaken some counselling training/ education and who want to develop further a base for the effective use of counselling skills

continued...

Star System: * *Introductory course only* • ** *2-3 yr pt-time course to Cert/Dip level* •
*** *Professional development for trained counsellors*
For added help, see section 'Essential Information for Students', page 1

*   **7) Certificate in Counselling Theory**

Duration   2.5 hrs/week for 1 year

Entry   For students who have undertaken some counselling training/ education previously and are wanting to build a theoretical base for effective counselling

*   **8) Further Counselling Skills**

Duration   approx 22 hrs over 11 weeks

Entry   For those who have completed the basic counselling skills course or who have relevant counselling experience

*   **9) Basic Counselling Skills**

Duration   approx 22 hrs over 11 weeks

Entry   For anyone interested in learning counselling skills

*   **10) Introduction to Counselling Children and Adolescents**

Duration   30 hrs over 10 weeks

Entry   For people interested/involved in counselling/working with young people

Apply To: Louise MacKinney

KENT INSTITUTE OF MEDICINE & HEALTH SCIENCES
01227 827663

Kent Research & Development Centre, University Of Kent At Canterbury, CANTERBURY, CT2 7PD,

*   **1) Certificate in Counselling Studies**

Duration   2 years, min, 4 years, maximum. Modular, 8 units: 5 compulsory core + 3 options

Entry   By interview after successful completion of two modules + assignments

**   **2) Diploma in Counselling**

Core Model   Integrative

Duration   2 years, part-time

Entry   Evidence of ability to study at undergraduate level 2/3; completion of Certificate in Counselling Studies (HE level 1); professional qualification + basic counselling training considered. Programme requirement of 40 weekly sessions in counselling required

Star System: ** Introductory course only • ** 2-3 yr pt-time course to Cert/Dip level •*
*** Professional development for trained counsellors
For added help, see section 'Essential Information for Students', page 1

210

*** **3) MSc in Supervision for the Helping Professions** (subject to approval)

Duration   To be offered from January 2000. 2 years, part-time

Entry   Training in counselling or psychotherapy & have practised for a min of
              6 months as a supervisor, or have a relevant professional qualification
              and min of 1 year relevant practice as a supervisor. Selection by
              interview

*** **4) Stand Alone Modules**

Duration   Please enquire

Core Model   A wide choice of specialised areas in the counselling field, e.g. Family
              Therapy, Counselling Children & Adolescents, TA, Group Leading
              Skills, Change, Loss & Bereavement

Entry   Open entry. Credit can be gained by attending 80% of the module
              contact time and successful completion of the assignment.

Apply To: Mrs Susan Longley, Tel. 01227 827663

MID-KENT COLLEGE OF H & FE,   01634 830633

Horsted, Maidstone Road, CHATHAM, Kent, ME5 9UQ,

No response received to our enquiries for 2000, entry details as of November 1998

*   **1) Introductory Courses in Counselling Skills**

*   **2) Certificate in Counselling Skills** (CSCT/AEB)

*   **3) Certificate in Counselling Theory** (CSCT/AEB)

**   **4) Diploma in Counselling** (CSCT/AEB)

TRAINING SOUTH EAST ENGLAND,   01580 852 414

The Old Farm House, Biddenden Road, Frittenden, CRANBROOK, Kent, TN17 2BE,

No response received to our enquiries for 2000. Entry details as of Nov 1998

*   **1) Introductory TA Course '101'** (ITAA)

*   **2) Intermediate Training in TA**

**   **3) Advanced Training in TA**

---

*Star System: * Introductory course only • ** 2-3 yr pt-time course to Cert/Dip level •*
*** Professional development for trained counsellors
For added help, see section 'Essential Information for Students', page 1

211

CENTRE FOR COUNSELLING & PSYCHOTHERAPY STUDIES
01322 622 078
FAX: 01322 622 082

Thames Gateway NHS Trust, Stone House Hospital, Cotton Lane, DARTFORD, DA2 6AU,

**	**The Thames Gateway Diploma in Counselling (BAC Acc, East London Univ)**
Duration	2 years, part-time, 1 afternoon to evening/week, for 36 weeks/year (450 hrs+)
Entry	Selection by interview; no formal entry requirements, suitable for those with foundation level training and/or previous helping experience professionally or voluntarily.
Apply To:	Marian Smith, Counselling Diploma Administrator

COUNSELLING TRAINING INITIATIVES LTD,(CTI) 0115 944 7849

Galtee House, 1 Heanor Road, ILKESTON, Derbyshire, DE7 8DY,

Please see National Section entry for full details of courses offered

♿ No response received to our enquiries for 2000, entry details as of Nov 1998

CENTRAL SCHOOL OF COUNSELLING & THERAPY,
0800 243463

80 Paul Street, LONDON, EC2A 4UD,
See National Section entry for full details.

COUPLES COUNSELLING NETWORK,   01689 850 726

43 North Drive, ORPINGTON, Kent, BR6 9PG,
No response to our enquiries for 2000. Entry details as of Nov 1998

***   **1) Foundation Course in Counselling Couples**

***   **2) Certificate in Couples and Marriage Counselling**

***   **3) Diploma in Couples and Marriage Counselling**

ORPINGTON COLLEGE,   01689 899 700

The Walnuts, ORPINGTON, Kent, BR6 0TE,
No response received to our enquiries for 2000, entry details as of Nov 1998

*   **1) Introduction to Counselling Skills**

---

*Star System: * Introductory course only • ** 2-3 yr pt-time course to Cert/Dip level •*
*** Professional development for trained counsellors*
For added help, see section 'Essential Information for Students', page 1

*   2) Transactional Analysis Workshop

*   3) Transactional Analysis Workshop (Intensive)

*   4) Introduction to Bereavement Counselling

*   5) Certificate in Counselling Skills (CENTRA)

KENT ADULT EDUCATION CENTRE,   01843 292013
Ramsgate Centre, 35 Chapel Place, RAMSGATE, Kent, CT11 9SB,
No response received to our enquiries for 2000, entry details as of November 1998

*   1) Introduction to Basic Counselling Skills

*   2) Basic Counselling Skills

*   3) Developing Counselling Skills

*   4) Certificate in Counselling (CPCAB)

WEST KENT COLLEGE,FACULTY OF SERVICES TO PEOPLE
01732 358 101
Brook Street, TONBRIDGE, TN2 2PW
No response received to our enquiries for 2000, entry details as of Nov 1998

**   Advanced Diploma in Humanistic Counselling (BAC Acc)

TUNBRIDGE WELLS COUNSELLING CENTRE,   01892 548750
St Georges Centre, 7 Chilston Road, TUNBRIDGE WELLS, Kent, TN4 9LP,
Workshops in counselling and counselling skills, psychodynamic concepts

♿ Very limited as many stairs in our building

*   1) Is Counsellor Training for You?
Duration   0.5 day workshop
Entry   None

*   2) Introduction to Counselling
Duration   10x2 hr sessions
Entry   None

continued...

Star System: ** Introductory course only • ** 2-3 yr pt-time course to Cert/Dip level •*
*** Professional development for trained counsellors
For added help, see section 'Essential Information for Students', page 1
213

*   **3) WPF Certificate in Counselling Theory & Skills**

Duration   a) 1 yr 4.5 hrs/week, 30 weeks, workshops, individual tutorials OR b) 2 yrs, 3 hrs/week, 30 weeks/year, workshops, individual tutorials

Entry   Interview and detailed application form

**   **4) WPF Diploma in Psychodynamic Counselling**

Duration   2 yr, part-time. 1 eve/week (30 wks/yr), workshops, individual tutorials, weekly clinical work and supervision form part of course

Entry   Certificate in Counselling Theory and Skills or equivalent + year training, interview, individual and group, detailed application form. Personal therapy throughout the course

**   **5) WPF Advanced Diploma in Psychodynamic Counselling**

Duration   2 yr, part-time, 0.5 day per week (4.5 hrs), 30 wks/yr, weekly clinical work and supervision form part of the course

Entry   WPF Diploma in Psychodynamic Counselling (or equivalent); individual and group interviews, detailed application forms, personal therapy throughout the course

Apply To: Marilyn Foster (Administrator)

*Star System: * Introductory course only • ** 2-3 yr pt-time course to Cert/Dip level •
*** Professional development for trained counsellors*
For added help, see section 'Essential Information for Students', page 1

214

TAMESIDE COLLEGE,   0161 908 6868

Library & Learning Centre, Beaufort Road, ASHTON-UNDER-LYNE, Lancashire, OL6 6NX,

No response received to our enquiries for 2000. Entry details as of Nov 1998

*   **1) Introduction to Counselling** (CENTRA Level 1)

**   **2) Certificate in Counselling** (CENTRA Level II)

**   **3) Diploma in Counselling**

BLACKPOOL & THE FYLDE COLLEGE,   01253 352352 X2321

Ashfield Road, Bispham, BLACKPOOL, FY2 0HB,

In-house/tailor-made training and counselling workshops eg: Sexuality; TA; counselling skills in organisational context

♿ Most areas of the college are accessible; after assessment can provide, where appropriate, resources.

*   **1) Introductory Counselling Skills Course** (CENTRA)
Duration	10 weeks, part-time, day or evening
Entry	For those in the caring professions and relevant voluntary organisations

*   **2) RSA Certificate, Counselling Skills in the Development of Learning**
Duration	36 weeks, part-time, evenings
Entry	By interview after completion of introductory module

**   **3) Advanced Diploma in Counselling** (CENTRA)
Duration	2 yrs, part-time, afternoon and evening/week
Entry	Completion of Level 2 and meet course criteria; selection by application and interview

***   **4) Higher National Diploma in Counselling** (BTEC)
Duration	2 years full time course
Entry	Level 2 and interview
Apply To:	Ms Patricia Roche

Star System: *Introductory course only* • *** 2-3 yr pt-time course to Cert/Dip level* •
*** Professional development for trained counsellors
For added help, see section 'Essential Information for Students', page 1

215

BOLTON COLLEGE,   01204 453441

Manchester Road, BOLTON, BL2 1ER,

In-house/tailor-made training and workshops in counselling and counselling skills.

♿ Ground floor entry for wheelchair lift to all floors, specialsed toilet facilities. Support workers eg: Visual Impaired Unit

* 1) Level 1 An Introduction to Counselling (CENTRA)

Duration	30 hrs (10 weeks 3hrs/week) Saturday morning, day, evening
Entry	No formal requirements — just an interest in counselling
Core Model	Person Centred

* 2) Level 2 Certificate in Counselling Skills (CENTRA)

Duration	100 hrs (34 weeks 3hrs/week) + weekend residential day and evening
Entry	Level 1 Certificate of Attendance or equivalent qualification
Core Model	Person centred with Egan structure

*** 3) Level 3 Diploma in Counselling (CENTRA)

Entry	Level 2 Certificate Interview + references. Example of counselling skills
Duration	200 hrs (68 weeks 3hrs/week) + 2 residential weekends and Saturday workshops — Day and evening
Core Model	Integrative approach with Person Centred base
Apply To:	Meg Gough, Elisabeth Long

BOLTON COMMUNITY EDUCATION SERVICE,   01204 525500

Clarence Street Centre, Clarence Street, BOLTON, BL1 2ET,

Courses run at various venues

* 1) Introduction to Counselling Skills Level 1 (CENTRA)

Duration	20+ hrs day or evening (course Sept — Dec & Jan — March terms at present)
Entry	None
Apply To:	Liz Perry ext 3912, Rachel Jones

* 2) Certificate in Counselling skills — Level II (CENTRA)

Duration	34 wks, 3hrs/day & evening + 1 compulsory residential (120 hrs)
Entry	Completion of 1); min 25 yrs of age at commencement of course; selection by application form and group/individual interview
Apply To:	Liz Perry, Rachel Jones

*Star System: * Introductory course only • ** 2-3 yr pt-time course to Cert/Dip level •*
*** Professional development for trained counsellors*
For added help, see section 'Essential Information for Students', page 1

216

BURY COLLEGE,   0161 280 8280 X 642
FAX 0161 280 8228

Market Street, BURY, Lancashire, BL9 0BG,

In-house and tailor-made courses for companies and organisations also workshops in counselling

♿ Ramp access to building — disabled and wheelchair access; lift, toilet facilities

*   **1) Introduction to Counselling Level 1** (CENTRA)

Duration   8 weeks, (24 hrs)

Entry   Open access

*   **2) Counselling Skills Certificate Level 2** (CENTRA)

Duration   102 hrs, over 34 weeks + residential

Entry   Level 1 or part of training meets level 1 criteria

**   **3) Diploma in Counselling Level 3**

Duration   2 years, part-time

Entry   Level 2 or equivalent; selection by interview

EARLY BREAK DRUGS SERVICE   0161 797 0108

17 Parsons Lane, BURY, Lancashire, BL9 0LY,

The Project provides counselling support & information for young people & their families about drug abuse

♿ All venues will have access, those with visual or aural impairment should discuss their needs with the Project Trainers

*   **1) Level 1 Counselling Skills Course** (Drugs Focus) (CENTRA)

Duration   6-8 weeks, 3 hrs/week (24 hrs)

Entry   None stated

**   **2) Level II Counselling Skills Certificate Course** (CENTRA)

Duration   34 weeks, 3hrs/weeks + 1 residential weekend

Entry   None stated

Apply To: Barbara Jack, Service Directory

Star System: * Introductory course only • ** 2-3 yr pt-time course to Cert/Dip level •
*** Professional development for trained counsellors
For added help, see section 'Essential Information for Students', page 1

217

ADULT COLLEGE — LANCASTER, THE,   01524 60141
PO Box 603, White Cross Education Cnt, Quarry Road, LANCASTER, LA1 3SE,
Workshops in counselling and counselling skills

♿ Access for disabled/wheelchair users. Support for visual and hearing impairment.
Learning support for specific learning needs.

*   **Level 1 certificate Intorduction to Counselling** (CENTRA)

Duration	10 weeks 3hrs/week, Wed eve or Wed morning
Entry	Open access suitable for anyone who has or intends to have to use listening/counselling skills in their lives.
Core Model	Person centred approach — Carl Rogers

*   **Level 2 Certificate in Counselling Skills** (CENTRA)

Duration	33 weeks 3.5 hrs/week + Residential Weekend (15 hrs). Two courses — Mon eve or Fri morning
Entry	Adult College Level 1 Certificate in Counselling, OR equivalent plus interview.
Core Model	Person centred approach — Carl Rogers

LANCASTER & MORECAMBE COLLEGE,   01524 66215 X 237
Student Services Unit, Morcambe Road, LANCASTER, LA1 2TY,
No response received to our enquiries for 2000, entry details as of November 1998

*   **1) Introduction to Counselling** (CENTRA)

*   **2) RSA Certificate in Counselling Skills in the Development of Learning**

**   **3) Diploma in Counselling**

LANCASTER THERAPY CENTRE,   01524 39443
49 Westbourne Road, LANCASTER, LA1 5DX,
No response received to our enquiries for 2000. Entry details as of Nov 1998

**   **Transactional Analysis Psychotherapy Training** (EATA, UKCP)

UNIVERSITY COLLEGE, OF ST MARTIN   01524 384 384
Department Of Applied, Social Sciences, LANCASTER, LA1 3JD,

**   **Diploma** (HE) in Counselling (BAC Acc)

Star System: ** Introductory course only • ** 2-3 yr pt-time course to Cert/Dip level •*
*** Professional development for trained counsellors
For added help, see section 'Essential Information for Students', page 1

RUNSHAW COLLEGE,   01772 622 677
Langdale Road, Wigan Road, LEYLAND, Lancs, PR5 2DQ,
No response to our enquiries for 2000, entry details as of Nov 1998

*   **1) Counselling Skills Level II** (CENTRA)

**   **2) Diploma in Counselling** (CENTRA)

NELSON & COLNE COLLEGE,   01282 440 200
Scotland Road, NELSON, Lancashire, BB9 7YT,

 ♿ Disabled people should contact the college to discuss their needs

*   **1) Introduction to Counselling**
Duration   17 weeks, 3 hrs/week, evening (2 courses per year)
Entry   Open, Adult entry

*   **2) RSA Counselling Certificate**
Duration   1 year, part-time, evenings; 3.5 hs + 1 weekend
Entry   Selection by interview
Apply To: Thelma Thornton, College Counsellor

PRESTON COLLEGE,   01772 772200
Dept of Business & Information, Technology, St Vincent's Road, Fulwood, PRESTON, PR2 9UR,
No response was received to our enquiries for 2000. Entry details as of Nov 1998

*   **1) Introduction Counselling Skills — Level 1** (CENTRA)

*   **2) Counselling Skills Level II** (CENTRA)

**   **3) Advanced Certificate in Counselling** (CENTRA)

UNIVERSITY OF CENTRAL LANCASHIRE,   01772 893400/893413
Faculty Of Health, PRESTON, PR1 2HE,
In-house tailor-made and short counselling courses also available

 ♿ Ramp access, toilet facilities, parking facilities, lifts in main building

*   **1) Certificate in Introductory Counselling Skills** (CENTRA Level 1)
Duration   12 weeks, part-time, morning/afternoon or eve
Entry   Open access
Apply To: Peter Cardew

continued...

Star System: ** Introductory course only • ** 2-3 yr pt-time course to Cert/Dip level •*
*** Professional development for trained counsellors
For added help, see section 'Essential Information for Students', page 1

* 2) Certificate in Counselling Skills & Health Promotion

Duration   1 academic year, part-time, morning/afternoon/eve
Entry   Open access
Core Model   Person-Centred
Apply To: Jim Martin

* 3) Advanced Certificate in Counselling Skills (CENTRA Level 2)

Duration   30 weeks, part-time, afternoon or eve, 1 residential & 1 non-residential weekend
Entry   Completion of 1) Introductory skills course and/or using counselling skills within their occupation/private life, application by CV

** 4) Graduate Diploma in Professional Counselling (CENTRA Level 3)

Duration   2 yrs, part-time, afternoon/eve, 1 residential/year
Entry   Completion of Certificate/Advanced Certificate, selection by interactive interview, over 24 yrs of age, those who have completed Level 1/2 elsewhere may need to complete Dip in Couns studies
Core Model   Person-Centred
Apply To: Peter Cardew

*** 5) Post-graduate Certificates in Counselling Studiies (Aspects of Sexuality)

Duration   1-2 yrs, part-time, afternoon/evening
Entry   Qualified, practising counsellor, Dip/Graduate Diploma, ability to study at postgraduate level, non-standard entrants are admitted on the basis of a portfolio showing experience, personal development & learning
Apply To: Peter Cardew/Jim Martin

*** 6) Post-graduate Certificate in Counselling Studies (Bereavement)

Duration   1-2 yrs, part-time, afternoon/eve
Entry   Qualified, practising counsellor, Dip/Graduate Diploma, ability to study at postgraduate level, non-standard entrants admitted on the basis of portfolio showing experience, personal development & learning

*** 7) Post-graduate Certificate in Counselling Studies (Supervision)

Duration   1-2 yrs, part-time, afternoon/eve
Entry   As 5) above

*** 8) Post-graduate Certificate in Counselling Studies (Substance Misuse)

Entry   As 5) above
Duration   1-2 yrs, part-time, afternoon/eve

Star System: * Introductory course only • ** 2-3 yr pt-time course to Cert/Dip level •
*** Professional development for trained counsellors

For added help, see section 'Essential Information for Students', page 1

220

***   **9) Post-graduate Diploma in Counselling Studies**

Duration	2-3 yrs, part-time, afternoon/eve
Entry	As 5) above
Apply To:	Peter Cardew/Jim Martin

WIGAN & LEIGH COLLEGE,   01942 761600

Counselling Section, Wigan Business School, Wigan & Leigh College, WIGAN,
Lancashire, WN1 1RS,

♿ Building partially ramped; no lift facility; visual and aural aids

*   **1) Introduction to Counselling** (CENTRA Level 1)

Duration	8 weeks, part-time day or evening
Entry	None specified

*   **2) Certificate in Counselling** (CENTRA Level 2)

Duration	1 year, part-time, day or evening + 1 weekend residential + 1 Saturday workshop
Entry	An introduction to counselling course

**   **3) Advanced Diploma in Counselling (BAC Acc; CENTRA)**

Duration	1 year, full-time, with residential OR 2 years, part-time with 2 residentials
Entry	100 hours counsellor education or equivalent

***   **4) Advanced Diploma in Casework Supervsion** (CENTRA)

Duration	1 year, part-time, meeting weekly + 1 Saturday workshop
Entry	2 years since training and currently in a position to supervise at least 2 caseworkers
Apply To:	Anita Warhurst, Curiculum Manager — Care and Counselling, Faculty of Art, Image and Care

*Star System: * Introductory course only • ** 2-3 yr pt-time course to Cert/Dip level •*
*** Professional development for trained counsellors*
For added help, see section 'Essential Information for Students', page 1

221

COUNSELLING TRAINING INITIATIVES LTD,(CTI)   0115 944 7849

Galtee House, 1 Heanor Road, ILKESTON, Derbyshire, DE7 8DY,

Please see National section for fuller details of courses offered

♿ No response received to our enquiries for 2000, entry details as of Nov 1998

SECOND GENESIS,   0116 235 6569

58C St Stephens Road, LEICESTER, LE2 1GG,

No response received to our enquiries for 2000, entry details as of Nov 1998

*   **Counselling from an African/Caribbean, Asian & Mixed Race Perspective**

UNIVERSITY OF LEICESTER,   0116 251 7368

Dept of Adult Education, Vaughan College, St Nicholas Circle, LEICESTER, LE1 4LB,

Workshops in counselling/counselling skills, e.g. Endings, Dreamwork, Therapeutic Stories, Intrauterine Experience

 Full access — lifts, toilets, etc

*   **1) Counselling Skills**

Duration	20 hours, part-time day/evening (Sept, Jan, April start), also as 3 linked Saturdays, one week (5 days)
Entry	None

**   **2) Certificate in Counselling Studies**

Duration	At least 2 years — 180 hours (modular)
Entry	Completion of 1)/equivalent elsewhere; current involvement in counselling/caring work is useful. Non-certificate students can attend most of the modules.

**   **3) Advanced Certificate in Counselling**

Duration	Additional 90 hours
Entry	Successful completion of 2), currently counselling under supervision & acceptable tutor's & supervisor's report, selection process

**   **4) Diploma in Counselling**

Duration	Additional 180 hours
Entry	Successful completion of 3)

Star System: ** Introductory course only* • *** 2-3 yr pt-time course to Cert/Dip level* •
*** Professional development for trained counsellors

For added help, see section 'Essential Information for Students', page 1

222

** **5) PG Diploma in Psychodynamic Counselling, and MA in Psychodynamic Counselling (BAC Acc)**

Core Model	Psychodynamic
Duration	2 years, (450 hours)
Entry	By selection (limited places available); at least one year's training in counselling & preferably experience in counselling

** **6) Certificate in Alcohol and Drug Counselling**

Duration	1 year, part-time, (180 hours)
Entry	Degree/professional qualification; suitable experience

** **7) Diploma in Alcohol and Drug Counselling**

Duration	1 year, part-time (240 hrs)
Entry	Successful completion of 6)

*** **8) Diploma in Psychodynamic Studies** (Psychotherapy training)

Duration	Foundation year (one session a week), then 2 years, 1 day/week + further year minimum for UKCP registration
Entry	By selection (limited places available); at least 2 years previous training to high level of counselling; at least 3 years counselling and/or psychotherapy practice

*** **9) Certificate in Psychodynamic Supervision**

Core Model	Psychodynamic
Duration	180 hours (including home based learning) including practice of supervision
Entry	Attendance on 2 'Supervision of Counselling & Therapy' residential courses at University of Leicester
Apply To:	Michael Jacobs, Director of Counselling & Psychotherapy Prog.

*Star System: * Introductory course only • ** 2-3 yr pt-time course to Cert/Dip level •*
*** *Professional development for trained counsellors*
For added help, see section 'Essential Information for Students', page 1

223

GRANTHAM COLLEGE,

01476 400200
FAX 01476 400291

Stonebridge Road, GRANTHAM, Lincolnshire, NG31 9AP,

* 1) Basic Counselling Skills Stage 1 (EMFEC)

Duration	30 hrs, 1 morning or evening/week (Autumn & Spring terms); OR 1 evening/week in Sleaford
Entry	Open access

* 2) Basic Counselling Skills Stage 2 (EMFEC)

Duration	36 hrs
Entry	Stage 1/equivalent; selection by interview
Apply To:	Carol Short

NORTH LINCOLNSHIRE COLLEGE,   01522 876000 X798

Professional Development Unit, Cathedral Building, Monk's Road, LINCOLN, LN2 5HQ,
Also offers in-house & tailor-made training and short courses

♿ Student Co-workers/deaf/visually impaired — auditory loop, audiotape course books, large print copies

* 1) Introduction to Counselling

Duration	10 weeks, day/eve (30 hrs)
Entry	None stated

* 2) Certificate in Counselling Theory (CSCT/AEB)

Duration	30 weeks, evening (75 hrs)
Entry	None

* 3) Certificate in Counselling Skills (CSCT/AEB)

Duration	30 weeks, day (75 hrs)
Entry	None

** 4) Advanced Certificate in Counselling Skills & Theory (CSCT/AEB)

Duration	150 hrs, 1 afternoon + same evening
Entry	Certificates in Counselling Skills & Theory or APL

** 5) Diploma in Therapeutic Counselling (Psychodynamic route) (CSCT/ AEB)

Core Model	Psychodynamic
Duration	215 hours, half day + same evening
Entry	CSCT/AEB Advanced Certificate or APL
Apply To:	Liz Came, Counselling Courses Co-ordinator

Star System: * Introductory course only • ** 2-3 yr pt-time course to Cert/Dip level •
*** Professional development for trained counsellors
For added help, see section 'Essential Information for Students', page 1

224

CENTRAL SCHOOL OF COUNSELLING & THERAPY,
0800 243463
80 Paul Street, LONDON, EC2A 4UD,
See National Section entry for full details.

STAMFORD COLLEGE,   01780 484300
Drift Road, STAMFORD, Lincolnshire, PE9 1XA,

♿ Disabled access, individual needs of all students assessed at enrolment

*   1) **Introduction to Counselling** (CSCT/AEB)
Duration   15 weeks, 2 hrs/week, eve/daytime
Entry   Open

*   2) **Certificate in Counselling Theory** (CSCT/AEB)
Duration   30 weeks, 3 hrs/week, daytime/eve
Entry   Open

*   3) **Certificate in Counselling Skills** (CSCT/AEB)
Duration   30 weeks, 3 hrs/week, daytime/eve
Entry   Open

*   4) **Introduction to Counselling Children & Adolescents** (CSCT/AEB)
Duration   15 weeks, 2 hrs/week, eve
Entry   Open

**   5) **Advanced Certificate in Counselling Skills & Theory** (CSCT/AEB)
Duration   180 hrs, daytime
Entry   Interview, successful completion of Certs in Couns Skills & Theory or
                APL

**   6) **Diploma in Therapeutic Counselling** (CSCT/AEB)
Duration   200 hrs, eves
Entry   Successful completion of Advanced Certificate in Counselling Skills &
                Theory or APL
Apply To: Patricia Page

---

*Star System: * Introductory course only • ** 2-3 yr pt-time course to Cert/Dip level •*
*** Professional development for trained counsellors*
For added help, see section 'Essential Information for Students', page 1

225

J.I. LITTLE TRAINING AGENCY,   0151 666 1383

2nd Floor, 54 Hamilton Square, BIRKENHEAD, Merseyside, L41 5AS,

No response received to our enquiries for 2000, entry details as of November 1998

*   **1) Basic Course**

*   **2) Counselling Skills — Level 2** (Relational Counselling) (CENTRA)

**   **3) Diploma in Counselling, Level 3** (Psychodynamic & Relational Counselling) (CENTRA)

***   **4) Diploma in Case Work Supervision**

***   **5) Art Therapy**

***   **6) Couple & Family Counselling** (CENTRA)

WIRRAL METROPOLITAN COLLEGE,   0151 551 7501

Borough Road Campus, Borough Road, BIRKENHEAD,

 ♿ No wheelchair access in main training room

*   **1) Introduction to Counselling Skills** (CENTRA)

Duration   ﹨   10 weeks, part-time, (30 hours)
Entry   None

**   **2) Intermediate Counselling Skills** (CENTRA)

Duration   36 weeks, part-time, (150 hours)
Entry   Satisfactory completion of 1) or equivalent + interview

**   **3) Diploma in Counselling** (CENTRA)

Duration   72 weeks, part-time (300 hours)
Entry   Satisfactory completion of 2) or equivalent + interview. Counselling placement (min 100 hours during the year)
Apply To: Jude Wood

HUGH BAIRD FURTHER EDUCATION COLLEGE,   0151 934 4410

Balliol Road, BOOTLE, Merseyside, L20,

No response received to our enquiries for 2000, entry details as of Nov 1998

*   **1) Introduction to Counselling Skills** (Merseyside Open College)

*   **2) Intermediate Certificate in Counselling** (CENTRA)

---

*Star System: * Introductory course only • ** 2-3 yr pt-time course to Cert/Dip level •*
*** Professional development for trained counsellors
For added help, see section 'Essential Information for Students', page 1

COMPASS,   **0151 7086688**

25 Hope Street, LIVERPOOL, L1 9BQ,

Will run tailor-made courses for specific needs

♿ Full access and facilities for wheelchair users at Hope Street. Taps etc for blind/visually impaired trainees.

*   **1) Basic Counselling Skills** (Level 1 CENTRA)

Duration	36 hours, aprt-time, day or evening
Entry	No qualifications required

**   **2) Foundation Counselling Course**

Duration	1 year, part-time, (150 hours)
Entry	Completion of 1) or equivalent

**   **3) Counsellor Training Course, Diploma (BAC Acc, CENTRA)**

Duration	450 hours, part-time, over 3 years, including foundation and client practice with COMPASS clients (Sept start)
Entry	Those who have completed 36 hr basic course; selection procedure; commitment required to be a voluntary COMPASS counsellor for a minimum 2 years post qulaification
Apply To:	The Training Administrator

***   **4) Advanced Diploma in Counselling in Primary Care**

Duration	122 hours, Fridays, Jan — July + 1 weekend + minimum of 100 hrs supervised counselling practice in GP setting
Entry	Diploma in Counselling, preferably BAC Acc, or equivalent + post-qualifying counselling experience

JOHN MOORES UNIVERSITY,   **0151 231 4054**

School of Human Sciences, Trueman St Building, 15-21 Webster Street, LIVERPOOL, L3 2ET,

No response received to our enquiries for 2000, entry details as of Nov 1998

**   **1) Postraguate Diploma in Counselling**

***   **2) MA in Counselling Studies**

CENTRAL SCHOOL OF COUNSELLING & THERAPY,
0800 243463

80 Paul Street, LONDON, EC2A 4UD,

See National Section entry for full details.

Star System: ** Introductory course only • ** 2-3 yr pt-time course to Cert/Dip level •*
*** Professional development for trained counsellors
For added help, see section 'Essential Information for Students', page 1

227

CENTRE TRAINING INTERNATIONAL SCHOOL OF
HYPNOTHERAPY AND PSYCHOTHERAPY **01772 617663**
FAX: 01772 614211

145 Chapel Lane, Longton, PRESTON, PR4 5NA,
See National Section entry for full details

*Star System: * Introductory course only • ** 2-3 yr pt-time course to Cert/Dip level •*
**** Professional development for trained counsellors*
For added help, see section 'Essential Information for Students', page 1

228

TDA CONSULTING LTD,   0181 568 3040
4 Thameside Centre, Kew Bridge Road, BRENTFORD, Middlesex, TW8 0HF,
No response received to our enquiries for 2000. Entry details as of Nov 1998

** **Diploma in Counselling at Work** (Roehampton Institute)

ENFIELD COLLEGE,   0181 443 3434
Dept of Health & Social Care, 73 Hertford Road, ENFIELD, Middlesex, EN3 5HA,
In-house training for organisations & short courses in dealing with stressed employees,
anger & change

♿ Equipped as fully as possible for students with disabilities

* **1) Introduction to Counselling** (LOCF)
Duration   10 weeks (4 courses per year, 2 daytime & 2evening)
Entry   No prior experience necessary, for those who wish to explore
              counselling as a career & as an adjunct to their current profession

* **2) Counselling Skills** (CSCT/AEB)
Duration   30 weeks, 1 morning, afternoon or eve/week
Entry   Those interested in improving their counselling skills and/or interested
              in professional training in counselling

* **3) Certificate in Counselling Theory** (CSCT/AEB)
Duration   30 weeks, 1 morning, afternoon or evening/week
Entry   Those interested in improving their counselling theory and/or
              embarking on professional training in counselling

** **4) Advanced Certificate in Counselling Skills & Theory** (CSCT/AEB)
Duration   150 hrs, day or evening (2 courses)
Entry   Successful completion of CSCT Counselling Skills & Theory at
              foundation level or APL for applicants with substantial prior training

** **5) Diploma in Theraputic Counselling-Humanistic Approaches** (CSCT/
     AEB)
Duration   33 weeks (210 hrs), day and twilight (2 courses)
Entry   Successful completion of Advanced Certificate in Counselling Skills/
              Theory (CSCT) or APL with prior training at the appropriate standard
Apply To: Maureen Moore, Programme Manager

---

*Star System: * Introductory course only • ** 2-3 yr pt-time course to Cert/Dip level •*
*** Professional development for trained counsellors*
For added help, see section 'Essential Information for Students', page 1
229

ENFIELD COUNSELLING SERVICE, 0181 367 2333
St Pauls Centre, 102a Church Street, ENFIELD, Middlesex, EN2 6AR,
No response received to our enquiries for 2000, entry details as of November 1998

** **1) Introduction to Counselling Course** (WPF)

** **2) Certificate in Psychodynamic Counselling** (WPF)

GREENHILL COLLEGE, 0181 869 8651
Lowlands Road, HARROW, Middlesex, HA1 3AQ,
No response received to our enquiries for 2000. Entry details as of Nov 1998

* **1) Introduction to Counselling Skills**

* **2) Bereavement Counselling**

WPF COUNSELLING, NORTH WEST MIDDLESEX, STUART WILSON, TRAINING OFFICE
1 Orley Court, 93 Greenford Road, HARROW, Middlesex, HA1 3QD,
No response received to our enquiries for 2000, entry details as of November 1998

* **1) Introductory Counselling Skills Course**

** **2) Diploma in Psychodynamic Counselling** (WPF) (Agency Practice)

HESTON ADULT EDUCATION AND TRAINING CENTRE
0181 577 1166
Heston Community School, Heston Road, Heston, HOUNSLOW, TW17 0SL,
In-house and tailor-made training also offered

♿ Ramps, disabled toilets, minicom & typetalk service. Some staff are trained up to British Sign Language — Stage 2

* **1) Counselling** (AEB) — Introduction
Duration   12 weeks — Monday 6.30pm-9pm
Entry   None

* **2) Counselling Skills** (AEB/CSCT)
Duration   30 weeks, Monday 6.45pm-9.15pm
Entry   None

---

*Star System: * Introductory course only • ** 2-3 yr pt-time course to Cert/Dip level •*
*** Professional development for trained counsellors*
For added help, see section 'Essential Information for Students', page 1
230

*   **3) Counselling Children and Adolescents** (AEB)

Duration	15 weeks, Monday 7pm — 9pm
Entry	None
Apply To:	Anne Lloyd

HOUNSLOW MANOR ADULT ED,   0181 572 1828

Prince Regent Road, HOUNSLOW, Middlesex, TW3 1NE,

No response received to our enquiries for 2000. Entry details as of Nov 1998

*   **1) Introduction to Counselling**

*   **2) Counselling Skills** (AEB)

*   **3) Counselling Skills** (AEB)

BRUNEL UNIVERSITY,   0181 891 0121
FAX: 0181 891 0487

Dept Health Studies, Osterley Campus, Borough Road, ISLEWORTH, Middlesex, TW7 5DU,

Short courses available eg: Client centred, Creative Imagination, Relationships and Intimacy

♿ Access to most areas

***   **MSc Counselling in Health Care and Rehabilitation**

Duration	1 day/week over 4 semesters + minimum 3 months to complete dissertation
Entry	Professional Diploma/Degree/equivalent preferably in health care field or with experience in voluntary organiations/pastoral care/education
Apply To:	Pamela Griffiths, Course Leader

WEST THAMES COLLEGE,   0181 326 2337

Heath House, London Road, ISLEWORTH, Middlesex, TW7 6HS,

♿ Ramps/Easy access to all buildings, lift available to the library

*   **1) Introduction to Counselling Skills**

Duration	10 weeks, 1 eve/week (Sept and Jan start)
Entry	None stated

continued...

Star System: * *Introductory course only* • ** *2-3 yr pt-time course to Cert/Dip level* •
*** *Professional development for trained counsellors*
For added help, see section 'Essential Information for Students', page 1

231

*   **2) Certificate in Counselling Theory** (AEB)
Duration   32 weeks, part-time, 1 evening or morning/week (Sept start)
Entry   None stated

*   **3) Counselling Skills** (CSC/AEB)
Duration   33 weeks, part-time, 1 morning or evening/week (Sept start)
Entry   None stated

**   **4) Advanced Certificate in Counselling Skills & Theory**
Duration   1 year, 2 eves/week (150 hours)
Entry   Certificate in Counselling Skills and Theory

**   **5) Diploma in Therapeutic Counselling** (CSCT/AEB)
Duration   1 year, (33 weeks), 200 hours, Wednesdays
Entry   Succesful completion of Certificate in Counselling Skills and Theory
               courses + the Advanced Certificate in Theory and Skills
Core Model   Humanistic or Pyschodynamic Route

**   **6) Certificate in Counselling Skills in Organisations** (CSCT/AEB)
Duration   75 hours evening/day
Entry   None stated
Apply To: Ms Jill Lopez

RICHMOND ADULT & COMMUNITY COLLEGE,   0181 940 0170
Social Science & Interpersonal, Skills, Parkshot, RICHMOND, Surrey, TW9 2RE,
No response received to our enquiries for 2000. Entry details as of Nov 1998

*   **1) Basic Person-Centred Counselling Skills**

*   **2) Introduction to Counselling Skills Level 2** (Intermediate, SOCN)

*   **3) Psychology & Counselling Theory**

*   **4) Theory & Practice of Counselling Level 3** (SOCN)

*   **5) RSA Certificate in Counselling Skills**

*   **6) Certificate in Counselling Skills** (CPCAB)

**   **7) Certificate in Therapeutic Counselling** (CPCAB)

**   **8) Advanced Certificate in Therapeutic Counselling**

**   **9) Diploma in Therapeutic Counselling** (CPCAB)

---

*Star System: * Introductory course only • ** 2-3 yr pt-time course to Cert/Dip level •*
*** Professional development for trained counsellors
232   **For added help, see section 'Essential Information for Students', page 1**

ROYAL BROMPTON & HAREFIELD NHS TRUST,   01895 822819
Harefield Hospital, Hill End Road, Harefield, UXBRIDGE, Middlesex, UB9 6JH,
Short courses in Counselling Skills offered

♿ Assistance with most requirements. Because of the age of the building access is
limited; minicom number: 01895 828 534, 9-5 pm

*   **1) Introduction to Counselling Skills**
Duration   10 weeks, 3 hrs/week, times by arrangement
Entry   Interest in the subject

**   **2) Certificate in Professional Development in Integrative Counselling**
        (Univ of North London) (46 CATS points, Level 1)
Duration   Module — 1 Skills: 3 terms Mon eve (90hrs); Module 2 — Theory: 3
                terms Tues eve (90 hrs)
Entry   Selection By Interview

**   **3) Diploma in Professional Development in Integrative Counselling**
        (Univ of North London) (45 CATS points, Level 2)
Duration   3 terms, 2 evenings/week(Wed & Thurs) (150 hrs)
Entry   Successful completion of the Certificate on Professional Development
                in Integrative Counselling or equivalent
Core Model   Integrative
Apply To: Diane Hunt or Linda Hill

UXBRIDGE COLLEGE,   01895 853 333
Park Road, UXBRIDGE, Middlesex, UB8 1NQ,
No response received to our enquiries for 2000, entry details as of Nov 1998

*   **1) Certificate in Counselling Skills & Theory**

Star System: * Introductory course only • ** 2-3 yr pt-time course to Cert/Dip level •
              *** Professional development for trained counsellors
        For added help, see section 'Essential Information for Students', page 1
                                                                                    233

GREAT YARMOUTH COLLEGE OF FURTHER EDUCATION
01493 419270
Centre for Counselling, Psychology, GREAT YARMOUTH, Norfolk, NR31 0ED,

* 1) NOCW Intermediate Certificate in Counselling Skills
Duration 1 year, daytime 9.30am — 4.30 pm
Entry Those in the caring professions, and relevant voluntary organisations; selection by interview

** 2) Edexcel Higher National Certificate in Counselling Skills
Duration 2 years, either daytime 9.30am — 4.30pm or afternoon & evening 2pm — 9pm
Entry Those in caring professions and voluntary organisations. Selection by interview
Apply To: Dr. J. Cockburn

CENTRAL SCHOOL OF COUNSELLING & THERAPY,
0800 243463
80 Paul Street, LONDON, EC2A 4UD,
See National Section entry for full details.

CENTRE FOR COUNSELLING STUDIES, 01603 592651
Counselling Service, University Of East Anglia, NORWICH, NR4 7TJ,
Courses leading to professional qualifications in counselling

♿ Well adapted for disabled people in its buildings & facilities

** 1) Diploma in Counselling (BAC Acc)
Duration 1 year, full time (600+ hrs)
Entry Degree preferred but other professional qualifications/evidence of academic competence accepted. Written statement, personal reference, interview,counselling skills desirable

** 2) Diploma in Education and Professional Development (inc. Counselling Skills)
Duration 125 hrs, weekend attendance
Entry Degree or advisory responsibility, written application, references, interview

*** 3) MA in Counselling Studies
Duration 2 years, part-time
Entry Diploma in Counselling (minimum) and at least 1 year's practice

Star System: * Introductory course only • ** 2-3 yr pt-time course to Cert/Dip level •
*** Professional development for trained counsellors
For added help, see section 'Essential Information for Students', page 1
234

***   **4) Person Centred Counselling Supervision** (UEA Master's Level Award
Programme)

Duration	80 hrs, weekends
Entry	Diploma in Counselling, 2 years post-diploma experience with at least 450 supervised counselling hours
Apply To:	Professor Brian Thorne
Core Model	Person Centred

CENTRE FOR HEALTH, NURSING & SOCIAL WORK,
01603 773 225

City College, Norwich, Ipswich Road, NORWICH, NR2 2LJ,

No response received to our enquiries for 2000, entry details as of November 1998

*   **1) Introduction to Counselling Skills** (OCN)

**   **2) Diploma of Higher Education** (Counselling)

RUTH WRIGHT & ASSOCIATES,   01603 408390

33 Woodview Road, Hellesdon, NORWICH, NR6 5QD,

Workshops in Counselling Skills and Bereavement

♿ Wheelchair Access — Can cater for all disabilities

*   **1) Basic Counselling Skills**

Duration	12 weeks, 2 hrs/week, evenings
Entry	For those in the caring professions/ charieties/voluntary carers/carers of the elderly

*   **2) Loss, Change & Bereavement**

Duration	12 weeks, 2hrs/week,evenings
Entry	For those in the caring professions/charities/voluntary carers/carers of the elderly
Apply To:	Ruth Wright

*Star System: * Introductory course only • ** 2-3 yr pt-time course to Cert/Dip level •
*** Professional development for trained counsellors*
For added help, see section 'Essential Information for Students', page 1
235

CENTRAL SCHOOL OF COUNSELLING & THERAPY,
0800 243463

80 Paul Street, LONDON, EC2A 4UD,
See National Section entry for full details.

UNIVERSITY CENTRE,   **01604 251 803**

Barrack Road, NORTHAMPTON, NN2 6AF,

Non-Certificate students can attend modules, e.g. Couples Counselling, Counselling Skills, Bereavement

♿ Access and toilets for disabled students

*   1) Counselling Skills

Duration   20 hours, part-time, day or evening
Entry   None

*   2) Counselling Theory & Practice

Duration   66 hours, part-time, day/evening (33 sessions)
Entry   Completion of 1)

**   3) Counselling & Personal Development

Duration   66 hours, part-time, day/evening (33 sessions); comprises teaching
            followed by personal awareness group
Entry   Completion of 1) and 2)

**   4) Certificate in Counselling Studies

Duration   2-3 years on a modular format — min attendance 180 hours.
            Comprises 1) 2) 3) + optional modules (28 hours)
Entry   None

**   5) Advanced Certificate in Counselling

Duration   Additional 90 hours
Entry   Successful completion of 4) & 6 months practice as a counsellor, 25
            hrs client contact & acceptable supervisor's report

**   6) Diploma in Counselling

Duration   Additional 150 hours
Entry   Successful completion of 5) + 150 hours counselling practice in total
Apply To: Aileen Coupe, Consultant to Counselling Programme

Star System: * Introductory course only • ** 2-3 yr pt-time course to Cert/Dip level •
*** Professional development for trained counsellors
For added help, see section 'Essential Information for Students', page 1

236

TRESHAM INSTITUTE OF FURTHER & HIGHER ED,
01933 224165

Wellingborough Campus, Church Street, WELLINGBOROUGH, Northamptonshire, NN8 4PD,

No response received to our enquiries for 2000. Entry details as of Nov 1998

*   **1) Introduction to Counselling Skills**

*   **2) RSA Certificate, Counselling Skills in the Development of Learning**

---

*Star System: * Introductory course only • ** 2-3 yr pt-time course to Cert/Dip level •*
*** Professional development for trained counsellors
For added help, see section 'Essential Information for Students', page 1

237

FRANK DANIELS ASSOCIATES,   01773 532195

103 Hands Road, Heanor, HEANOR, Derbyshire, DE75 7HB,
No response received to our enquiries for 2000, entry details as of November 1998

*   1) NLP Introductory Seminar

*   2) Ericksonian Language Patterns & Hypnosis

**   3) NLP Practitioner Certification Training (ANLP, INLPTA)

**   4) NLP Master Practitioner Training (ANLP)

COUNSELLING TRAINING INITIATIVES LTD,(CTI) 0115 944 7849

Galtee House, 1 Heanor Road, ILKESTON, Derbyshire, DE7 8DY,
Please see National Section for fuller details of courses offered

♿ No response received to our enquiries for 2000, entry details as of Nov 1998

CENTRAL SCHOOL OF COUNSELLING & THERAPY,
0800 243463

80 Paul Street, LONDON, EC2A 4UD,
See National Section entry for full details.

WEST NOTTINGHAMSHIRE COLLEGE,   01623 27191

Chesterfield Road, MANSFIELD, Nottinghamshire, NG19 7BB,
No response received to our enquiries for 2000, entry details as of Nov 1998

*   1) Taster in Basic Counselling Skills (NEMAP)

*   2) Counsellong Skills Certificate (CPCAB)

*   3) Certificate in Therrapeutic Counselling (CPCAB)

*   4) Combined Certificate in Counselling Skills & Therapeutic
         Counselling (CPCAB)

**   5) Advanced Certificate in Therapeutic Counselling (CPCAB)

---

*Star System: * Introductory course only • ** 2-3 yr pt-time course to Cert/Dip level •*
*** Professional development for trained counsellors
For added help, see section 'Essential Information for Students', page 1

238

CENTRE FOR THE STUDY OF HUMAN RELATIONS,   0115 951 4420

School of Education, University of Nottingham, NOTTINGHAM, NG7 2RD,
No response received to our enquiries for 2000, entry details as of November 1998

**   1) Diploma/MEd in Human Relations

***   2) Diploma/MA in Counselling Studies

NOTTINGHAM TRENT UNIVERSITY,   0115 848 5527

Dept of Health & Human Services, Burton Street, NOTTINGHAM, NG1 4BU,
Foundation, professional & post professional training in counselling/psychotherapy & in Trauma Management. For in-house/tailor-made training please discuss with Richard Broadley on 0115 948 6809

♿ Ramps/lifts with full access; toilet on the Health & Human Services floor (7th)

*   1) Foundation Certificate in Counselling Studies

Duration	30 weeks, part-time, 0.5 day or 1 evening/week (120 hrs); 3 courses per annum (Oct, Jan & April start)
Entry	Those whose current work or voluntary role includes one-one helping/caring; selection by interview

**   2) Professional Diploma in Counselling & Psychotherapy (BAC Acc)

Duration	2 years, part-time, 1 afternoon & evening/week (360 hrs) (Oct start)
Entry	Those seeking training at professional level, strongly influenced by Person Centred Approach. FCCS/equivalent & evidence of ability to work at university level (could include sound relevant experience); Selection by interview.

**   3) Postgraduate Diploma in Counselling & Psychotherapy (BAC Acc)

Duration	2 years, part-time, 1 afternoon & evening/week (360 hrs). (Oct start)
Entry	Those seeking professional training at post grad level, strongly influenced by Person-Centred Approach. Degree or evidence of equivalent academic achievement + FCCS/equivalent & relevant work experience. Selection by interview

continued...

Star System: * Introductory course only • ** 2-3 yr pt-time course to Cert/Dip level •
*** Professional development for trained counsellors
For added help, see section 'Essential Information for Students', page 1
239

*** **4) MA in Counselling & Psychotherapy**

Duration	1 year, part-time, equivalent to 0.5 day/week (120 hrs)
Entry	Completion of 2) or equivalent + appropriate current work experience (paid of voluntary); selection by interview; BAC Accred graduate counsellors may be considered for direct entry to the MA year.
Apply To:	Programme Administrator on 0115 848 5527, or discuss with Admissions Tutor on 0115 948 6809

*** **5) Diploma & Advanced Diploma in The Management of Psychological Trauma**

Duration	Modular; Module 1: Psychosocial & Psychological Aspects of Trauma & Post Traumatic Stress. Module 2: Interventions
Entry	Professionals in the Human Services; those with a teaching or counselling qualification; evidence of academic ability; relevant work record
Apply To:	Lesley Warren, tel. 0115 848 5554

SHERWOOD PSYCHOTHERAPY TRAINING,INSTITUTE
0115 924 3994

Thiskney House, 2 St James Terrace, NOTTINGHAM, NG1 6FW,
No response received to our enquiries for 2000, entry details as of November 1998

** **1) Diploma in Counselling Using the Person-Centred Approach (BAC Acc)**

** **2) MA Integrative Psychotherapy** (Univ of Derby, UKCP)

** **3) MA Gestalt Psychotherapy** (Univ Derby, UKCP)

** **4) MA Transactional Analysis Psychotherapy** (UKCP, EATA, Univ of Derby)

SOUTH NOTTINGHAM COLLEGE,   0115 914 6400

Greythorn Drive, West Bridgford, NOTTINGHAM, NG2 7GA,
No response was received to our enquiries for 2000. Entry details as of Nov 1998

* **Certificate in Continuing Professional Development — Counselling & Guidance Skills** (City & Guilds 7402)

*Star System: * Introductory course only • ** 2-3 yr pt-time course to Cert/Dip level •
*** Professional development for trained counsellors*
For added help, see section 'Essential Information for Students', page 1
240

UNIVERSITY OF NOTTINGHAM, SCHOOL OF CONTINUING EDUCATION   0115 956 6466

Jubilee Campus, Wollaton Road, NOTTINGHAM, NG8 1BB,

Workshops offered, e.g. Introduction to and Building on Basic Counselling Skills, Assertiveness

♿ Applicants with Special needs should contact the Degree Programmes Unit, Tel. 0115 956 6466

*   **1) Certificate in Higher Education** (Counselling)

Duration	2 years, part-time evening/day (330 hrs)
Entry	Selection by interview

**   **2) Diploma in Professional Counselling Practice**

Duration	2 years, part-time evenings/day (300 hrs). Starting October 1999
Entry	Selection by interview. Certificate in Higher Education — Counselling/equivalent; counselling practice experience minimum of 35 hours
Apply To:	Val Watson, Counselling Tutor

Star System: ** Introductory course only •*   *** 2-3 yr pt-time course to Cert/Dip level •*
*** Professional development for trained counsellors
For added help, see section 'Essential Information for Students', page 1

241

ABINGDON COLLEGE, 01235 555585 X 225
Northcourt Road, ABINGDON, Oxfordshire, OX14 1NN,
Tailor-made courses for commerce & industry on request

* **1) Certificate in Basic Counselling Skills — An Introductory Course** (NCFE 3702)

Duration	60 hrs over 20 weeks, 1 eve/week
Entry	Informal interview with course tutor. For those wanting to find out more about counselling/listening/and/or using counselling skills as part of their role.

** **2) Certificate in Counselling** (NCFE 3703)

Duration	1 year, half day + 1 eve/week OR mornings (9.30-12.30pm)
Entry	Counselling skills training and/or experience; application form and interview
Apply To:	Ms K Slade

COUNSELLING CONSULTANCY OXFORD (CCO), 01865 863705
19 Eaton Village, ABINGDON, Oxfordshire, OX13 5PR,

** **Diploma in Counselling Principles & Practice** (Oxford Brookes Univ)

Duration	3 years, part-time, evenings. Yr 1 can be taken as a free-standing Foundation year
Entry	Selection by interview, entry at Yr 2 is possible for those with appropriate experience
Apply To:	Co-ordinator CCO

CENTRAL SCHOOL OF COUNSELLING & THERAPY,
0800 243463

80 Paul Street, LONDON, EC2A 4UD,
See National Section entry for full details.

INTEGRA, 01865 723 613
West Oxford Centre for, Counselling & Psychotherapy, 32 Westminster Way, OXFORD, OX2 0LW,
No response to our enquiries for 2000, entry details as of Nov 1998

*** **Towards Integrative Practice**

Star System: *Introductory course only • ** 2-3 yr pt-time course to Cert/Dip level •*
*** Professional development for trained counsellors
For added help, see section 'Essential Information for Students', page 1
242

ISIS CENTRE,   01865 556648

Oxfordshire Mental Healthcare, NHS Trust, Little Clarendon Street, OXFORD, OX1 2HS,

In house/tailor-made training available

***   **1) MSc & Post Graduate Diploma in Counselling Practice** (Oxford Brookes University)

Duration	2/3 yrs, 12+ hrs/week, programme includes supervised clinical practice
Entry	First degree or equivalent, some previous training & supervised clinical experience essential, preference given to members of helping professions and those with experience of personal therapy
Core Model	Psychodynamic

***   **2) Associate Programme**

Duration	10 hrs+/week
Entry	Open to experienced counsellors wishing to consolidate clinical experience under supervision
Apply To:	Isis Centre Co-ordinator

OXFORD CENTRE FOR PSYCHOTHERAPY,   01865 725 588
PAMARMITAGE@OXFORD CENTRE.FREESERVE.CO.UK

38 Rectory Road, OXFORD, Oxfordshire, OX4 1BU,

Introduction to Counselling. Also offer workshops in counselling/skills

*   **Introduction to Counselling**

Duration	4 Saturdays, afternoon Jan-May with 8 evening counselling skills training group
Entry	For those looking for a basic introduction to counselling
Apply To:	Pamela Armitage

OXFORD PSYCHODRAMA GROUP,   01865 747 604

8 Rahere Road, Cowley, OXFORD, OX4 3QG,

No response received to our enquiries for 2000, entry details as of Nov 1998

**   **Diploma in Psychodrama Training Programme** (leading to UKCP accred)

Star System: ** Introductory course only • ** 2-3 yr pt-time course to Cert/Dip level •*
*** Professional development for trained counsellors
For added help, see section 'Essential Information for Students', page 1

243

OXFORD SCHOOL OF COUNSELLING,   01865 515 470

Mill House, Mill Road, Wolvercote, OXFORD, OX2 8PR,
No response to our enquiries for 2000, entry details as of Nov 1998

*   **Certificate in Counselling** (C&G 3703)

OXFORDSHIRE COUNTY COUNCIL COMMUNITY EDUCATION
01865 772198

Community Education, Staff Development Unit, Cricket Road Centre, OXFORD,
OX4 3PU,
Introduction to counselling. The couse is held in a variety of locations each term.

*   **Introduction in Counselling Skills 370/1/2 NCFE**
Duration   40 hrs, evenings + Saturday
Entry   None stated
Apply To: Rosemary Napper

UNIVERSITY OF OXFORD, DEPT OF CONTINUING
EDUCATION   01865 270 360

Rewley House, 1 Wellington Square, OXFORD, OX1 2JA,
No response to our enquiries for 2000, entry details as of Nov 1998

**   **1) Postgraduate Certificate in Psychodynamic Coun**

**   **2) Postgraduate Diploma in Psychodynamic Practice**

***   **3) Master of Studies** (M.St) in Psychodynamic Pract

FOCUS (FEDERATION OF CHRISTIAN CARING &
COUNSELLING)   0118 957 5120

32 Western Elms Avenue, READING, RG30 2AN,
For further information, see entry in Bucks

WANTAGE COUNSELLING SERVICE,   01235 769744

2a Newbury Street, WANTAGE, Oxfordshire, OX12 8BL,
No response received to our enquiries for 2000, entry details as of November 1998

*   **1) Introduction to Counselling — Skills & Attitude**

**   **2) Diploma in Psychodynamic Counselling Part 1** (Stage 2)

---

*Star System: * Introductory course only • ** 2-3 yr pt-time course to Cert/Dip level •*
*** Professional development for trained counsellors
For added help, see section 'Essential Information for Students', page 1

**   **3) Diploma in Psychodynamic Counselling — Part 2** (Stage 3)

Star System: ** Introductory course only • ** 2-3 yr pt-time course to Cert/Dip level •*
*** Professional development for trained counsellors
For added help, see section 'Essential Information for Students', page 1

245

UNIVERSITY OF BIRMINGHAM,   0121 4145602
Edgbaston, BIRMINGHAM, B15 2TT,
Course is run in Birmingham, Shrewsbury & Worcester, Please see Hereford &
Worcester entry for full details

NORTH SHROPSHIRE COLLEGE,   01691 684813 01691 684800
School of Professional Studies, Upper Brook Street Campus, OSWESTRY, Shropshire,
SY11 2TQ,
Short courses available, e.g. Introduction to Counselling Skills

♿ Wheelchair and toilet facilities for disabled people, lift to some floors, visually
impaired students welcomed

*   **1) OCR Certificate in Counselling Skills in the Development of Learning**
Duration   120 hrs, eves + 3 Saturdays
Entry   Open Access

**   **2) CPCAB Advanced Certificate in Therapeutic Counselling**
Duration   1 yr, eves & 6 Saturdays (210 hrs)
Entry   Certificate in counselling

**   **3) Diploma in Therapeutic Counselling**
Duration   1 yr, eves & 6 Saturdays (210 hrs)
Entry   2) above
Apply To: Ms P Sheldon, Lecturer in Counselling

CONFIDE — COUNSELLING SERVICE,   01743 351319
The Roy Fletcher Centre, 12-17 Cross Hill, SHREWSBURY, SY1 1JE,
Affiliate of WPF Counselling — Courses available in Shrewsbury. Workshop
programme available.

**   **1) Certificate in Counselling Skills & Theory;** (leading to Certificate in
        Psychodynamic Counselling)
Duration   2 years, part-time, 1 eve/week + 4 days/year + 2 residential weekends
                (+100 supervised hrs of client work)
Entry   Anyone over 25 who has or intends to have a counselling role in their
                lives; who has completed a Foundation Certificate in Counselling Skills
                or equivalent, and wish to become counsellors/use advanced
                counselling skills in their work; interview

***   **2) 1 day workshops for qualified psychodynamic counsellors**
Apply To: The Administrator tel: 01743 351319

---

*Star System: * Introductory course only • ** 2-3 yr pt-time course to Cert/Dip level •*
*** Professional development for trained counsellors
For added help, see section 'Essential Information for Students', page 1

246

AGE CONCERN, BATH & N.E SOMERSET,   01225 429 720
Mobile Counselling Services, 2 Hetling Court, BATH, BA1 1SH,
No response received to our enquiries for 2000, entry details as of Nov 1998

*   **Induction Course in Counselling Older People**

BATH CENTRE FOR PSYCHOTHERAPY &,COUNSELLING
BCPC   01225 429720
1 Walcot Terrace, London Road, BATH, BA1 6AB,
No response to our enquiries for 2000, copy current as of 1998 Please send a large
sae

**   **1) Foundation Stage 1**

**   **2) Foundation Stage 2**

**   **3) Counselling Diploma Stage 3 (BAC Acc)**

**   **4) Basic Psychotherapy 3P**

**   **5) Psychotherapist in Training Stage 4**

***   **6) Final Psychotherapy Stage 5**

CENTRE FOR STAFF TEAM DEVELOPMENT,   01225 333 737
FAX: 01225 333 738
24 Gay Street, BATH, BA1 2PD,
Also supervision courses for counsellors/psychotherapists, social workers etc.

***   **CORE, Therapeutic, Advanced, Group Supervision Courses, Certificate**
      in Supervision

Duration   CORE: 3 days; Therapeutic; 3 days; Group Supervision 3 days;
             Advanced: 3 days.
Entry   CORE: Currently supervising/about to do so; Therapeutic: Have
             supervised for 1 year; Advancd: Those who have completed the
             Therapeutic course.
Apply To: Robin Shohet, Joan Wilmot, Peter Hawkins

---

*Star System: * Introductory course only • ** 2-3 yr pt-time course to Cert/Dip level •*
*** Professional development for trained counsellors*
For added help, see section 'Essential Information for Students', page 1

247

BRIDGWATER COLLEGE,   01278 455464 EXT 257

Bath Road, BRIDGWATER, Somerset, TA6 4PZ,
In-house/tailor-made training

♿ Fully accessible building, awareness training to all staff, wide range of learning support

*   **1) First Steps in Counselling**

Duration	10 weeks, part-time, day (20 hrs), 3 courses — Sept, Jan, May
Entry	None stated

*   **2) First Steps in Counselling**

Duration	10 weeks, part-time, eves, (20 hrs) Jan, April and Sept start
Entry	None stated

*   **3) RSA Certificate, Counselling Skills in the Development of Learning**

Duration	Sept-May, part-time, morning, afternoon or evening + residential weekend (106 hrs)
Entry	By interview; for those with no experience; completion of 1) required

**   **4) Advanced Certificate in Counselling** (3 units towards modular MA Counselling)

Duration	Sept-June, aprt-time, afternoon or evening + residential weekend (106 hrs)
Entry	By interview and previous training and experience such as 2) and 3)

**   **5) Diploma in Counselling** (8 units towards modular MA Counselling)

Duration	2 years, part-time, 1 day/week (min 480 hrs) (Sept-June)
Entry	By interview; also significant counselling qualification and training; ongoing counselling practice; ongoing supervision
Apply To:	Trish Edwards

WESSEX COUNSELLING SERVICE,   01373 453355

The Old Bakery, Saxonvale, FROME, Somerset, BA11 1PS,
Short courses and workshops offered eg: addiction, transference/counter transference. Affliate of WPF

♿ Access is limited by stairs

*   **1) WPF Certificate in Counselling Skills**

Duration	1 year, part-time, 3.5 hours/morning (Tues) (starts Sept)
Entry	Interviews required

Star System: * Introductory course only • ** 2-3 yr pt-time course to Cert/Dip level •
*** Professional development for trained counsellors
For added help, see section 'Essential Information for Students', page 1

**   2) WPF Diploma in Psychodynamic Counselling (Agency)
Duration   2 years, part-time, 3.5 hours/morning (Monday) (starts Sept)
Entry   1) above or equivalent; in therapy with an approved therapist, clients/
supervision provided by Wessex

**   3) WPF Advanced Diploma in Psychodynamic Counselling
Duration   2 years, part-time, 3.5 hrs/morning (Fridays) (starts January)
Entry   2) above or equivalent, over 25, minimum 150 hours supervised
counselling experience, in therapy with an approved therapist
Apply To: The Administrator

STRODE COLLEGE,   01458 844400
Church Road, STREET, BA6 8AF,

♿ Lifts, ramps for some ground floor rooms, toilet facilities for disabled, other
facilities on request

*   1) Helping Others — Introduction to Counselling
Duration   11 weeks, 2 hrs/eve, Autumn & Spring start
Entry   Interview only

**   2) Combined Certificate in Counselling Skills & Therapeutic
Counselling (CPCAB)
Duration   210 hrs, 3.5 hrs/week, term-time, over 4 terms. 2 courses, 1 morn, 1
eve
Entry   Completion of 1) and/or some experience of counselling. Interview
required

**   3) Advanced Certificate in Therapeutic Counselling (CPCAB)
Duration   210 hrs, 3.5 hrs/session, morning or eve, 4 terms
Entry   Completion of 2) or equiv, interview required
Core Model   Integrative

**   4) Diploma in Therapeutic Counselling (CPCAB)
Duration   210 hrs, 1 day/week for 1 yr
Entry   Completions of 3) or equivalent
Apply To: Heather Price

---

*Star System: * Introductory course only • ** 2-3 yr pt-time course to Cert/Dip level •*
*** Professional development for trained counsellors*
For added help, see section 'Essential Information for Students', page 1
249

SOMERSET COLLEGE OF ART & TECHNOLOGY,   01823 366438

School of Health & Social Care, Studies, 94 Staplegrove Road, TAUNTON, Somerset, TA1 1DN,

No response received to our enquiries for 2000. Entry details as of Nov 1998

**   **1) Combined Certificate in Counselling Skills & Therapeutic Counselling** (CPCAB)

**   **2) Advanced Certificate in Therapeutic Counselling** (CPCAB)

**   **3) Diploma in Therapeutic Counselling** (CPCAB)

**   **4) Advanced Diploma in Therapeutic Counselling**

SOMERSET COUNSELLING CENTRE (TAUNTON),   01823 337 049

38 Belvedere Road, TAUNTON, Somerset, TA1 1HD,

Affiliated member of WPF, Supervised, integrated clinical practice on site following successful entry to stage 2

♿ Wheelchair access for stage 1

*   **1) Certificate in Counselling Skills** (WPF)

Duration	1 year, part-time 108 hrs. 2 courses; 1) General; 2) for those in a medical setting
Entry	By interview

**   **2) Stage 2 Diploma in Psychodynamic Counselling, Agency** (WPF)

Apply To:	Training Co-ordinator
Duration	171 hrs
Entry	Completion of year 1 and interview; previous training required

---

Star System: ** Introductory course only* • *** 2-3 yr pt-time course to Cert/Dip level* •
*** Professional development for trained counsellors

For added help, see section 'Essential Information for Students', page 1

250

BURTON UPON TRENT COLLEGE,   01283 545401
Lichfield Street, BURTON-ON-TRENT, Staffordshire, DE14 3RL,
No response received to our enquiries for 2000, entry details as of November 1998

*   **1) Introductory Counselling** (CENTRA)

*   **2) RSA Certificate in Counselling Skills in the Development of Learning**

NEWCASTLE-U-LYME COLLEGE,   01782 715 111
Liverpool Road, NEWCASTLE, Staffordshire, ST5 2DF,
No response received to our enquiries for 2000, entry details as of November 1998

*   **Counselling Skills 1 & 2**

UNIVERSITY OF KEELE,   01782 621 111 X8035
Dept Applied Social Studies, NEWCASTLE, Staffordshire, ST5 5BG,
No response received to our enquiries for 2000, entry details as of November 1998

*   **1) Certificate in Counselling Skills/Human Relations**

*   **2) Certificate in Bereavement Counselling**

**   **3) Post Graduate Certificate in Counselling**

**   **4) Post Graduate Diploma in Counselling**

***   **5) MA in Counselling** (by research)

***   **6) Post Graduate Certificate in Counselling Supervision**

***   **7) MA in Counselling Studies —** (Overseas Students only)

***   **8) MPhil/PhD in Counselling Studies** (by research)

***   **9) MSc in Counselling Supervision** (by research) **—** Subject to Approval
        by University Senate

Star System: * Introductory course only • ** 2-3 yr pt-time course to Cert/Dip level •
               *** Professional development for trained counsellors
For added help, see section 'Essential Information for Students', page 1
                                                                          251

STAFFORD COLLEGE,   **01785 223800**
Earl Street, STAFFORD, ST16 2QR,
In-house/tailor-made training may be negotiated

♿ Learning support is available and appropriate access can be organised

*   **1) Counselling Level 1** (Open College Network)
Duration   24 hrs, day & eve
Entry   No formal entry requirements

*   **2) Counselling Level 2** (OCN)
Duration   24 hrs eve/daytime
Entry   Level 1 or equivalent

*   **3) Counselling Level 2 Continuation** (OCN)
Duration   24 hrs
Entry   Completion of Level 2 or equivalent
Apply To: Iora Dawes

STOKE ON TRENT COLLEGE,   **01782 208 208**
Faculty of Caring Services, Cauldon Campus, Stoke Road, Shelton, STOKE ON
TRENT, ST4 2DG,
In-house/tailor-made training available

♿ Disabled access, lift, learning support for students with dyslexia, etc.

*   **1) Understanding Substance Misuse** (Open College Network)
Entry   Open
Duration   3 hrs/week, 10 weeks, eves
Core Model   Person-Centred

*   **2) Substance Misuse in a Specialist Environment** (OCN)
Duration   3 hrs/week, 10 weeks, eves
Entry   Individuals working in a a professional capacity wishing to further their
                knowledge concerning substance misuse issues
Core Model   Person-centred

*   **3) Building Self Confidence** (OCN)
Duration   24 hrs, 2 hrs/week for 12 weeks, day & eve
Entry   Open

---

*Star System: * Introductory course only • ** 2-3 yr pt-time course to Cert/Dip level •*
*** Professional development for trained counsellors*
For added help, see section 'Essential Information for Students', page 1
252

*   **4) Introduction to Counselling Skills** (OCN)

Duration	3 hrs/week, 24 weeks, day or eve
Entry	Open, students must be willing to participate in self awareness exercises, skills practice & discussions
Core Model	Person Centred

*   **5) Certificate in Counselling** (Univ of London)

Duration	4 hrs/week for 36 sessions + additional workshops and tutorial support, day and eve attendance
Entry	Completion of minimum 20 hrs couns skills training (or equiv) during previous 5 yrs
Core Model	Person-Centred

*   **6) Certificate in Loss & Bereavement Support** (Univ of London)

Entry	Open to those who either work within the field of loss & bereavement or aspire to do so
Duration	4 hrs/week for 36 weeks, + additional tutorial support, day attendance
Core Model	Person-Centred

**   **7) Diploma in Counselling** (Univ of London)

Duration	2 yrs part-time, 6 hrs/week for 72 sessions + additional workshops & tutorial support
Entry	Applicants will have completed a Cert in Couns or equivalent (150 training hrs) and have experience of using counselling skills
Core Model	Person-Centred

***   **8) Continuing Professional Development for Counsellors**

Duration	A series of issues-based workshops & seminars, Sat mornings,9.30-12.30
Entry	Applicants will normally have achieved a Diploma in Counselling or have extensive experience of working in a professional capacity as a counsellor.
Apply To:	Cathy Crabtree, Lecturer in Counselling

Star System: * Introductory course only • ** 2-3 yr pt-time course to Cert/Dip level •
*** Professional development for trained counsellors
For added help, see section 'Essential Information for Students', page 1

253

WEST SUFFOLK COLLEGE,,   01284 716348

Dept of Continuing Education, Out Risbygate, BURY ST. EDMUNDS, Suffolk, IP33 3RL,

♿ Wheelchair access to most venues, extra support on request

*   1) Short Introductory Courses
Duration   1-2 terms
Entry   None stated

*   2) Basic Counselling (Open College Network)
Duration   3 terms
Entry   No formal requirements

**   3) Counselling Course
Duration   3 years, part-time, 500+ hrs including 2x3 day residentials each year
Entry   No specifc requirements
Apply To: Department of Continuing Education

IPSWICH CONCERN COUNSELLING CENTRE,   01473 212788

Gainsborough House, 20 Bolton Lane, IPSWICH, IP4 2BT,

Affiliate of Westminster Pastoral Foundation. In-house training in a wide range of
subjects, also personal development and tailor-made courses

♿ Wheelchair access to ground floor but no disabled toilet

*   1) WPF Certificate in Counselling Skills
Duration   1 yr, part-time, 30 seminars of 1.5hrs each + 30 self-awareness
              groups of 1.5hrs each
Entry   By interview, for those who use counselling skills

**   2) WPF Diploma in the Application of Psychodynamic Theory to the Basic Principles of Counselling
Duration   1 yr, part-time, 30 weeks extended seminars 2.5 hrs + self awareness
              group 1.5 hrs
Entry   By interview. For those who wish to enhance counselling skills who
              have completed 1) or equivalent

**   3) WPF Diploma in Psychodynamic Counselling
Duration   2 yrs part-time, one eve/week seminar/group work + clinical practice
              with Centre clients + weekly supervision work
Entry   By interview, for those who wish to have or have a counselling role
              and have completed 2) or equivalent
Apply To: The Training Co-ordinator

---

*Star System: * Introductory course only • ** 2-3 yr pt-time course to Cert/Dip level •*
*** Professional development for trained counsellors*

For added help, see section 'Essential Information for Students', page 1

254

UNIVERSITY COLLEGE SUFFOLK,   **01473 296555**
Rope Walk, IPSWICH, IP4 1TL,
No response was received to our enquiries for 2000. Entry details as of Nov 1998

*   **1) Certificate in Counselling Theory** (CSCT/AEB)

*   **2) Certificate in Counselling Skills** (CSCT/AEB)

LOWESTOFT COLLEGE,   **01502 583 521**
St Peter's Street, LOWESTOFT, Suffolk, NR32 2NB,
No response received to our enquiries for 2000, entry details as of Nov 1998

*   **1) Introduction to Counselling Skills** (North Anglia Open College
        Network) 1 credit at level 1

*   **2) Counselling Skills** (North Anglia Open College Network) 2 credits at
        level 2

**   **3) Certificate in Counselling Skills** (North Anglia Open College Network)
        10 credits level 3

---

*Star System: * Introductory course only • ** 2-3 yr pt-time course to Cert/Dip level •*
*** Professional development for trained counsellors
For added help, see section 'Essential Information for Students', page 1

255

SURREY YOUTH & ADULT EDUCATION SERVICE -,
01306 883351/881849

Dorking Adult Education Centre, Dene Street, DORKING, Surrey, RH4 2DA,
No response received to our enquiries for 2000. Entry details as of Nov 1998

*   1) Counselling — An Introduction OR Counselling Is It For Me (Univ Surrey)

**   2) Certificate in Counselling (Univ Surrey)

**   3) Counselling Certificate

NORTH EAST SURREY COLLEGE OF TECHNOLOGY,
0181 394 1731

Reigate Road, Ewell, EPSOM, Surrey, KT17 3DS,
No response received to our enquiries for 2000. Entry details as of Nov 1998

*   1) Introduction to Counselling

*   2) Advanced Certificate in Counselling Skills & Theory (BTEC)

**   3) Diploma in Psychodynamic Counselling (BAC Acc)

GUILDFORD — SURREY ADULT EDUCATION,SERVICE
01483 560978

Adult Education Centre, Sydenham Road, GUILDFORD, Surrey, GU1 3RX,
No response received to our enquiries for 2000, entry details as of November 1998

*   1) Preliminary Certificate in Counselling — Module

*   2) Preliminary Certificate in Counselling — Module

*   3) Preliminary Certificate in Counselling Year 2

GUILDFORD COLLEGE OF FURTHER &,HIGHER EDUCATION
01483 448500

Stoke Park, GUILDFORD, Surrey, GU1 1EZ,
No response received to our enquiries for 2000, entry details as of November 1998

*   1) Counselling Skills Certificate (CSCT/AEB)

*   2) Counselling Theory Certificate (AEB/CSCT)

---

*Star System: * Introductory course only • ** 2-3 yr pt-time course to Cert/Dip level •*
*** Professional development for trained counsellors
For added help, see section 'Essential Information for Students', page 1

*   3) Combined Certificate in Counselling Skills and

**   4) Weekend Humanistic Diploma in Counselling

**   5) Diploma in Humanistic Counselling

**   6) Diploma in Integrative Counselling

**   7) Diploma in Psychodynamic Counselling

***   8) Teacher Training for Counsellors

HUMAN POTENTIAL RESEARCH GROUP,   01483 300 800
School of Educational Studies, University of Surrey, GUILDFORD, Surrey, GU2 5XH,
No response received to our enquiries for 2000, entry details as of November 1998

*   1) Introduction to Facilitating Learning Groups

*   2) Facilitating Groups: A Process Approach

*   3) Working with Gestalt: An Inquiry into the Gestalt Approach in
         Counselling & Group Faciliatation

*   4) Dimensions of Facilitator Style

*   5) Interpersonal Skills for Helping the Client

*   6) Interpersonal Skills for Helping The Client: Training the Trainer

*   7) Assertiveness at Work

*   8) Assertiveness Teacher Training

*   9) Co-Counselling — Fundamental Skills

---

*Star System: * Introductory course only • ** 2-3 yr pt-time course to Cert/Dip level •
*** Professional development for trained counsellors*
For added help, see section 'Essential Information for Students', page 1

257

UNIVERSITY OF SURREY,   01483 300 800 X3143/3164

MATER Project, School of Educational Studies, GUILDFORD, Surrey, GU2 5XH,

A wide range of shorter courses including supervision is available. Consultancy & in-house training also available.

  ♿ Wheelchair access

**   1) Module: Counselling for Occupational Health (10 credits)

Duration	5 days, + home/practice based study (can count towards Adv Dip/MSc Occupational Health
Entry	Professional qualification & experience in the work place

**   2) Postgraduate Cert in Counselling & Psychotherapy as a Means to Health (Client Centred)

Duration	5 day block, then 1 year, 1 afternoon & evening/week
Entry	Professionals &/or graduates from statutory, voluntary & private health/social service organisations/functions

**   3) Postgraduate Dip in Counselling & Psychotherapy as a Means to Health

Duration	5 day block, then 1 year, part-time, 1 day/week
Entry	Successful completion of 2); or 40 credits at Level M in an appropriate subject. Course involves: Existentialism/Phenomonology/Post-modernism
Core Model	Existentialism/Phenomonology/Post-modernism

***   4) MSc in Counselling & Psychotherapy as a Means to Health

Duration	1 year, 1 day/week
Entry	Successful completion of 2)

***   5) MPhil/PhD in Counselling/Psychotherapy as a form of Education/ Learning

Duration	Full OR part-time
Entry	Relevant MSc or degree
Apply To:	Helen McEwan/Dr Del Loewenthal

KINGSTON COLLEGE,   0181 268 3041

Counselling Training, Kingston Hall Road, KINGSTON UPON THAMES, Surrey, KT1 2AQ,

No response received to our enquiries for 2000, entry details as of November 1998

**   Diploma in Professional Counselling (BAC Acc)

Star System: * Introductory course only • ** 2-3 yr pt-time course to Cert/Dip level • *** Professional development for trained counsellors

For added help, see section 'Essential Information for Students', page 1

258

MERTON COLLEGE,   0181 640 3001 X 204

London Road, MORDEN, Surrey, SM4 5QX,
No response received to our enquiries for 2000, entry details as of November 1998

* **1) An Introduction to Counselling** (Cert of Attendance)

* **2) Certificate in Counselling Skills** (CSCT/AEB)

* **3) Certificate in Counselling Theory** (CSCT/AEB)

** **4) Advanced Skills Certificate** (CSCT/AEB)

EAST SURREY COLLEGE,   01737 772 611

Faculty of Services to People, Gatton Point, North Claremont Road, REDHILL,
RH1 2JX,
No response received to our enquiries for 2000, entry details as of Nov 1998

* **1) Introduction to Counselling**

* **2) Foundation Course in Counselling**

* **3) Group Dynamics & Interpersonal Skills**

** **4) Diploma in Counselling** (Surrey Open College Federation)

SUTTON COLLEGE OF LIBERAL ARTS,   0181 770 6901

St Nicholas Way, SUTTON, Surrey, SM1 1EA,
No response received to our enquiries for 2000. Entry details as of Nov 1998

* **1) Introduction to Basic Counselling Skills**

* **2) RSA Certificate in Counselling Skills**

SUTTON PASTORAL FOUNDATION LTD,   0181 6617869

21A Cheam Road, SUTTON, Surrey, SM1 1SH,
Offers in-house and tailor-made training and workshops in counselling/counselling
skills

♿ Access to building

* **1) Communication Skills — an Introduction to Counselling Skills**
Duration   10 weeks, 2hrs/week, evenings

continued...

---

*Star System: * Introductory course only • ** 2-3 yr pt-time course to Cert/Dip level •*
*** Professional development for trained counsellors*
For added help, see section 'Essential Information for Students', page 1

*   **2) Certificate in Counselling Skills** (WPF Certificate given)
Duration   1 year Foundation Course, part-time, evening
Entry   Selection takes place from March

**   **3) Certificate in Theory of Psychodynamic Counselling** (SPF Certificate given)
Duration   2 years, part-time, evening
Entry   Completion of 2) or equivalent and selection by SPF

**   **4) Certificate in Psychodynamic Counselling** (WPF Certificate given)
Duration   Minimum 100 hours counselling practice
Entry   Completion of 2) and 3) or equivalent and selection for counselling
                  placement at SPF

***   **5) Diploma in Psychodynamic Counselling**
Duration   Minimum 200 hours counselling practice
Entry   Completion of 2), 3) and 4) or equivalent
Apply To: Ms T A Lipscombe, Administrator

ESHER COLLEGE,   0181 398 0291
Weston Green Road, THAMES DITTON, Surrey, KT7 0JB,
No response received to our enquiries for 2000, entry details as of November 1998

*   **1) Certificate in Counselling Skills** (CSCT/AEB)

*   **2) Certificate in Counselling Theory** (CSCT/AEB)

**   **3) Advanced Certificate in Counselling**

**   **4) Diploma in Counselling** (CSCT/AEB)

CETS,   0181 6656737/ 0181 6840231
Ambassador House, Brigstock Road, THORNTON HEATH, Surrey, CR7 7JG,
Workshops are also offered as part of whole courses eg: HIV/AIDS, Loss and
Bereavement. Alcohol and Drug Use, Domestic Violence

*   **Bilingual Counselling Skills Certificate** (LOCN) equivalent to a
       Foundation Course in Cross Cultural Counselling)
Duration   30 days, 1/week (120 hrs)
Entry   Two languages; basic understanding of counselling; awareness of
                  cross cultural issues
Apply To: Christina Pusceddu, Course Co-ordinator

Star System: * Introductory course only • ** 2-3 yr pt-time course to Cert/Dip level •
*** Professional development for trained counsellors
For added help, see section 'Essential Information for Students', page 1
260

GOLD TRAINING & COUNSELLING SERVICES,   0181 657 7845

Mayday Healthcare NHS Trust, THORNTON HEATH, Surrey, CR7 7YE,

No response received to our enquiries. Entry details as of Nov 1998

**   **Bereavement Counselling Diploma** (Greenwich Univ) (60 Credits at Level 2)

BROOKLANDS COLLEGE,   01932 7997 863

Faculty of Prof. Studies, Heath Road, WEYBRIDGE, Surrey, KT13 8TT,

No response received to our enquiries for 2000, entry details as of November 1998

*   **1) RSA Certificate in Counselling Skills in the Development of Learning**

**   **2) Diploma in Counselling Training** (BTEC Higher National Certificate/ Diploma)

Star System: * Introductory course only • ** 2-3 yr pt-time course to Cert/Dip level •
*** Professional development for trained counsellors
For added help, see section 'Essential Information for Students', page 1

261

BRIGHTON COLLEGE OF TECHNOLOGY,   01273 667709
Pelham Street, BRIGHTON, BN1 4FA,
No response received to our enquiries for 2000, entry details as of November 1998

**   **Advanced Certificate in Counselling Skills**

UNIVERSITY OF BRIGHTON,   01273600900 X 3494 FAX
                                                      01273 643473
School of Applied Social Science, Falmer, BRIGHTON, BN1 9PH,

**   **1) Postgraduate Diploma in Counselling**
Duration   2 yrs, part-time, 1 day/week + 1 weekend/term
Entry   Degree or professional qualification, have prior counselling experience
                       & continuing counselling practice during training

***   **2) MA Counselling Studies**
Duration   1 year, part-time
Entry   Degree or professional qualification + Postgraduate Diploma in
                       Counselling, continuing counselling practice during training

***   **3) Gestalt: A Post-qualifying Course for Counsellors**
Duration   1 year, 1 eve/week + 1 weekend/term
Entry   Diploma in Counselling
Core Model   Gestalt
Apply To: Administration Assistant, School of Applied Social Science

---

UNIVERSITY OF SUSSEX,   01273 678156
Cllg & Psychotherapy Unit, Health Centre Building, Falmer, BRIGHTON, BN1 9RW,
No response received to our enquiries for 2000, entry details as of November 1998

*   **1) Pre-Diploma in Counselling**

*   **2) Certificate in Psychodynamic Counselling**

**   **3) Post Graduate Diploma in Counseling** (Univ Sussex)

***   **4) Certificate in Clinical Supervision** (Univ Sussex)

Star System: *Introductory course only • ** 2-3 yr pt-time course to Cert/Dip level •*
*** *Professional development for trained counsellors*
For added help, see section 'Essential Information for Students', page 1

262

CHICHESTER COUNSELLING SERVICE,   01243 789200

Fernleigh Centre, 40 North Street, CHICHESTER, West Sussex, PO19 1LX,
Programme of 1 day workshops and short courses for qualifies counsellors also
available

♿ Unable to accommodate people in wheelchairs who cannot manage stairs, but
otherwise disabled people are welcome

**   Diploma Course in Psychodynamic Counselling (BAC Acc)

Duration	a) 3 years, part-time, daytime or evening seminars and Saturday workshops b) 2 years, part-time via APL
Entry	Application form and interview; selection procedure
Apply To:	Helen Botterill, Office Administrator

UNIVERSITY COLLEGE CHICHESTER,   01243 816000 X 6284
FAX: 01243 816080

Bishop Otter Campus, College Lane, CHICHESTER, West Sussex, PO19 4PE,
Also offers in-house/tailor made and short counselling courses

♿ Parking; access to teaching rooms, library, refectory; accommodation for
whhelchair users (integrated with that for able-bodied students)

*   1) Foundation Certificate in Counselling Skills

Duration	300 hours directed time, part-time, evening + 2 Sats
Entry	No formal entry requirements

**   2) Diploma in Professional Studies (Counselling)

Duration	240 hours, day/evening + 2 weekends, part-time + practice, personal counselling and supervision
Entry	Personal counselling; 120 level 1 points or portfolio route introductory level counselling course

**   3) BA in Professional Studies (Counselling) (BAC Acc)

Duration	576 hours, day/evening + 2 weekends
Entry	120 level 1 points or portfolio route; introductory level counselling course; personal counselling
Apply To:	Jill Hayes, Senior Lecturer in Social Studies

Star System: ** Introductory course only* • *** 2-3 yr pt-time course to Cert/Dip level* •
*** Professional development for trained counsellors
For added help, see section 'Essential Information for Students', page 1
263

CRAWLEY COLLEGE,   01293 442345

Service Industries, College Road, CRAWLEY, West Sussex, RH10 1NR,
No response received to our enquiries for 2000, entry details as of November 1998

*   **1) Introduction to Counselling & Communication Skills Part 1 & 2**
        (NCFE)

*   **2) Certificate in Counselling Skills in Bereavement & Loss** (in partnership
        with St. Catherine's Hospice)

*   **3) College Certificate in Person-Centred Art Therapy**

*   **4) RSA Certificate in Counselling Skills in The Development of Learning**

**   **5) Diploma in Therapeutic Counselling (BAC Acc)**

WEALDEN COLLEGE,   01892 655195

2 Quarry View, Whitehill Road, CROWBOROUGH, East Sussex, TN6 1JT,
No response received to our enquiries for 2000. Entry details as of 1998

*   **1) Certificate in Counselling Skills**

**   **2) Diploma in Counselling (BAC Acc)**

**   **3) Training in Transactional Analysis** (EATA)

**   **4) Certificate/Diploma in Applied Professional Studies or Masters in TA
        Psychotherapy** (Proposed)

***   **5) Diploma in Supervision**

BIOGRAPHY & SOCIAL DEVELOPMENT TRUST,   01342 810221

Coombe Hill Road, EAST GRINSTEAD, West Sussex, RH19 4LZ,
No response received to our enquiries for 2000, entry details as of November 1998

*   **1) Biography Work — Introductory Course with Groups**

*   **2) Introductory Courses to Counselling out of Anthroposophy —
        Counselling & the Planets**

**   **3) Biographical Counselling** (Certificate)

Star System: * Introductory course only • ** 2-3 yr pt-time course to Cert/Dip level •
*** Professional development for trained counsellors

For added help, see section 'Essential Information for Students', page 1

EASTBOURNE COLLEGE OF ARTS AND,TECHNOLOGY
013323 644 711

ECAT House, Crosslevels Way, EASTBOURNE, East Sussex, BN21 2UF,
No response received to our enquiries for 2000, entry details as of November 1998

*   **1) Introductory Counselling Modules 1, 2 & 3** (OCN)

*   **2) Certificate in Counselling Skills** (CSCT/AEB)

*   **3) Certificate in Alcohol/Drugs Counselling Skills**

*   **4) Certificate in Counselling Theory** (CSCT/AEB)

**   **5) Advanced Certificate in Skills & Theory** (CSCT/A

**   **6) Diploma in Counselling** (CSCT/AEB)

THE FOREST SCHOOL,
01403 261088

Compton Lane, HORSHAM, RH13 5NW,

♿ Downstairs classroom

*   **Counselling Skills**

Duration	1 yr, part-time, 3 hrs/week, 30 weeks
Entry	Introductory day, preparation/selection prior to starting
Apply To:	Adult Education Department

LEWES TERTIARY COLLEGE,
01273 483 188

Mountfield Road, LEWES, East Sussex, BN7 2XH,
No response received to our enquiries for 2000, entry details as of November 1998

*   **1) Groupwork Skills**

*   **2) Foundation in Counselling** (Certificate of Attendance) (OCN)

*   **3) Intermediate Certificate in Counselling** (Certificate of Attendance)
      (OCN)

*   **4) RSA Counselling Skills in the Development of Learning**

**   **5) Diploma in Counselling** (BAC Acc)

---

*Star System: * Introductory course only • ** 2-3 yr pt-time course to Cert/Dip level •*
*** Professional development for trained counsellors*
For added help, see section 'Essential Information for Students', page 1

265

PSYCHOSYNTHESIS UK,   01273 473113 ALSO FAX

4 Offham Terrace, LEWES, East Sussex, BN7 2QP,

Courses in Brighton, W Yorkshire & London. Residential Summer School : Gender, Sexuality & the Transpersonal. Short courses and residentials = 2). Adv Certs = Dip in Transpersonal Psychotherapy

♿ Brighton only has full Access for disabled who are most welcome

*** 1) Advanced Certificate in Applied Transpersonal

Duration   200 hrs, weekend and some evenings. Brighton September Start; London January start

Entry   Training in counselling and/or psychotherapy and be in practice

*** 2) Advanced Certificate in the Art of Therapy

Entry   Selection of pick & mix short courses & residentials. For practicing counsellors and psychotherapists

Duration   None Stated

HASTINGS COLLEGE OF ARTS AND TECHNOLOGY,
01424 442222 X229

Dept of Adult & Community Education, Archery Road, ST. LEONARDS-ON-SEA, East Sussex, TN38 0HX,

No response received to our enquiries for 2000, entry details as of November 1998

* 1) Basic Counselling Skills Introduction (NCFE/C&G)

* 2) Certificate in Basic Counselling Skills (NCFE/C&G)

* 3) Certificate in Basic Counselling Skills (Intensive Route) City & Guilds 3701/3702)

* 4) Certificate in Counselling (NCFE/C&G)

COUNSELLORS' GUILD,   01825 712802

Archdown Natural Health Centre, Royal Oak Cottage, High Street, Nutley, UCKFIELD, East Sussex, TN22 3NN,

No response received to our enquiries for 2000, entry details as of Nov 1998

* 1) Use Your Voice

* 2) Assertiveness Training

* 3) Emotional Literacy (Cert of Attendance)

Star System: * *Introductory course only* • ** *2-3 yr pt-time course to Cert/Dip level* •
*** *Professional development for trained counsellors*

*   **4) Communication Skills** (Cert of Attendance)

*   **5) How Christians can Help** (Cert of Attendance)

*   **6) Skills for Therapists** (Cert of Attendance)

*   **7) Interface between Drama & Therapy** (Cert of Attendance)

*   **8) Counselling Skills Level 1** (Cert of Attendance)

*   **9) Counselling Skills Level 2**

*   **10) Counselling Skills Level 3** (Cert of Attendance

*   **11) Voice Work**

NORTHBROOK COLLEGE OF F & HE,   01903 830057

Dept Prof & Managerial Studies, Littlehampton Road, Goring by the Sea, WORTHING, West Sussex, BN12 6NU,

No response received to our enquiries for 2000. Entry details as of Nov 1998

*   **1) RSA Certificate, Counselling Skills**

**   **2) Advanced Diploma in the Psychology of Counselling & Therapy**
(WPF)

---

*Star System: * Introductory course only • ** 2-3 yr pt-time course to Cert/Dip level •*
*** Professional development for trained counsellors
For added help, see section 'Essential Information for Students', page 1

267

GATESHEAD COLLEGE,　　　　　　　　0191 490 2373

Broadway Centre, Elgin Road, GATESHEAD, Tyne and Wear, NE9 5PA,
No response received to our enquiries for 2000, entry details as of November 1998

*　　　1) **Certificate in Counselling Skills** (AEB/CSCT)

*　　　2) **Certificate in Counselling Theory** (AEB/CSCT)

*　　　3) **Combined Certificate in Counselling Skills & Theory** (AEB/CSCT)

**　　4) **Diploma in Counselling** (AEB/CSCT)

SOUTH TYNESIDE COLLEGE,　　　　0191 427 3629

Hebburn Centre, Mill Lane, HEBBURN, Tyne and Wear, NE31 2ER,
Also run tailor-made short couselling courses according to demand

♿ Lifts, ramps, Lifts, ramps, reserved parking, toilet facilities with wheelchair access

*　　　1) **Certificate in Basic Counselling Skills** (NCFE)
Duration　　　42 hrs, part-time
Entry　　　　For those interested in developing skills for use in a variety of work
　　　　　　　and personal situations

*　　　2) **Certificate in Counselling** (NCFE)
Duration　　　88 hrs part-time, day or evening
Entry　　　　Those who have previous counselling skills, experience and/or
　　　　　　　training, to be discussed at interview

*　　　3) **HNC in Counselling Skills** (BTEC)
Duration　　　Day release for two years
Entry　　　　Foundation counselling skills/theory qualification, qualifications in
　　　　　　　caring professions
Core Model　　Psychodynamic, Humanistic, Cognitive Behavioural perspectives
Apply To:　　Juliet Higdon

CENTRAL SCHOOL OF COUNSELLING & THERAPY,
0800 243463

80 Paul Street, LONDON, EC2A 4UD,
See National Section entry for full details.

Star System:　* Introductory course only • ** 2-3 yr pt-time course to Cert/Dip level •
*** Professional development for trained counsellors
For added help, see section 'Essential Information for Students', page 1

268

UNIVERSITY OF NORTHUMBRIA,   **0191 227 3453**

Faculty Of Health, Soc Work & Education, C/O Manor House, Coach Lane Campus, Coach Lane, NEWCASTLE UPON TYNE, NE7 7XA,

Workshops offered, e.g. Personal Construct Theory in Career Counselling/Decision Making

♿ Good access for wheelchair users. Student Advisor to help with specific needs.

**   Post Graduate Diploma/MA in Guidance and Counselling

Duration	1 yr PG Certificate, 2 yrs PG Diploma, 3 yrs MA via dissertation, part-time, 1 day per week
Entry	Degree of recognised university
Apply To:	Peter Beven

JESMOND CENTRE FOR PSYCHODRAMA & COUNSELLING
0191 281 6243

94 St George's Terrace, Jesmond, NEWCASTLE-UPON-TYNE, NE2 2DL,

No response received to our enquiries for 2000, entry details as of November 1998

**   1) Diploma in Advanced Counselling & Therapy (Person-Centred Approach)

***   2) Certificate in Supervision (Person-Centred Approach)

NEWCASTLE CITY HEALTH NHS TRUST,   **0191 282 4547**

Dept of Psychotherapy, Claremont House, Off Framlington Place, NEWCASTLE-UPON-TYNE, NE2 4AA,

**   1) Dynamics at Work: A Psychodynamic Understanding of Mental Health Practice

Core Model	Psychodynamic
Duration	18 months, part-time, 1 half day/week
Entry	People working the Mental Health and related fields with an interest in the psychodynamic model of working in, and understanding mental health.

**   2) North of England Association for Training in Psychoanalytic Psychotherapy

Core Model	Psychoanalytic
Duration	Minimum 4 years, part-time
Entry	Please enquire

continued...

Star System: * Introductory course only • ** 2-3 yr pt-time course to Cert/Dip level •
*** Professional development for trained counsellors
For added help, see section 'Essential Information for Students', page 1

269

** 3) **Practitioner Level Training in Psychodynamic Psychotherapy**

Core Model Psychodynamic Psychotherapy
Duration 2-4 years, part-time (modules)
Entry Mental Health Professionals with some experience of psychotherapy
Apply To: Ms V Gore, Training Committee

NEWCASTLE COLLEGE, 0191 200 4600

Sandyford Campus, Sandyford Road, NEWCASTLE-UPON-TYNE, NE1 8QE,
No response received to our enquiries for 2000. Entry details as of Nov 1998

* 1) **Basic Counselling Skills** (NCFE)

** 2) **Certificate in Counselling** (NCFE)

** 3) **Further Counselling Skills** (NCFE)

** 4) **Diploma in Counselling — Humanistic Approach** (NCFE)

REDCAR & CLEVELAND COLLEGE, 01642 474841

Connections Campus, Redcar Lane, REDCAR, TS10 2PB,

♿ Wheelchair Access. Toilets for the disabled

* 1) **Certificate in Basic Counselling Skills** (NCFE 3701/02)
Duration 3 hrs per week, 12 weeks, evening or daytime
Entry None
Core Model Person-Centred

* 2) **Further Counselling Skills** (NCFE 3704)
Duration 3 hrs per weel, 1year, evening or daytime
Entry 1 year training, experience in helping profession

* 3) **Certificate in Counselling** (NCFE 3703)
Duration 3 hrs per week, 1 year, evening or daytime, 1 residential
Entry NCFE Certificate in Basic Skills or equivalent
Core Model Egan
Apply To: Denise Hardy

---

*Star System: * Introductory course only • ** 2-3 yr pt-time course to Cert/Dip level •
*** Professional development for trained counsellors*
For added help, see section 'Essential Information for Students', page 1
270

** **4) Advanced Diploma in Counselling** (CTI/NOCN/OU)

Duration	5 hrs per week, daytime, 2 years
Entry	Minimum 120 hrs previous training. Able to demonstrate appropriate academic ability to work at level 3, personal maturity.
Core Model	Person Centred
Apply To:	David Collingwood

CITY OF SUNDERLAND COLLEGE,   0191 511 6246

Dept of Care & Development, Hylton Centre, North Hylton Road, SUNDERLAND, SR5 5DB,

♿ Full facilities available

* **1) Introduction to Counselling Skills** (TROCN)

Duration	11 weeks, 1 evening or daytime/week (22 hours)
Entry	Open

* **2) Counselling Continuation** (TROCN)

Duration	11 weeks, 1 daytime/week (22 hours)
Entry	Introduction to Counselling

* **3) Certificate in Counselling Theory — 901** (CSCT/AEB)

Duration	30 weeks, 1 eve/week, (75 hrs)
Entry	Open access

* **4) Certificate in Counselling Skills — 900** (CSCT/AEB)

Duration	30 weeks,1 eve/week (75 hours)
Entry	Open access

* **5) Certificate in Counselling** (3703 NCFE)

Duration	25 weeks, 1 daytime/week, 75 hours
Entry	Introduction to Counselling

* **6) Introduction to Counselling Children and Adolescents** (NCFE)

Duration	11 weeks, 1 daytime or evening/week (22 hour)
Entry	Open access
Apply To:	Natalie Johnson, Counselling Course Team Leader

Star System: * *Introductory course only* • ** *2-3 yr pt-time course to Cert/Dip level* •
*** *Professional development for trained counsellors*
For added help, see section 'Essential Information for Students', page 1

271

WARWICK UNIVERSITY,, 01203 523841

Continuing Education Dept, Westwood Site, COVENTRY, CV4 7AL,
No response received to our enquiries for 2000. Entry details as of 1998

** **1) Certificate in Person Centred Rogerian Counselling**

** **2) Diploma in Person Centred Rogerian Counselling**

WARWICKSHIRE COLLEGE, ROYAL LEAMINGTON SPA & MORETON MORRELL 01926 318161

11 Warwick New Road, LEAMINGTON SPA, Warwickshire, CV31 5JE,
Offers in-house and tailor-made training

♿ Most buildings are accessible for wheelchairs, toilets in main buildings and Conference Centre; minicom; loop; screen reader, please contact college to discuss particular needs

* **1) Introduction to Counselling Skills** (Open College Network Level 1 and 2)

Duration	10 weeks, run termly, part-time day and evening
Entry	For people new to counselling skills

* **2) Intermediate Counselling Skills** (National Open College Network Level 1, 2 or 3)

Duration	10 weeks, run termly, part-time, day and evening
Entry	Those who have completed an introductory course

* **3) Games people play — An introduction to Transactional Analysis** (Open College Network Level 1, 2 or 3)

Duration	10 weeks, run termly, part-time, day and evenings
Entry	For people new to Transactional Analysis

* **4) Know Yourself Better — Personal Empowerment** (National Open College Network Level 1 or 2)

Duration	10 weeks, run termly, part-time, day or evening
Entry	For people who would like to know themselves better and tap into their own personal potential

*Star System: * Introductory course only • ** 2-3 yr pt-time course to Cert/Dip level •*
* *Professional development for trained counsellors*
For added help, see section 'Essential Information for Students', page 1

272

*   5) Certificate in Counselling Skills and Theory (CENTRA)

Core Model   Person Centred

Duration   36 weeks, mornings or evenings + 3 Saturdays (124 hrs) (Sept start)

Entry   Those who are interested in developing their counselling skills and
               want to explore personal development within a Person Centred
               framework. Applicants need to have completed an introductory
               counselling course or equivalent.

**   6) Diploma in Person Centred Counselling (CENTRA)

Duration   2 years, 36 weeks each year, evening + 4 Saturdays (Sept Start). Year
               One — 150 hours, Year Two 182 hours + counselling placement +
               supervision

Entry   Those who have completed a minimum of 90 hours counselling
               training at certificate level and can cope with the academic level of
               work involved at this level. Also applicants need to be able to adopt a
               person centred approach to their own learning & practice

Apply To: Patience O'Neill tel 01926 318161

NORTH WARWICKSHIRE & HINCKLEY COLLEGE,
01203 243000

Hinckley Road, NUNEATON, Warwickshire, CV11 6BH,

Also offers in-house & tailor-made courses & workshops

♿ Wheelchair access/lifts; special parking facility; special toilet facility, support from
guidance unit including carers, study support etc

***   1) Introductory Courses in Couns Skills; Stress Management;
       Assertiveness; TA; Gestalt; Personal Development**

Duration   Each course: 10 weeks

Entry   None stated

*   2) OCR (formerly RSA) Certificate in Counselling Skills

Duration   1 year, part-time, afternoon or evening

Entry   By interview

**   3) Advanced Certificate in Counselling Skills (Humanistic)

Duration   1 year, part-time

Entry   Successful completion of a 1 year counselling skills course. Selection
               by interview

Core Model   Humanistic

continued...

*Star System: * Introductory course only • ** 2-3 yr pt-time course to Cert/Dip level •
*** Professional development for trained counsellors*
For added help, see section 'Essential Information for Students', page 1

273

**   4) Diploma in Counselling** (Humanistic) — proposed for Sept 2000

Core Model	Humanistic
Duration	18 months, part-time
Entry	Successful completion of advanced certificate in counselling skills or equivalent. Selection by interview
Apply To:	Information Office for interview

LIFE SKILLS TRAINING SERVICES,   01788 547516, 0585 823046

163 Clifton Road, RUGBY, Warwickshire, CV21 3QN,

In-house/tailor-made training and workshops in counselling skills also offered, e.g. 2 day seminar in stress management

♿ Wheelchair access, BSL signing if required

***   1) Certificate in Counselling Children & Families

Duration	2 yrs, 1 day/month (120 hrs)
Entry	Be in regular contact with children & families, be in professional supervision, be in personal therapy (recommended)

***   2) Safety in the Consulting Room

Duration	1 day workshop in safety issues and practical self-defence
Entry	For counsellors, psychotherapists and other 'caring' professions
Apply To:	Roger Day, Trainer

RUGBY COLLEGE OF FURTHER EDUCATION,   01788 338800

Lower Hillmorton Road, RUGBY, Warwickshire, CV21 3QS,

No response received to our enquiries for 2000, entry details as of November 1998

*   **1) Introduction to Counselling Skills** (Open College Network)

**   **2) Combined Certificate in Counselling Skills & Therapeutic Counselling** (CPCAB)

**   **3) Advanced Certificate in Therapeutic Counselling** (CPCAB)

**   **4) Diploma in Therapeutic Counselling** (CPCAB)

**   **5) Advanced Diploma in Therapeutic Counselling** (CPCAB)

***   **6) Certificate in Counselling Supervision** (CPCAB)

***   **7) Diploma in Counselling Supervision** (CPCAB)

---

*Star System: * Introductory course only • ** 2-3 yr pt-time course to Cert/Dip level •*
*** Professional development for trained counsellors
For added help, see section 'Essential Information for Students', page 1

BILSTON COMMUNITY COLLEGE,   01902 821700
Westfield Road, BILSTON, West Midlands, WV14 6ER,
Details of a range of short courses available on application

♿ Facilities for stuidents with physical and sensory disabilities

*   **1) College Certificate in Counselling** (OCN)
Duration   1 year, part-time, 1 eve/week, weekend
Entry   None

*   **2) Professional Development Certificate in Counselling** (BTEC)
Duration   6 approved units which can be done individually. 1 year (day), 2 years
              (evening)
Entry   Over 21 and relevant experience (Units include TA, Egan, Rogerian
              approaches)

**   **3) Professional Development Diploma in Counselling** (BTEC)
Duration   7 approved units wich can be done individually. 2 years evening or 1
              year day.
Entry   Over 21, completion of 2) or equivalent involved in counselling with
              counselling supervision

***   **4) Counselling Supervision** (BTEC)
Duration   Varied, 120 hrs in total
Entry   A programme fr practising counsellors who have trained to Diploma
              level

***   **5) Postgraduate Diploma: Counselling in Primary Care Setting**
Duration   60 Fridays over 2 years
Entry   Experienced counsellors with diploma
Apply To: Colin Tatton

BIRMINGHAM INSTITUTE FOR TRANSACTIONAL A,
                                               0121 477 2420
62 Lightwoods Hill, Warley Woods, BIRMINGHAM, West Midlands, B67 5EB,
No response received to our enquiries for 2000, entry details as for Nov 1998

*   **1) '101' Introductory Courses** (Certificate of Attendance)

**   **2) Ongoing Programme leading to Preparation for Clinical TA
Examination**

Star System: ** Introductory course only • ** 2-3 yr pt-time course to Cert/Dip level •*
*** Professional development for trained counsellors
For added help, see section 'Essential Information for Students', page 1
       275

BOURNVILLE COLLEGE OF FURTHER EDUCATION,
0121 411 1414

Bristol Road South, BIRMINGHAM, B31 2AJ,
Variety of in-house/tailor-made programmes to suit different needs. Will offer
counselling workshops and courses on request to organisations.

♿ Physical access for wheelchair uses; loop; signers; note-takers.

*   **1) Introduction to Interpersonal and Counselling Skills** (OCN)
Duration   30 hrs, run at times to suit workplace and client requirements
Entry   Open; especially useful for workplace counselling

*   **2) Introduction to Counselling Skills** (AEB)
Duration   10 weeks, 22.5 hrs, 2.5 hrs/week, evening, run termly
Entry   Interest in developing interpersonal and counselling skills

*   **3) Introduction to Counselling Skills** (AEB)
Duration   10 weeks, 2.25 hrs/week, (22.5 hrs) twice termly (Saturdays)
Entry   Interest in developing interpersonal skills

*   **4) Certificate in Competence in the Use of Counselling Skills** (AEB)
Duration   2.5 hrs/week, (Tues), (75 hrs)
Entry   Introductory programme or in-house workshops in counselling skills,
                and/or appropriate experience.
Apply To: Celia Howell-Jones, Ruth Felstead

CARRS LANE COUNSELLING CENTRE,   **0121 643 6363**
Carrs Lane Church, Carrs Lane, BIRMINGHAM, B4 7SX,
No response received to our enquiries for 2000, entry details as of November 1998

*   **1) Counselling Skills Course**

EAST BIRMINGHAM COLLEGE,   **0121 743 4471**
Learning Resources Centre, Garretts Green Lane, BIRMINGHAM, B33 0TS,
No response received to our enquiries for 2000, entry details as of November 1998

*   **1) Initial Counselling** (Open College Network)

*   **2) RSA Certificate in Counselling Skills in the Development of Learning**

---

*Star System: * Introductory course only • ** 2-3 yr pt-time course to Cert/Dip level •*
*** Professional development for trained counsellors*
For added help, see section 'Essential Information for Students', page 1

276

NORTH BIRMINGHAM COLLEGE,   **0121 360 3543**

Aldridge Road, Great Barr, BIRMINGHAM, B44 8NE,

In-house/tailor-made training offered, also workshops in counselling/counselling skills

♿ Access to venue/lifts/toilets. Canteen facilities. Equal Opportunities policy

*   1) Crisis Counselling Skills (AEB)

Duration	30 hours (5 days)
Entry	Caring Professions/emergency services/voluntary organisations/ counsellors/social workers/anyone involved in education
Core Model	Humanistic

*   2) Grief and Bereavement Counselling Skills (AEB)

Duration	30 hours (5 days)
Entry	Caring professions/counsellors/anyone involved in education/voluntary organisations
Core Model	Humanistic

***   3) Certificate in Counselling Supervision (AEB)

Duration	18 hours (3 days/weekend)
Entry	This is an introduction to supervision skills, principles and models, and will interest any counsellor in supervision and offering supervision to other counsellors

*   4) Certificate in Counselling Skills (OCN, West Midlands)

Duration	78 hours over 26 weeks. One day/evening per week
Entry	Introduction to Counselling foundation course. Health care workers/ teachers/social workers/volunteers
Apply To:	Mrs Chris Hughes
Core Model	Humanistic

*   5) Certificate in Counselling Theory (OCN, West Midlands)

Duration	78 hours over 26 weeks, one day/evening per week
Entry	Health care workers/teachers/social workers/volunteers/counsellors
Apply To:	Mrs Chris Hughes

---

*Star System: * Introductory course only • ** 2-3 yr pt-time course to Cert/Dip level •*
*** Professional development for trained counsellors*
For added help, see section 'Essential Information for Students', page 1

SOUTH BIRMINGHAM COLLEGE,   0121 694 5086
                                            0121 694 6288

Cole Bank Road, BIRMINGHAM, B28 8ES,

♿ Access and facilities fo disabled people

*   **RSA Counselling Skills in the Development of Learning**
Duration   30 weeks, part-time, day or eve (120 hrs)
Entry   Anyone using or wanting to use counselling skills in paid or voluntary
              work.
Apply To: Helen Miller/Sumar Kang

UNIVERSITY OF BIRMINGHAM   0121 414 5593
Dept of Theology, P O Box 363, BIRMINGHAM, B15 2TT,
No response received to our enquiries for 2000, entry details as of November 1998

**   **Diploma/MA in Pastoral Studies**

UNIVERSITY OF BIRMINGHAM,   0121 4145602
Edgbaston, BIRMINGHAM, B15 2TT,
Course is run in Birmingham, Shrewsbury, Worcester, please see the Hereford &
Worcester entry for details

UNIVERSITY OF BIRMINGHAM,   0121 4145602
School of Continuing Studies, Edgbaston, BIRMINGHAM, B15 2TT,

*   **1) Introduction to Counselling Skills**
Duration   10 wks, 1 eve/week
Entry   Over 21 years of age

*   **2) Post Experience Certificate in Psychodynamic Groupwork**
Duration   1 yr, 1 eve/week
Entry   Over 21 years of age, a commitment to developing self-awareness
Core Model   Psychodynamic

**   **3) Diploma of Higher Education in Integrative Counselling**
Duration   2 yrs, 1 eve/week + 6 Saturdays/Sundays/year
Entry   120 hrs counselling training at level one
Core Model   Integrative
Apply To: Angela Webb

---

*Star System: * Introductory course only • ** 2-3 yr pt-time course to Cert/Dip level •*
*** Professional development for trained counsellors*
For added help, see section 'Essential Information for Students', page 1

278

**   **4) MA/Postgraduate Diploma/BPhil in Counselling (BAC Acc)**

Duration	2 years, 1 day/week
Entry	Degree/equivalent (MA/PG Dip), 240 credits (level 1+2) (BPhil), 5 years professional experience
Core Model	Psychodynamic
Apply To:	Susannah Izzard

***   **5) Advanced Certificate/Post Graduate Certificate in the Supervision** (leading to MA/BPhil in Professional Studies)

Duration	Modular — series of two and three day blocks.
Entry	BAC individual counsellor accreditation/equivalent or 5 years professional experience
Apply To:	Sue Wheeler

***   **6) PhD & MPhil by research**

Duration	PhD: minimum 4 years part-time, MPhil: nimimum 2 years part-time
Entry	PhD: a good honours degree, or postgraduate degree in an appropriate discipline, MPhil: degree from an approved university or other qualification judged satisfactory
Apply To:	Sue Wheeler

UNIVERSITY OF BIRMINGHAM, WESTHILL,   0121 4727245

Hamilton Drive, Weoley Park Road, BIRMINGHAM, B29 6 QW,

♿ Loop system

*   **1) Certificate in Counselling** (Univ Birmingham)

Duration	1 year, part-time
Entry	Experience of using counselling skills, able to demonstrate capacity to study at this level

*   **2) Certificate in Culturally Centred Counselling Skills** (Univ Birmingham)

Duration	1 year, part-time
Entry	Experience of using counselling skills & ability to demonstrate capacity to study at this level.

**   **3) Diploma/BPhil Counselling** (Univ Birmingham)

Duration	2 years, part-time
Entry	Degree/professional qualification + 2 years experience and completion of basic counselling skills training

---

*Star System: * Introductory course only • ** 2-3 yr pt-time course to Cert/Dip level •*
*** *Professional development for trained counsellors*
For added help, see section 'Essential Information for Students', page 1

279

UNIVERSITY OF CENTRAL ENGLAND AT BIRMINGHAM
0121 331 5000/6208
UCE Student Services, Franchise Street, Perry Barr, BIRMINGHAM, B42 2SU,

No response received to our enquiries for 2000, entry details as of November 1998

***   **Postgraduate Diploma/MSc in Counselling & Psychotherapy**

COVENTRY TECHNICAL COLLEGE,   024 7652 6700
The Butts, COVENTRY, CV1 3GD,

♿ Wheelchair access to ground floor accommodation

*   **1) Certificate in Therapeutic Counselling**
Duration   22 weeks, 3hrs/week, evenings or day + 4 Saturday mornings
Entry   Certificate in Counselling Skills

*   **2) Certificate in Counselling Skills**
Duration   22 weeks, 3 hrs/week, evenings or day + 4 Saturday mornings

---

COVENTRY UNIVERSITY,   01203 838 018
Admissions & Placements Unit, School of Health/Soc. Sciences, Room A116, Priory Street, COVENTRY, CV1 5FB,

No response received to our enquiries for 2000, entry details as of Nov 1998

*   **1) Introduction to Counselling — Short Courses**

***   **2) BSc** (Hons) Counselling

TILE HILL COLLEGE OF FE,   01203 694200
Tile Hill Lane, COVENTRY, CV4 9SU,

♿ Extensive Learning Support, Wheelchair accessibility, IT or Amanuensis facilities

*   **1) Introduction to Counselling** (OCN) (Person Centred)
Duration   22 hours, various formats eg: 4 days or 7 evenings
Entry   None
Apply To: Sandra Grainger/Richard Worsley

*   **2) Certificate in Counselling — Person Centred** (Coventry Univ, OCN)
Duration   1 year, part-time, 35 weeks, 3.5 hours/week
Entry   Introductory course or equivalent
Apply To: Sandra Grainger

---

*Star System: * Introductory course only • ** 2-3 yr pt-time course to Cert/Dip level •*
*** Professional development for trained counsellors
For added help, see section 'Essential Information for Students', page 1
280

**   **3) Diploma in Humanistic Counselling** (Warwick Univ)

Duration	2 years, part-time, 36 weeks, 6 hrs/week
Entry	Contact college for further details
Apply To:	Richard Worsley

***   **4) Counselling Supervision** (OCN)

Duration	22 hrs, 3 days over 2 weekends
Entry	Involvement in counselling; interest in improving knowledge of supervision

***   **5) The Theory and Practice of Counselling Supervision** (OCN)

Duration	140 hours, 35 evenings (Weds), 4hrs/eve
Entry	Diploma in counselling or similar; experienced counsellors wishing to improve their knowledge of the theory and practice of counselling supervision
Apply To:	Janet McNaught

HALESOWEN COLLEGE,   0121 550 1451

Whittingham Road, HALESOWEN, West Midlands, B63 3NA,
No response received to our enquiries for 2000, entry details as of Nov 1998

*   **1) Counselling** (Basic Counselling Skills)(City & Guilds)

*   **2) Certificate in Counselling** (City & Guilds)

**   **3) Diploma in Counselling**

COUNSELLING TRAINING INITIATIVES LTD,(CTI)   0115 944 7849

Galtee House, 1 Heanor Road, ILKESTON, Derbyshire, DE7 8DY,
Please see the National Section for fuller details of courses offered

♿ No response received to our enquiries for 2000, entry details as of Nov 1998

CENTRAL SCHOOL OF COUNSELLING & THERAPY,   0800 243463

80 Paul Street, LONDON, EC2A 4UD,
See National Section entry for full details.

NAFSIYAT,   0171 263 4130

278 Seven Sisters Rd, Finsbury Park, LONDON, N2,
Please see entry in the National Section, apply to Yvonne Wright, The Administrator

---

Star System: * Introductory course only • ** 2-3 yr pt-time course to Cert/Dip level •
*** Professional development for trained counsellors
For added help, see section 'Essential Information for Students', page 1

281

NAFSIYAT,   0171 263 4130

Inter-Cultural Therapy Centre, 278 Seven Sisters Rd, Finsbury Park, LONDON, N4 2HY,

No response received to our enquiries for 2000, entry details as of November 1998

***   **MSc in Inter-Cultural Psychotherapy** (ULC/London Univ)

BIRMINGHAM COUNSELLING CENTRE,   0121 429 1758

62 Lightwoods Hill, Bearwood, SMETHWICK, West Midlands, B67 5EB,

No response received to our enquiries for 2000, entry details as of November 1998

*   **1) Introduction to Counselling** (OCN)

*   **2) Certificate in Counselling Skills** (CPCAB)

**   **3) Certificate in Therapeutic Counselling** (CPCAB)

**   **4) Certificate in Humanistic & Integrative Counselling** (CPCAB)

**   **5) Advanced Certificate in Therapeutic Arts**

**   **6) Diploma in Therapeutic Counselling** (CENTRA)

**   **7) Fundamentals of Co-counselling**

**   **8) Fundamentals of Gestalt**

***   **9) Supervision & Support Group for Practitioners**

SANDWELL COLLEGE,   0121 556 6000

Dept Teacher Ed & Counselling, Smethwick Campus, Crocketts Lane, SMETHWICK, West Midlands, B66 3BU,

*   **1) Introduction to Counselling** (OCNWM)

Duration	5 weeks
Entry	Open

*   **2) Foundation in Counselling Skills** (CTI) Part I

Duration	18 weeks, part-time, evening or day
Entry	Basic or introductory course

Star System: ** Introductory course only • ** 2-3 yr pt-time course to Cert/Dip level •*
*** Professional development for trained counsellors
For added help, see section 'Essential Information for Students', page 1

282

*   **3) Foundation in Counselling Skills** (CTI) Part II
Duration   18 weeks, part-time, evening or day
Entry   Basic or introductory course

**   **4) Advanced Diploma in Counselling** (CTI)
Duration   2 years, part-time, day
Entry   Foundation Courses in Counselling Skills and Theory
Apply To: Hash Patel, Head Teacher Education & Counselling Studies

---

SOLIHULL COLLEGE,   **0121 678 7000**

Student Counselling Service, Blossomfield Road, SOLIHULL, West Midlands, B91 1SB,
Workshops & in-house/tailor-made training in counselling & counselling skills also
offered

♿ Disabled students students should discuss their suitability with the course tutor;
ground floor accomodation or lift access; funding available for help with a range of
disabilities

*   **1) Introduction to Working with Individuals** (OCN LEVEL 3)
Duration   12 X 3 hr sessions day or evening
Entry   First stage course for anyone interested in helping people through the
                 development of a range of listening skills applied in context. Suitable
                 for those involved in advice, guidance, tutoring or considering
                 counselling training

*   **2) Certificate in Counselling Skills part one** (OCN Level 2)
Duration   12 x 2.5 hr sessions day or evening
Entry   First stage experiential counselling skills for anyone who has some
                 basic training in listening skills

*   **3) Certificate in Counselling Skills part two** (OCN Level 3, Validated by
        Coventry University at 30 CATS points)
Duration   12 x 3hr sessions day or evening
Entry   For anyone who has completed part two and uses counselling skills as
                 a component of their work. The course takes the person-centred
                 perspective
Core Model   Person Centred

*   **4) Groupwork Skills for Helpers** (OCN Level 2/3)
Duration   30 hrs class time, 3 hrs x 10 week days
Entry   Introductory level — Anyone interested in findng out more about
                 themselves as a group member; Further: currently facilitating group,
                 previous experience of a process/personal development group

continued...

Star System: * Introductory course only • ** 2-3 yr pt-time course to Cert/Dip level •
*** Professional development for trained counsellors
For added help, see section 'Essential Information for Students', page 1
283

**   **5) Diploma in Person-Centred Counselling** (Warwick University)

Duration	2 years, part-time, (2-00-8.15pm) + 10 full days
Entry	Those who are working in counselling settings, in regular supervision & who have completed an advanced skills training course (eg Cert in Counselling); selection by interview
Apply To:	Estelle Seymour, Co-ordinator or Counselling Courses

SUTTON COLDFIELD COLLEGE,   0121 355 5671
FAX: 0121 355 0799

Lichfield Road, SUTTON COLDFIELD, West Midlands, B74 2NW,

*   **1) Certificate in Basic Counselling Skills** (3701/2) (NCFE)

Duration	20 weeks, 1 evening/week or Saturday mornings
Entry	Open

*   **2) Certificate in Counselling** (NCFE)(3703)

Duration	33 weeks, 1 eve/week
Entry	Completion of 1) above

*   **3) Certificate in Counselling Skills** (CSCT/AEB)

Duration	1 year, part-time, 1 evening/week

*   **4) Certificate in Counselling Theory** (CSCT/AEB)

Duration	1 year, part-time, 1 evening/week
Entry	None although completion of 3) above is helpful

**   **5) Advanced Certificate in Counselling Skills & Theory** (CSCT/AEB)

Duration	1 year, part-time, 1 evening/week
Entry	Completion of 3) and 4) above

**   **6) Diploma in Therapeutic Counselling** (CSCT/AEB)

Duration	Proposed course details to be confirmed

**   **7) Diploma in Counselling** (NCFE/C&G) (3704)

Duration	Proposed course, details to be confirmed
Apply To:	Jackie Stratford, Programme Manager

THANET CENTRE FOR THERAPEUTIC STUDIES,   0121 354 4042

63 Victoria Road, SUTTON COLDFIELD, West Midlands, B72 1SN,
No response received to our enquiries for 2000, entry details as of Nov 1998

*   **1) Certificate in Humanistic Counselling** (Transactional Analysis Core approach)

*Star System: * Introductory course only • ** 2-3 yr pt-time course to Cert/Dip level •*
*** Professional development for trained counsellors*
For added help, see section 'Essential Information for Students', page 1

284

**   2) Diploma in Humanistic Counselling (Transactional Analysis Core Approach)

UNIVERSITY OF WOLVERHAMPTON,   01902 321 101

Psychology Division, School of Health Sciences, Lichfield Street, WOLVERHAMPTON, WV1 1DJ,

No response received to our enquiries for 2000. Entry details as of Nov 1998

***   MSc Counselling Psychology/Diploma in Counselling

WULFRUN COLLEGE OF FE,   01902 317700
FAX: 01902 423070

Division Of Humanities And Social Scienc, Paget Road, WOLVERHAMPTON, WV6 0DU,

A range of counselling courses and workshops run on a regular basis. Tailor-made training for organisations

♿ Access for disabled people, experience with training deaf people in counselling skills, blind people should discuss needs with the college.

*   1) Introduction to Counselling (OCN)

Duration	10 weeks, 2.5 hrs/week daytime and evenings
Entry	For those interested in discovering some basics about counselling

*   2) Certificate in Counselling Skills (RSA)

Duration	32 weeks, 3hr/week, daytime, evenings, start Sept, Jan and April
Entry	For those in caring, professional and voluntary organisations, selection by interview

**   3) Professional Development Certificate in Counselling (EDEXEL/BTEC)

Duration	Either 1 year (34 sessions 7hr/week) OR 2 years (34 sessions 3.5 hrs/week) Sept start
Entry	For those in caring, professional and voluntary organisations who wish to deepen their knowledge and practice of counselling and counselling skills. Must have completed either 2) or equivalent and have access to using couns skills, selection by interview

continued...

*Star System: * Introductory course only • ** 2-3 yr pt-time course to Cert/Dip level •*
*** Professional development for trained counsellors
For added help, see section 'Essential Information for Students', page 1

285

*** 4) Advanced Diploma in Counselling

Duration	2 year part-time, afternoon, evenings + Sat Morning (Yr 1) Sept start
Entry	For those who wish to pursue a career in counselling. Have completed eith 2) with additional core module in counselling theories (50hrs min) or 3). Need to arrange placement, supervision and personal therapy
Apply To:	Peter Creagh, Co-ordinator, Counselling Training

Star System: *Introductory course only • ** 2-3 yr pt-time course to Cert/Dip level •*
**** Professional development for trained counsellors*
For added help, see section 'Essential Information for Students', page 1

286

CHIPPENHAM COLLEGE,   01249 464 644
Cocklebury Road, CHIPPENHAM, Wiltshire, SN15 3QD,
No response received to our enquiries for 2000, entry details as of Nov 1998

* 1) **Counselling Skills** (CSCT/AEB)

* 2) **Counselling Theory** (CSCT/AEB)

** 3) **Advanced certificate in Counselling** (CSCT/AEB)

** 4) **Diploma in Counselling** (CSCT/AEB)

COUNSELLING TRAINING INITIATIVES LTD,(CTI) 0115 944 7849
Galtee House, 1 Heanor Road, ILKESTON, Derbyshire, DE7 8DY,
Please see National Section for fuller details of the courses offered

♿ No response received to our enquiries for 2000, entry details as of Nov 1998

SWINDON COLLEGE,   01793 498401
Regent Circus, SWINDON, SN1 1PT,
Workshops in counselling/counselling skills

♿ The main college sites are wheelchair accessible. The college has a support
service for students with hearing or sight impairment

* 1) **Introduction to Counselling**
Duration   6 weeks, 2hrs/week — evenings
Entry   Open

* 2) **Certificate in Basic Counselling Skills** (C+G/NCFE 3702)
Duration   36 hours, 2 day workshops + 8x3hr evening/afternoon sessions
Entry   Subject to interview by course tutors

* 3) **Certificate in Counselling** (C+G/NCFE 3703)
Duration   76 hrs, 4 full days + 16x3hrs sessions each week
Entry   Selection interview, completion of 3702 or equivalent
Core Model   Person Centred
Apply To: Marianne Northam

*Star System: * Introductory course only • ** 2-3 yr pt-time course to Cert/Dip level •*
*** Professional development for trained counsellors*
For added help, see section 'Essential Information for Students', page 1
287

SWINDON COUNSELLING SERVICE, 01793 514550
23 Bath Road, SWINDON, SN1 4AS,
No response received to our enquiries for 2000, entry details as of November 1998

* **1) WPF Certificate in Counselling Skills**

* **2) WPF Certificate in Psychodynamic Counselling Practice)**

TROWBRIDGE COLLEGE, 01225 766241 X303
College Road, TROWBRIDGE, BA14 0ES,
In-house and tailor-made training, workshops in counselling and counselling skills
♿ We offer to make is possible to attend any course on offer.

* **1) Introduction to Counselling Skills — Module One** (Open College)
Duration   18 weeks, 1 evening/week (2 groups), 2 daytime groups
Entry   By interview, suited to people wishing to incorporate the use of
              counselling skills in their professional lives or those with a personal
              interest.

* **2) Introduction to Counselling Skills — Module 2** (Open College)
Duration   18 weeks, 2hrs/evening (1 group), 2 daytime groups
Entry   Completion of 1)

* **3) Developing a Counselling Approach to Working with Learning
Difficulties**
Duration   24 weeks, 3hrs sessions
Entry   By interview, for those working in the field of learning difficluties

* **4) Certificate in Therapeutic Counselling** (CPCAB)
Duration   1 group, Monday per month
Entry   Introduction to counselling skills course, Parts 1 & 2 or equivalent eg:
              obtained as part of another professional training, such as social work,
              nursing etc.

** **5) Advanced Certificate in Theraputic Counselling** (CPCAB)
Duration   36 weeks, 210 guided learning hours
Entry   Succesful completion of CPCAB Certificate course or APL
              equivalence, Sept start

---

*Star System: * Introductory course only • ** 2-3 yr pt-time course to Cert/Dip level •
*** Professional development for trained counsellors*
For added help, see section 'Essential Information for Students', page 1
288

** **6) Diploma in Therapeutic Counselling** (CPCAB)

Duration   Fridays mornings, 4 hrs

Entry   Completion of earlier Certificate and Advanced Certificate levels or APL of equivalent training and experience.

Apply To: Garry Hutchinson, School of Community Studes tel ex: 303

Star System: ** Introductory course only* • *** 2-3 yr pt-time course to Cert/Dip level* • **** Professional development for trained counsellors*

For added help, see section 'Essential Information for Students', page 1

289

BARNSLEY COLLEGE,   01226 730 191
Old Mill Lane Site, Church Street, BARNSLEY, South Yorkshire, S70 2YW,
No response received to our enquiries for 2000, entry details as of Nov 1998

*   **1) Introduction to Counselling Skills** (AEB/CSCT)

*   **2) Certificate in Counselling Skills** (AEB/CSCT)

*   **3) Certificate in Counselling Theory** (AEB/CSCT)

**   **4) Diploma in Counselling** (AEB/CSCT)

PERSON-CENTRED APPROACH INSTITUTE (GB),   01924 468 998
32 Commonside Batrey, BATLEY, West Yorkshire, WF17 6JZ,
No response to our enquiries for 2000, entry details as of Nov 1998

**   **Diploma in Person-Centred Therapy & Application of the Person
        Centred Approach**

BEVERLEY COLLEGE OF FURTHER EDUCATION,   01482 868362
Longcroft Hall, Gallows Lane, BEVERLEY, North Humberside, HU17 7DT,
No response to our enquiries for 2000, copy current as of 1998

**   **1) Certificate in Basic Counselling Skills** (NCFE)

*   **2) Certificate in Counselling** (NCFE)

STOCKTON & BILLINGHAM COLLEGE OF FURTHER
EDUCATION   01642 865566
The Causeway, BILLINGHAM, TS23 2DB,
In-house, tailor-made training available

♿ Facilities available, please enquire

*   **1) Certificate in Basic Counselling Skills** (NCFE)
Duration   13 weeks, 3 hrs/week
Entry   18 yrs or over with a willingness to participate in practical exercises

*   **2) Certificate in Counselling** (NCFE)
Duration   30 weeks, 3 hrs/week
Entry   Minimum age 18 yrs, basic counselling skills training
Apply To: Information & Guidance Department

Star System: ** Introductory course only • ** 2-3 yr pt-time course to Cert/Dip level •*
              *** Professional development for trained counsellors
290   **For added help, see section 'Essential Information for Students', page 1**

BRADFORD & ILKLEY COMMUNITY COLLEGE,   01274 753118/ 753204
FAX: 01274 753198

School of Teaching & Community, Studies, Great Horton Road, BRADFORD, West Yorkshire, BD7 1AY,

Venue: Counselling and Group Work Unit, Bradford. General enquiries to John Aldcroft

♿ Most college buildings have disabled access, though the current building does not, provision can be made

*   1) RSA Counselling Skills in the Development of Learning

Duration	30 weeks, part-time, day or evening + 2 non-residential weekends (114 hrs)
Entry	Those in an appropriate work context eg: caring or voluntary work
Apply To:	Malcolm Coward tel: 01274 753118/John Aldcroft tel: 01274 753204

**   2) Diploma in Counselling & Human Relations

Duration	2 years, part-time, day or evening (478 hrs including 2 residential weekends)
Entry	Prior counselling skills; over 24 years of age; access to counselling clients
Apply To:	Malcolm Coward tel: 01274 753118/John Aldcroft tel: 01274 753204

***   3) MA Counselling in the Community

Duration	2 years, part-time, 1 day/week
Entry	Relevant first degree or Diploma in Counselling/formal equivalent; minimum 2 years supervised counselling practice
Apply To:	Jean Davidson tel: 01943 602347

DEWSBURY COLLEGE,   01924 465916

Halifax Road, DEWSBURY, West Yorkshire, WF13 2AS,

♿ Learning support to suit needs to individuals

*   1) Introduction to Counselling

Duration	10 weeks (3 courses per year)
Entry	None

*   2) Certificate, Foundation Course

Duration	34 weeks, part-time, evening and day (Sept start)
Entry	Completion of !) or equivalent and intends to have or has a counselling role in their lives, Selection by interview
Core Model	Person Centred

continued...

Star System: * Introductory course only • ** 2-3 yr pt-time course to Cert/Dip level •
*** Professional development for trained counsellors
For added help, see section 'Essential Information for Students', page 1

291

**   3) Diploma in Counselling

Duration	2 years, part-time, half day/early evening + weekend (Sept start)
Core Model	Person Centred
Entry	Completion of at least 120 hrs or recognised counselling training (including skills and theory) For those who are over 25 years and working in the caring professions or voluntary sector. Selection by interview
Apply To:	Jenny Humphreys

DONCASTER COLLEGE,   01302 553 741

Faculty of Client Services, Waterdale, DONCASTER, South Yorkshire, DN1 3EX,
No response received to our enquiries for 2000, entry details as of Nov 1998

*   1) Foundation Course: Counselling Skills (OCN)

*   2) Certificate in Counselling Skills (CSCT/AEB)

*   3) Certificate in Counselling Theory (CSCT/AEB)

*   4) Introduction to Counselling in the Workplace (AEB)

*   5) Introduction to Counselling Children & Adolescents (CSCT/AEB)

**   6) Advanced Certificate in Counselling Skills & Theory (CSCT/AEB)

MIMIROSA: COUNSELLING, PSYCHOTHERAPY & SUPERVISION   1302 761 915

24 Sandringham Road, DONCASTER, South Yorkshire, DN2 5HU,
No response received to our enquiries for 2000, entry details as of Nov 1998

*   1) '101' Transactional Analysis Training

**   2) Ongoing Training in TA in Preparation for Clinical TA Examination

YORKSHIRE TRAINING CENTRE,   01422 366 356

27 Clare Road, HALIFAX, West Yorkshire, HX1 2JP,
No response received to our enquiries for 2000, entry details as of Nov 1998

*   1) '101' Introductory TA course (ITA/EATA)

**   2) Ongoing TA training (ITA/UKCP)

Star System: *Introductory course only • ** 2-3 yr pt-time course to Cert/Dip level •*
*** *Professional development for trained counsellors*

For added help, see section 'Essential Information for Students', page 1

292

HARROGATE COLLEGE,   01423 879 466

Hornbeam Park, Hookstone Road, HARROGATE, North Yorkshire, HG2 8QT,
In-house/tailor-made training & short courses, e.g. Stress Management through
Relaxation/Psychodrama; AEB/Relate couns

♿ Access for wheelchairs and specialised toilet facilities

*   **1) Counselling Skills** (NCFE)

Duration	6 weeks, 1 evening/week (core); 6 weeks, 1 eve/week, 3 hrs (Development)
Entry	None Stated

*   **2) RSA Certificate in Counselling & the Development of Learning**

Duration	35 weeks, 3 hrs/week + 2 days (Sats)
Entry	Some knowledge of counselling; access to counselling to be able to maintain a learning diary; commitment to working as part of a group
Apply To:	Angela Sansam

HARTLEPOOL COLLEGE OF FE,   01429 295000
ENQUIRIES@HARTLEPOOLFE.AC.UK
WWW.HARTLEPOOLFE.AC.UK

Stockton Street, HARTLEPOOL, Cleveland, TS24 7NT,

College has a non-smoking policy; Short courses, in-house & tailor-made courses
contact Business Services: 01429 292888

♿ Access for wheelchairs, students with learning difficulties & disabilities should
discuss needs with the Co-ordinator

*   **1) Certificate Basic Counselling Skills** (NCFE 3702)

Duration	2 modules of 18 hours each — evening or daytime
Entry	By interview, minimum age of entry: 18 yrs

*   **2) Certificate in Counselling** (NCFE 3703)

Duration	2 terms, part-time, evening or daytime
Entry	Completion of 1)/equivalent and/or adults working in related professional or voluntary work. Applicants invited to interview; reference requested; minimum age 18 yrs
Apply To:	Student Services

---

*Star System: * Introductory course only ● ** 2-3 yr pt-time course to Cert/Dip level ●*
*** Professional development for trained counsellors*
For added help, see section 'Essential Information for Students', page 1

293

KAIROS COUNSELLING STUDIES LTD,　　01482 649 839 FAX
01482 647 377

22 The Weir, HESSLE, North Humberside, HU13 0RU,
No response received to our enquiries for 2000, entry details as of Nov 1998

**　1) Diploma in Counselling

***　2) Advanced Diploma in Counselling

HUDDERSFIELD TECHNICAL COLLEGE,　　01484 536521

School of Caring, New North Road, HUDDERSFIELD, HD1 5NN,
No response received to our enquiries for 2000, entry details as of November 1998

*　1) Introduction to Counselling

*　2) RSA Certificate, Counselling Skills in the Deve

**　3) RSA Advanced Diploma in Counselling & Groupwork

NORTHERN TRUST FOR DRAMATHERAPY,　　01484 428427

41 Netheroyd Hill Road, Fixby, HUDDERSFIELD, HD2 2LS,
Dramatherapy certificates and 1-2 day introductions

♿ Usually accessible venues, please write for details. Diploma is at a disabled living centre

**　**Diploma in Dramatherapy** (validated Manchester Univ, approved by Brit Assoc Dramatherapists

Duration	3 years, part-time, weekends + 1 residential weekend
Entry	Over 23; Post basic, some experience in theatre or drama, working with client groups
Apply To:	The Registrar

HULL UNIVERSITY,　　01482 465406

Department of Psychology, HULL, HU6 7RX,
No response received to our enquiries for 2000, entry details as of November 1998

**　1) Postgraduate Diploma in Counselling

***　2) MSc in Counselling

***　3) MSc in Counselling Studies

Star System:　* Introductory course only • ** 2-3 yr pt-time course to Cert/Dip level •
*** Professional development for trained counsellors
For added help, see section 'Essential Information for Students', page 1

294

COUNSELLING TRAINING INITIATIVES LTD,(CTI)   0115 944 7849

Galtee House, 1 Heanor Road, ILKESTON, Derbyshire, DE7 8DY,

Please see National Section for fuller details of courses offered

♿ No response received to our enquiries for 2000, entry details as of Nov 1998

KEIGHLEY COLLEGE,   01535 618555

Cavendish Street, KEIGHLEY, West Yorkshire, BD21 3DF,

Applications welcome regardless of age, sex, race or disability. Workshops available on working with children & young people, TA, also introductory workshops and In house/ tailor-made trainings

♿ Individual support for people with various disabiliies. Some rooms wheelchair accessible and specialised equipment is available for visually impaired.

*   1) Introduction to Counselling/Cert. in Basic Counselling (NCFE)

Duration	20 weeks, part-time, 2 hrs/week, eve/daytime
Entry	No entry requirements. Particularly useful for those in the caring professions or working with people

*   2) RSA Certificate in Counselling Skills

Duration	110 hrs, over 3 terms, part-time, eves including 2 non-residential weekends & 1 Saturday School
Entry	Evidence of previous counselling courses or relevant experience preferred

3) Higher National Diploma in Counselling (BTEC)

Duration	2 yrs part-time, 1 afternoon/eve/week, 1 non-residential and 1 residential weekend/year
Entry	Over 25 with a counselling skills certificate of at least 90 hrs. Good level of education/literacy skills, mature attitude. Selection by interview
Core Model	Humanistic
Apply To:	Jayne Godward

---

*Star System: * Introductory course only • ** 2-3 yr pt-time course to Cert/Dip level •
*** Professional development for trained counsellors*
For added help, see section 'Essential Information for Students', page 1

295

LEEDS METROPOLITAN UNIVERSITY,   0113 283 2600
                                                 FAX 0113 283 3124

Fac. Health & Social Care, Calverley Street, LEEDS, LS1 3HE,

Application forms & full details for all courses from Counselling Courses Administrator tel ext 6755. In-house & tailor-made training, workshops in counselling/counselling skills

♿ University facilities quite extemsive

*   **1) Introduction to Counselling Skills**

Duration   30 hrs, various days/times
Entry   None

*   **2) Certificate** (HE) in Counselling Skills — in consortium with Park Lane College

Duration   1-2 yrs, part-time, morning/afternoon or eves — in various locations in West Yorkshire
Entry   Age 22/23+, minimum 30 hrs training in counselling skills, Yr 2 — qualifications appropriate for the point of entry, using counselling skills in paid/voluntary settings

**   **3) Diploma in** (HE) Therapeutic Counselling in consortium with Park Lane College

Duration   2 yrs, part-time, 6 hrs, afternoon & early eve/week
Entry   Successful completion of 2) above or equivalent, over 24, offering regular counselling for a minimum 2 hrs/week, evidence of appropriate academic ability
Apply To: Informal enquiries to Nina Wright, tel 0113 242 2648

**   **4) BSc Therapeutic Counselling**

Duration   1 yr, Wednesdays, 1.00-5.00 p.m.
Entry   3) or equivalent or evidence of 200 hrs skills training/240 hrs supervised client work, over 26
Apply To: Informal enquiries to Kate Kent, tel 0113 283 2600

**   **5) BSc Counselling and Therapeutic Studies**

Duration   3 yrs, full time (a pre-professional training course)
Entry   Apply through UCAS

Star System: *Introductory course only • ** 2-3 yr pt-time course to Cert/Dip level •
*** Professional development for trained counsellors*
For added help, see section 'Essential Information for Students', page 1

296

***   **6) Postgraduate Diploma/MA Scheme in a) Counselling** (Relational) b) Psychotherapy

Duration	1 or 2 yrs, part-time
Entry	3) above or equivalent or evidence of 200 hrs skills training/240 hrs supervised client work, over 26 (proposed course, contact university for confirmation of availability)
Apply To:	Informal enquiries to Geoff Pelham, tel 0113 283 2600

PARK LANE COLLEGE OF FURTHER EDUCATION,
0113 216 2320 FAX 0113 216 2321

Park Lane, LEEDS, LS3 1AA,

Informal enquiries to Nina Wright on the above number

♿ Access for wheelchair users. Other needs should be discussed with the colege

*   **1) Introduction to Counselling Skills** (OCN)

Duration	10 weeks, 3 hrs/week, morning or evening (offered 3 times per year
Entry	Aged 22+

*   **2) Counselling Skills in Transcultural Setting** (OCN)

Duration	12 weeks, 3 hrs/week, Wednesday evening (offered twice each year)
Entry	Aged 22+

3) Certificate (FE) in Counselling Skills (CENTRA)

Duration	1 year part-time 3 hrs/week + 2 weekends
Entry	Aged 23+; minimum 25 hrs counselling skills training; opportunity to practice counselling skills in a paid or voluntary setting
Apply To:	Course Administrator tel: 0113 283 6755

**   **4) Certificate** (HE) in Counselling Skills, (Iin collaboration with Leeds Met Univ)

Duration	1 year part-time, 4 hrs/week, morning + 2 weekends
Entry	Aged 23+; minimum 30 hrs training in counselling skills and qualification/experience appropriate for this point of entry into H/E; using counselling skills in paid or voluntary setting

**   **5) Diploma** (HE) in Counselling, (BAC Acc) (In collaboration with Leeds Met Univ)

Duration	2 years part-time, 6 hrs/week, afternoon — early evening (474hrs)
Entry	24+; completion of 4) above/ equivalent and experience of using conselling skills; able to offer regular counselling for a minimum of 2 hrs/week; evidence of appropriate academic ability

---

Star System: ** Introductory course only • ** 2-3 yr pt-time course to Cert/Dip level •*
*** Professional development for trained counsellors
For added help, see section 'Essential Information for Students', page 1

297

SWARTHMORE ADULT EDUCATION CENTRE,   0113 243 2210

3/7 Woodhouse Square, LEEDS, LS3 1AD,

No response received to our enquiries for 2000. Entry details as of Nov 1998

*   **1) Introduction to Counselling Skills & Brief Introduction to Counselling Skills** (Open College Network)

*   **2) RSA Certificate in Counselling Skills in the Development of Learning**

WPF COUNSELLING NORTH,(WESTMINSTER PASTORAL FOUNDATION)   0113 2450303

Leeds Bridge House, Hunslet Road, LEEDS, LS10 1JN,

No response received to our enquiries for 2000. Entry details as of Nov 1998

*   **1) Foundation Certificate in Counselling Skills**

**   **2) Diploma in Psychodynamic Counselling (BAC Acc)**

**   **3) Advanced Diploma in Psychodynamic Counselling**

PSYCHOSYNTHESIS UK,

LEWES, East Sussex, BN7 2QP,

Venues in London & West Yorkshire. Please see Sussex

MIDDLESBROUGH COLLEGE,   01642 333333

Middlesbrough Campus, Roman Road, MIDDLESBROUGH, Cleveland, TS5 5PJ,

No response received to our enquiries for 2000, entry details as of November 1998

*   **1) Certificate in Counselling Skills** (NCFE)

*   **2) Certificate in Counselling**

*   **3) Further Counselling Skills Certificate** (NCFE)

CLEVELAND TERTIARY COLLEGE,   01642 473132

Corporation Road, REDCAR, Cleveland, TS10 1EZ,

No response received to our enquiries for 2000, entry details as of November 1998

*   **1) Basic Counselling Course**

*   **2) RSA Certificate in Counselling Skills in the Development of Learning**

Star System: ** Introductory course only • ** 2-3 yr pt-time course to Cert/Dip level •*
*** Professional development for trained counsellors

For added help, see section 'Essential Information for Students', page 1

**   **3) Certificate in Counselling** (Teeside Univ)

**   **4) Advanced Diploma in Counselling & Groupwork Skills**

PROUDFOOT SCHOOL OF HYPNOSIS,& PSYCHOTHERAPY
01753 585960

Blinking Sike, Eastfield, SCARBOROUGH, North Yorkshire, YO11 3YT,
No response received to our enquiries for 2000, entry details as of November 1998

*   **1) Hypnotist Course** (Diploma Master Hypnotist awarded)

**   **2) Hypnotherapy Course** (Diploma, Hypnotherapist awarded)

**   **3) NLP Practitioner Course** (Diploma, NLP Practitioner)

**   **4) Master Practitioner NLP** (Diploma, NLP Master Practitioner)

CENTRE FOR PSYCHOTHERAPEUTIC STUDIES,   0114 222 2961/
2/3/4

University of Sheffield, 16 Claremont Crescent, SHEFFIELD, S10 2TA,
Workshops offered, e.g. Starting a private practice

♿ Ramp, disabled WC, special parking space

**   **1) Postgraduate Diploma in Art Psychotherapy** (giving eligibility for State Registered Status)

Core Model	Art Psychotherapy
Duration	2 years, full time, OR 3 years part time. This includes attendance at university & clinical placements
Entry	A relevant degree; pre-course experience of at least one year; commitment to personal art work & knowledge of psychotherapeutic work
Apply To:	Indira Samaraweera, Course Secretary

**   **2) MA/Diploma in Psychoanalytic Psychotherapy** (accredited by UKCP & UPA)

Core Model	Psychoanalytic Psychotherapy
Duration	4 years, 0.5 day/week in the university, additional time is required for clinical work, supervision and personal therapy
Entry	Good degree; some prior training; some clinical experience; 1 yr personal (analytic) therapy prior to starting the course
Apply To:	Trudy Coldwell (Course Secretary)

Star System: * Introductory course only • ** 2-3 yr pt-time course to Cert/Dip level •
*** Professional development for trained counsellors
For added help, see section 'Essential Information for Students', page 1

ROTHER VALLEY COLLEGE,   01909 550550
Doe Quarry Lane, Dinnington, SHEFFIELD, S25 2NF,
No response received to our equiries for 2000. Entry details as of Nov 1998

*   **1) Counselling Skills** (SYOCF) Level 2/3: 4 credits

*   **2) Counselling Theory** (SY0CF) Level 3: 6 credits

SHEFFIELD COLLEGE,   0114 260 2276
Sheffield College, The Loxley Centre, Myers Grove Lane, SHEFFIELD, S6 5JL,
No response received to our enquiries for 2000, entry details as of November 1998

*   **1) Basic Counselling Awareness + Skills**

*   **2) Introduction to Counselling Skills**

*   **3) Certificate in Counselling Skills** (City & Guilds)

**   **4) Bretton Hall Certificate in Counselling** (Leeds Univ)

SHEFFIELD HALLAM UNIVERSITY,   0114 272 0911 X 4401
Counselling Development Unit, School of Education, Collegiate Crescent, SHEFFIELD,
S10 2BP,
No response received to our enquiries for 2000, entry details as of Nov 1998

*   **1) Certificate in Counselling Skills**

**   **2) Diploma in Counselling**

***   **3) MA Counselling & Psychotherapy**

***   **4) Postgraduate Certificate in Counselling Supervision**

TEMENOS,   0114 266 3931
13A Penrhyn Road, Hunter's Bar, SHEFFIELD, S11 8UL,
No response received to our enquiries for 2000, entry details as of November 1998

*   **1) Counselling Skills Short Courses**

*   **2) Counselling Skills** (in conjunction with Sheffield Health Authority)

*   **3) Advanced Counselling Skills** (joint with Sheffield Health Authority)

Star System: * Introductory course only • ** 2-3 yr pt-time course to Cert/Dip level •
*** Professional development for trained counsellors
For added help, see section 'Essential Information for Students', page 1

**   **4) Diploma in Person-Centred Counselling**

SHIPLEY COLLEGE,   01274 757222
Exhibition Road, Saltaire, SHIPLEY, West Yorkshire, BD18 3JW,
No response to our enquiries for 2000. Entry details as of Nov 1998

*   **1) Introduction to Counselling Skills**

*   **2) Counselling Skills Certificate** (AEB)

**   **3) Counselling Theory Certificate** (AEB)

BRETTON HALL COLLEGE -COLLEGE OF UNIVERS,
01924 830261

West Bretton, WAKEFIELD, West Yorkshire, WF4 4LG,
No response received to our enquiries for 2000, entry details as of November 1998

*   **1) Certificate in Counselling** (Leeds Univ)

**   **2) Graduate Diploma in Counselling** (Leeds Univ)

***   **3) Postgraduate Diploma/MA in Counselling** (Leeds Univ)

***   **4) (Post Qualifying) Certificate in Counselling Supervision** (Leeds Univ)

MANYGATES EDUCATION CENTRE,   01924 303303/303302
Manygates Lane, Sandal, WAKEFIELD, West Yorkshire, WF2 7DQ,
Level I/II available at a range of venues in the Wakefield district, Level III runs in
Wakefield only at present.

♿ Most centres have access for those with mobility problems; extra support can be
negotiated where needs are identified.

*   **1) Basic Counselling Skills Level 1/11** (OCN)
Duration   2.05 hrs/weeks, day (24 hrs)
Entry   Open access

*   **2) Further Counselling Skills Level 111** (OCN)
Duration   2 compulsory units + 1 optional unit over 1 year
Entry   Completion of 1) above, or the equivalent
Apply To: Sandra Skuse, Adult & Community Education Officer

*Star System: * Introductory course only • ** 2-3 yr pt-time course to Cert/Dip level •*
*** Professional development for trained counsellors*
For added help, see section 'Essential Information for Students', page 1
301

COLLEGE OF RIPON & YORK ST JOHN 01904 716675
FAX 01904 716749

Individual & Organisation Development, Studies, Lord Mayors Walk, YORK, YO31 7EX, Extensive short course programme.

♿ People with special needs should discuss these with the college

*   1) Introduction to Counselling Skills (Cert Attendance)

Duration	5 weeks, part-time, evenings (term time). Weekend course, Saturday & Sunday (term time). 3-day summer course (July)
Entry	Anyone interested in developing counselling skills or enhancing communication skills

*   2) Certificate in Counselling

Duration	2 terms, part-time, 1 day/week or 1 evening/week + 4 Saturdays or 1 day/week (part afternoon/part evening)
Entry	Preferably completion of 1) and ability to obtain counselling practice outside the course; selection by interview

**   3) Graduate Diploma in Counselling (Leeds Univ, BAC Acc)

Duration	2 years, part-time, 1 day/week + 2 residential weekends/equivalent
Entry	First degree or equivalent; Cert Counselling or equivalent; selection by interview

***   4) Diploma in Counsellor Supervision (Leeds Univ)

Duration	1 year, part-time, 1 Thursday & Friday/month
Entry	Completion of recognised counselling training course normally to diploma level or equivalent of at least 40 credits at Level 2; ability to obtain supervision practice outside the course; selection by interview

***   5) Postgraduate Diploma/MA — Counselling (Leeds Univ)

Duration	2 years, part-time, or 1 year, full-time
Entry	Please contact the college for further details
Apply To:	Alison Perry, Course Administrator

YORK COLLEGE OF FURTHER & HIGHER ED, 01904 770251

Learning Resources Centre, Tadcaster Road, Dringhouses, YORK, YO2 1UA,
No response received to our enquiries for 2000. Entry details as of Nov 1998

*   RSA Certificate in Counselling in the Development of Learning

Star System: * Introductory course only • ** 2-3 yr pt-time course to Cert/Dip level •
*** Professional development for trained counsellors
For added help, see section 'Essential Information for Students', page 1

302

YORK PSYCHOTHERAPY TRAINING INSTITUTE,   01904 638 623

38 Millfield Road, YORK, YO2 1NQ,

No response received to our enquiries for 2000, entry details as of Nov 1998

*   1) Foundation Training in Gestalt Therapy (GPTI)

**   2) Diploma in Gestalt Psychotherapy (GPTI/UKCP)

Star System: * Introductory course only • ** 2-3 yr pt-time course to Cert/Dip level •
*** Professional development for trained counsellors
For added help, see section 'Essential Information for Students', page 1

303

ARMAGH COLLEGE OF FURTHER EDUCATION,   01861 522205
Lonsdale Street, ARMAGH, BT61 7HN,

♿ We have a Special Needs Unit (attended by clients from local Day Centres etc).
Ramps/lifts etc facilitate access to building.

*   **Introduction to Counselling**
Duration   12 weeks, 2hrs/week (1 evening/week)
Entry   No prior experience/qualifications
Apply To: Des McCready (Head of Adult Education)

BELFAST INSTITUTE OF FURTHER & HIGHER ED,
01232 265 050
College Square East Building, College Square, BELFAST, BT1 6DJ,
No response received to our enquiries for 2000, entry details as of November 1998

*   **1) Introduction to Counselling Skills**

*   **2) Certificate in Counselling Skills** (CSCT/AEB)

*   **3) Certificate in Counselling Theory** (CSCT/AEB)

*   **4) RSA Certificate in Counselling Skills & the Development of Learning**

*   **5) Certificate in Counselling** (Ulster Univ)

**   **6) Diploma in Counselling in Organisations** (Surrey Univ)

QUEEN'S UNIVERSITY,INST OF CONTINUING ED,   01232 245133
X 3801
School of Adult Education, BELFAST, BT7 1NN,
No response received to our enquiries for 2000. Entry details as of Nov 1998

*   **1) Introduction to Counselling**

*   **2) Abuse, Trauma & Counselling**

*   **3) Certificate in Counselling**

**   **4) Diploma in Counselling**

---

*Star System: * Introductory course only • ** 2-3 yr pt-time course to Cert/Dip level •*
*** Professional development for trained counsellors
For added help, see section 'Essential Information for Students', page 1

UPPER BANN INSTITUTE OF FURTHER & HIGHER,
01762 326135

Lurgan Campus, Kitchen Hill, Lurgan, CRAIGAVON, Co Armagh, BT66 6AZ,
No response received to our enquiries for 2000, entry details as of November 1998

*   **1) RSA Certificate in Counselling**

*   **2) Certificate in Counselling Skills** (CSCT/AEB)

*   **3) Certificate in Counselling Theory** (CSCT/AEB)

**   **4) Diploma in Counselling** (CSCT/AEB)

EAST TYRONE FURTHER EDUCATION COLLEGE,   028 8772 2323

Circular Road, DUNGANNON, Co Tyrone, BT71 6BQ,
No response received to our enquiries for 2000, entry details as of Nov 1998

*   **1) Introductory course in Counselling**

*   **2) Beyond Basic Counselling**

*   **3) Certificate in Counselling** (Queens Univ Belfast)

FERMANAGH COLLEGE,   01365 322431

Fairview, 1 Dublin Road, ENNISKILLEN, Co Fermanagh, BT74 6AE,
In-house & tailor-made training, workshops in listening skills & empathetic response

♿ Access for disabled people

*   **1) Bereavement & Loss Counselling** (OCN)
Duration   15 weeks, 2 hrs/week, evening
Entry   Open

*   **2) Introduction to Basic Counselling Skills** (OCN)
Duration   15 weeks, 2 hrs/week, evening
Entry   Open

*   **3) RSA Certificate in Counselling Skills & Learning Support**
Duration   32 weeks, 1 eve/week (Sept-June)
Entry   Open, by interview

*   **4) Stress Management**
Duration   10 weeks, 2 hrs/week, eves +10 hrs private study

continued...

Star System: ** Introductory course only* • *** 2-3 yr pt-time course to Cert/Dip level* •
*** Professional development for trained counsellors
For added help, see section 'Essential Information for Students', page 1
305

** **5) Certificate in Counselling** (Ulster Univ)

Duration   32 weeks, 5 hrs/week, afternoon to evening
Entry   5 GCSEs or equivalent, selection by interview

* **6) Introduction to Art as Therapy** (OCN)

Duration   10 weeks, 2 hrs/week, eves + 10 hrs private study
Entry   Open

** **7) Diploma in Counselling** (Ulster Univ)

Duration   2 yrs, 5 hrs/week, afternoon to evening
Entry   Certificate in counselling/equivalent & 5 GCSEs/equivalent, selection
             by interview
Apply To: Dr Jennifer Cornyn tel: 01365 342251

NORTH WEST INSTITUTE OF FURTHER & HIGHER EDUCATION   01504 374722

Strand Road, LONDONDERRY, BT48,

A variety of workshops offered, these include Contracts, Theoretical Perspectives, Boundary Issues, Support Systems in Counselling Practice. Also in-house and tailor-made training

♿ Wheelchair access, computer aids, interpreters, audio support for the partially sighted and blind

* **1) Counselling Skills — NVQ Level 3 , Underpinning knowledge** (City & Guilds)

Duration   10 weeks x 2 hrs x 3 terms (academic)
Entry   For those wishing to undertake NVQ in Counselling. Candidates must
             be recommended by their manager, and working in a counselling
             setting plus 2 references, relevant to counselling, to be provided

* **2) Introductory Counselling Course** (In-house Certificate of Attendance)

Duration   10 weeks/2 hrs evening
Entry   For those in caring professions/voluntary organisations or those
             working to acquire basic counselling knowledge & skills

* **3) Certificate in Counselling** (Validated by Univ Ulster)

Duration   10 weeks/3 hrs day/evening x 3 terms
Entry   Please enquire
Apply To: Helena McVeigh

*Star System: * Introductory course only • ** 2-3 yr pt-time course to Cert/Dip level •*
*** Professional development for trained counsellors*
For added help, see section 'Essential Information for Students', page 1

306

NEWRY COLLEGE OF FURTHER & HIGHER EDUCATION
01693 69359

Model School Campus, NEWRY, Co Down, BT35 6JG,

In-house/tailor-made training can be offered and short courses also offered

♿ Easy access ramps & special toilet

* **1) Introduction to Counselling** (CSCT/AEB)

Duration	90-140 hrs
Entry	None

* **2) Certificate in Counselling Skills** (CSCT/AEB)

Duration	30 weeks, 90-140 hrs
Entry	Good standard of education

* **3) Advanced Certificate in Counselling Skills & Theory**

Duration	30 weeks, 90-100 hrs
Entry	Skills & Theory Certificates

** **4) Diploma in Therapeutic Counselling**

Duration	250 hrs
Entry	Advanced Certificate in Counselling
Apply To:	Tom Torley, Head of School (Adult + Continuing Ed)

UNIVERSITY OF ULSTER AT JORDANSTOWN,   01232 365131

School of Behavioural &, Communication Sciences, Shore Road, NEWTOWNABBEY, Co Antrim, BT37 0QB,

No response received to our enquiries for 2000. Entry details as of Nov 1998

** **1) Diploma in Counselling**

*** **2) Postgraduate Certificate/Diploma/MSc in Counselling & Guidance**

GILEAD CENTRE & COUNSELLING COLLEGE,   01762 393909

The Elms, 72 Brownstown Road, PORTADOWN, BT62 3PY,

* **1) Certificate in Counselling Supervision Skills** (AEB)

Duration	One weekend (Friday evening, all day Saturday and all day Sunday; none residential
Entry	None stated

continued...

*Star System: * Introductory course only • ** 2-3 yr pt-time course to Cert/Dip level •
*** Professional development for trained counsellors*
For added help, see section 'Essential Information for Students', page 1

307

*   **2) Diploma in Counselling Supervision**

Duration   40 tutor hours contact plus 60 hours self-directed study = 100 hrs
Entry   None stated

**   **3) Diploma in Addictions Counselling**

Duration   100 contact hours in classroom, plus 40 hours practical placement
              with a further 60 hours approx for assessed written work, over one
              year.
Entry   Please enquire

Star System: * *Introductory course only* • ** *2-3 yr pt-time course to Cert/Dip level* •
               *** *Professional development for trained counsellors*
               For added help, see section 'Essential Information for Students', page 1
308

ABERDEEN COLLEGE,   01224 612000

Dept of Social Studies, The Gallowgate, ABERDEEN, Scotland,

No response received to our enquiries for 2000, entry details as of November 1998

*   **1) Introduction to Counselling**

UNIVERSITY OF ABERDEEN,CENTRE FOR CONTINUING
EDUCATION   01224 272447

Regent Building, Regent Walk, King'S College, ABERDEEN, AB23 8BD,

Courses may be offered throughout the Highlands and Islands if there is sufficient interest. In-house & tailor-made training and short courses also available

♿ Access, laptop computers where appropriate, individual consideration of learning needs.

*   **1) Certificate in Counselling Skills** (COSCA)

Duration	2 yrs part-time, day, eve, Saturday available, divided into 4 courses term time only (120 hrs)
Entry	For those who wish to know more about counselling skills, either for use in their work or for their own personal development; an interest in counselling

**   **2) Certificate in Counselling Skills Theory**

Duration	Several courses, term time only, day,eve, Saturday available 3-4 yrs part-time (240hrs)
Entry	Those wishing to know more about counselling skills, either for use in their work or for personal development
Apply To:	Dr. Deborah Simonton

WEST LOTHIAN COLLEGE,   01506 634 300

Marjorbanks Street, Morris Square, BATHGATE, West Lothian, EH48 1QJ,

No response received to our enquiries for 2000. Entry details as of Nov 1998

*   **1) Introduction to Counselling/Higher National Units in Counselling Approaches**

*   **2) Certificate in Counselling/COSCA endorsed**

---

*Star System: * Introductory course only • ** 2-3 yr pt-time course to Cert/Dip level •*
*** Professional development for trained counsellors
For added help, see section 'Essential Information for Students', page 1

309

COLLEAGUES IN INTEGRATIVE COUNSELLING (C,
01786 832 768

Camelon Community Project, Abercrombie Street, CAMELON,
No response received to our enquiries for 2000, entry details as of Nov 1998

** **Diploma in Integrative Counselling**

CLYDEBANK COLLEGE,
0141 527771 X 2193

Kilbowie Road, CLYDEBANK, G81 2AA,
In-house/tailor-made training and workshops in counselling/counselling skills

 ♿ Access and Loop System. Individual needs should be discussed with the College.

* **1) Introduction to Counselling** (SQA)

Duration	40 hours, Thursdays, Aug — Dec
Entry	An interest in counselling — no formal entry requirements

* **2) Counselling Skills** (SQA)

Duration	80 hours, Thursdays, Jan — June
Entry	Completion of SQA Introduction to Counselling Module
Apply To:	Stewart Moore

JEWEL & ESK VALLEY COLLEGE,
0131 669 8461

Newbattle Road, DALKEITH, Midlothian, EH22 3AE,
No response received to our enquiries for 2000, entry details as of November 1998

* **1) Introduction to Counselling** (SCOTVEC)

** **2) Certificate in Counselling**

** **3) Diploma in Counselling** (Person-Centred)

KINHARVIE, COUNSELLING, EDUCATION,,TRAINING
01387 850433 FAX 01387 850465

Kinharvie House, New Abbey, DUMFRIES, DG2 8DZ,
See National Section entry for full details

---

*Star System: * Introductory course only • ** 2-3 yr pt-time course to Cert/Dip level •*
*** Professional development for trained counsellors*
For added help, see section 'Essential Information for Students', page 1
310

DUNDEE COLLEGE,   01382 834834

Melrose Terrace Centre, Dundee College, DUNDEE, DD3 7QX,

A skills based approach to exploring he aims/methods of counselling, mixing theory & practical exercises

  ♿ Wheelchair access; people with sight/hearing impairment should discuss their needs with student advisor Ingrid Muir

*   **1) Introducing Counselling** (SCOTVEC)

Duration	12 weeks, 1 eve/week (30 hrs)
Entry	Open access, participants must be prepared to take part in group work & group exercises
Apply To:	Evening Class Bureau, Dundee College, tel. 01382 834800

*   **2) Certificate in Counselling Skills** (COSCA)

Duration	120 hrs. evening or 1 day/week for 20 weeks OR 1 eve/week for 30 weeks + 4 Saturdays
Entry	Selection will be from application form and reference
Apply To:	Corrine Reilly x 3130

UNIVERSITY OF DUNDEE,   01382 344442

Institute for Education &, Lifelong Learning, DUNDEE, DD1 4HN,

No response received to our enquiries for 2000. Entry details as of Nov 1998

*   **1) ACE Certificate in Counselling Skills**

*   **2) Transactional Analysis**

ANNE HOUSTON & COLIN WHITE,   0131 5550 0038

7 Coltbridge Terrace, EDINBURGH, EH12 6AB,

No response received to our enquiries for 2000, entry details as of Nov 1998

*   **Working with Men Who Have Been Sexually Abused**

Star System: ** Introductory course only • ** 2-3 yr pt-time course to Cert/Dip level •*
*** Professional development for trained counsellors
For added help, see section 'Essential Information for Students', page 1

311

EDINBURGH & GREATER GLASGOW NHS TRUSTS,
0131 537 6707

The Cottage, Royal Edinburgh Hospital, Morningside Terrace, EDINBURGH, EH10 5HF,

Half the teaching is held in Edinburgh (Royal Edinburgh Hospital) and half in Glasgow (Gartnavel Royal Hospital). In-house/tailor-made training offered, teaching days are specifically CBT related.

*** South of Scotland Cognitive Therapy Course

Core Model	Cognitive Behavioural
Duration	One Three-day full time module in March, followed by one full day a week from March to November
Entry	Should be a health care professional from psychiatry, psychology, occupational therapy, social work or nursing. Should be familiar with individual case work, history taking, caseload management.
Apply To:	Diane Matheson, Course Administrator

EDINBURGH'S TELFORD COLLEGE,   0131 332 2491

Department of Core Health & the Sciences, Crewe Toll, EDINBURGH, EH4 2NZ,

Short courses in Grief & Bereavement, Post Trauma, Addiction Counselling, Group Counsellor: Grants available for 5)

*   1) Introduction to Counselling (SQA)

Duration	12 weeks, part-time, day or evening (run each term)
Entry	None
Apply To:	Gus McFadzen (Course information ext 2317)

*   2) Counselling Skills (SQA)

Duration	80 hrs, part-time day or evening
Entry	Introduction to Counselling

*   3) Certificate in Counselling Skills (CSCT/AEB)

Duration	1 year, part-time, 1 evening/week — 75 hrs
Entry	Open Access

*   4) Certificate in Counselling Theory (CSCT/AEB)

Duration	1 year, part-time, 3 hrs/week, evening — 75 hrs
Entry	Open Access. (Students successfully completing Skills & Theory Certificate courses will receive the Combined Cert & may apply for Advanced Certificate Counselling Course)

*Star System: * Introductory course only • ** 2-3 yr pt-time course to Cert/Dip level •*
*** *Professional development for trained counsellors*
For added help, see section 'Essential Information for Students', page 1

312

** **5) Advanced Certificate in Counselling**

Duration	1 yr part-time evening
Entry	Skills & Theory Certificate. APL available

** **6) Transpersonal Psychology Certificate** (SQA)

Core Model	Transpersonal Psychology
Duration	12 weeks (evenings)
Entry	Basic counselling skills

** **7) Advanced Certificate in Gestalt Psychotherapy** (SQA)

Core Model	Gestalt
Duration	One year over 10 weekends, 6 units
Entry	Counselling skills and client base

** **8) Diploma in Therapeutic Counselling** (Humanistic) (CSCT/AEB)

Core Model	Humanistic
Duration	1 year, part-time, 3 hrs/week, evening
Entry	Completion of Advanced Certificate

** **9) Higher National Certificate** (Integrative Model) (SQA)

Core Model	Integrative
Duration	1 year full time or 2 yrs p/time, 12 units (480 hrs) day release or evenings
Entry	Basic counselling training of 120 hrs at Cert. level

*** **10) Diploma in Counselling** (SQA)

Duration	One and a half years, part-time, 10 units, day release (400 hrs)
Entry	For practitioners; HNC (SQA) AEB Diploma/equivalent

*** **11) Counselling Supervision** (SQA)

Entry	Part 1: Open; Part 2: for counsellors who are moving into a supervisory role
Duration	40 hrs, part-time (Part 1); 80 hrs, part-time (Part 2)
Apply To:	Roz Chetwynd (ext 27352)

*Star System: * Introductory course only • ** 2-3 yr pt-time course to Cert/Dip level •*
*** *Professional development for trained counsellors*
For added help, see section 'Essential Information for Students', page 1

313

MORAY HOUSE INSTIT. OF EDUCATION, FACULTY OF
EDUCATION   **0131 651 6229**
FAX 0131 651 6111

University of Edinburgh, Paterson's Land, Holyrood Road, EDINBURGH, EH8 8AQ,
The Faculty of Education is currently strengthening its research base, and welcomes
enquiries from those interested in doctoral research in counselling studies.

**   1) Postgraduate Certificate in Counselling Approaches
Duration   120 hours, part-time, in 4x30 hr modules delivered over 2 weekends or
                  1 afternoon/eve per week basis
Entry   Degree/equivalent for Module 1, then completion of previous module
                  in sequence for each subsequent module

**   2) Postgraduate Diploma in Counselling
Duration   2.5 years, part-time, 1 afternoon/evening per week (480 hrs)
Entry   Completion of first two modules of 1) above + interview

***   3) MSc in Counselling Studies by dissertation (15-20,000 words)
Duration   2 yrs part-time
Entry   Completion of 2) above at required level
Apply To: Colin Kirkwood, Senior Lecturer in Counselling Studies,
                  colin.kirkwood@ed.ac.uk

PETER BOWES CONSULTANCY, THE,   **0131 334 6412**
92 Broomfield Crescent, EDINBURGH, EH12 7LX,

Short courses in counselling skills, advice guidance, conflict stress. (In-house/tailor-
made training, mentoring/consultancy)

♿ Residential courses have access for disabled people; courses are open to all
without discrimination.

*   1) Certificate in Counselling Skills ((COSCA)
Duration   120hrs, residential in 4 modules, each Sunday eve — Friday lunchtime
Entry   Module 1 : Open; Module 2,3,4, requires evidence of completion of
                  previous modules

**   2) Diploma in Counselling & Spiritual Development
Duration   2 yrs, residential format, 3 weeks and 5 week-ends/yr 475hrs)
Entry   Certificate in Counselling (120 hrs); the opportunity for counselling
                  experience; interview
Core Model   Personal Contruct Psychology as intergrating Meta Psychology
Apply To: Peter Bowes

---

*Star System: * Introductory course only • ** 2-3 yr pt-time course to Cert/Dip level •*
*** Professional development for trained counsellors
For added help, see section 'Essential Information for Students', page 1

314

SCOTTISH CHURCHES OPEN COLLEGE,   0131 3114726

Annie Small House, 18 Inverleith Terrace, EDINBURGH, EH3 5NS,

Courses in Association with the Pastoral Foundation Counselling Service, Edinburgh

*   **1) Counselling Course: Certificate in Counselling Skills**

Duration	120 hrs, each module: 30hrs, evening & weekends
Entry	Those who want to listen/communicate more effectively, or enhance the skills they already have; self awareness and assessment

**   **2) Advanced Diploma in Counselling** (Napier Univ, COSCA)

Duration	3 years, evenings & weekends (460 hrs)
Entry	Selection by interview onto year 2, also completion of year 1 or equivalent
Apply To:	Martha Mount, Counselling Course Leader

SCOTTISH INSTITUTE OF HUMAN RELATIONS,   0131 556 0924

56 Albany Street, EDINBURGH, EH1 3QR,

No response received to our enquiries for 2000. Entry details as of Nov 1998

**   **1) Training of Psychoanalytical Psychotherapists**

**   **2) Training in Family Therapy** (CCETSW approved for funding)

**   **3) Diploma in Human Relations & Counselling**

**   **4) Training in Child & Adolescent Psychotherapy**

**   **5) Therapeutic Skills with Children & Young People**

***   **6) Advanced Diploma in Psychodynamic Counselling**

STEVENSON COLLEGE,   0131 535 4620

Carrickvale Centre, Stenhouse Street West, EDINBURGH, EH11 3EP,

Also offers in-house & tailor-made training

♿ Ramp access, wheelchair lift, toilet

*   **1) Introduction to Counselling** (SQA)

Duration	14 weeks, 2.75 hrs/week, eve or 0.5 day
Entry	None

continued...

Star System: ** Introductory course only* • *** 2-3 yr pt-time course to Cert/Dip level* •
*** Professional development for trained counsellors
For added help, see section 'Essential Information for Students', page 1   *315*

* 2) Certificate in Counselling Skills (COSCA)

Duration	120 hrs + tutorials, 1 eve or 0.5 day/week OR 1 block week followed by 1 day /week
Entry	Selection by application form and interview
Apply To:	Alison Harold/May Ross

TEAMWORK EDINBURGH GESTALT INSTITUTE, 0131 228 3841
51 Lothian Road, EDINBURGH, EH1 2DJ,

In-house psychotherapy training and short courses applying the gestalt approach. One and two day introductory short courses offered.

♿ Not accessible for wheelchairs

* 1) Gestalt Therapy Foundation Course — SQA Advanced Certificate in Professional Development

Duration	1 year part-time
Entry	Relevant working context; basic counselling skills and group/individual therapy experience; either degree in related subject or training in a helping profession

** 2) Gestalt Therapy Training Programme — leading towards Diploma in Gestalt Psychotherapy

Duration	3 years part-time
Entry	Gestalt Therapy Foundation Course or equivalent + see entry qualifications for foundation course

*** 3) Choice, change and creativity — a personal/professional development group

Duration	Ongoing monthly meetings (Friday eve & Saturday)
Entry	Professionals with a personnel or pastoral role, health care and social workers, counsellors and therapists in training or practice

FALKIRK COLLEGE OF FURTHER & HIGHER EDUCATION
01324 403 000
Faculty of Humanities, Grangemouth Road, FALKIRK, FK2 9AD,

Tailor-made training available

♿ For individual requirments please contact: Student Information & Guidance Office

** 1) Counselling Skills Modules: Levels 1,2,3,4 (COSCA)

Duration	36 hours modules, part-time, 1 eve/week or 1 full day/week OR 1.5 day/week, some weekends
Entry	Anyone who has or intends to have a counselling role in their life, selection by interview with COSCA tutor

Star System: * Introductory course only • ** 2-3 yr pt-time course to Cert/Dip level •
*** Professional development for trained counsellors
For added help, see section 'Essential Information for Students', page 1

**   **2) Post Certificate Courses in Counselling**

Duration   36 hour modules (Counselling supervision, Gestalt, Transpersonal,
                 Psychodynamic, etc), part-time, 1 session/week for 12 weeks
Entry   COSCA certificate or approved equivalent
Apply To: Francis Monaghan, Senior Lecturer

OPEN SECRET,   01324 630100

22 Newmarket St, FAULKIRK, FK1 1JQ,
In-house/tailor made training offered

*   **Working with Adult Survivors of Childhood Sexual Abuse**

Duration   50hrs, 4 full days + 1 eve/week for 8 weeks
Entry   Basic Counselling Skills and /or knowledge of Sexual Abuse Issues
Apply To: Catriona Laird

CARDONALD COLLEGE,   0141 883 6151

The Library, 690 Mosspark Drive, GLASGOW, G52 3AY,
No response received to our enquiries for 2000, entry details as of 1998

*   **1) Introduction to Counselling** (SQA)

*   **2) Higher National Certificate Units** (SQA)

COLLEGE OF HOLISTIC MEDICINE,   0141 554 5808

4 Craigpark, GLASGOW, G31 2NA,
No response received to our enquiries for Nov 1998, entry details as of Nov 1998

**   **1) Certificate in Therapeutic Counselling**

**   **2) Diploma in Therapeutic Counselling**

**   **3) Advanced Diploma in Therapeutic Counselling**

Star System: ** Introductory course only • ** 2-3 yr pt-time course to Cert/Dip level •*
*** Professional development for trained counsellors
For added help, see section 'Essential Information for Students', page 1

317

GARNETHILL CENTRE, 0141 333 0730

28 Rose Street, GLASGOW, G3 6RE,

Various short courses and workshops, including counselling skills & general groupwork and group psychotherapy training

♿ Access to basement, counselling rooms & toilets

*   **1) Introduction to Counselling Skills** (Cert of Attendance)

Duration	1 yr, part-time modular (Module 1 validated by COSCA)
Entry	Anyone wishing to make more use of counselling skills especially in counselling settings

**   **2) Training in Group-Analytic Psychotherapy** (IGA)

Duration	6yrs, part-time. Includes Introductory yr, 2 yr Advanced course (both available on their own), 3yr Diploma
Entry	Professionals who intend to work with groups or are already doing so
Apply To:	Mrs Marjorie McKenna, Course Administrator

HERONSFIELD PPD HUMANISTIC TRAINING, 0141 357 3371

Regression & Integration, Therapy in Scotland, 115 Dowanhill Street, GLASGOW, G12 9EQ,

No response received to our enquiries for 2000, entry details as of Nov 1998

**   **1) Advanced Humanistic Counselling & Therapy Training Course**

***   **2) Training in Regression & Integration: Pre & Peri-natal Therapy work**

PCT BRITAIN (SUPERVISION), 01324 840 575 ALSO FAX
LAMBERSMEARNS@COMPUSERVE.COM

40 Kelvingrove Street, GLASGOW, G3 7RZ,

In-house & tailor-made counselling training also offered

♿ No wheelchair access but if necessary an alternative suitabe venue will be arranged

***   **Certificate in Person Centred Counselling Supervision**

Duration	120 hrs, 4 non-resedential weekends + private study and distance learning. November — June
Entry	Practising counsellors, trained to diploma level; on-going supervision practice required
Core Model	Person Centred
Apply To:	Elke Lambers, C. Psychol; FBAC BAC AccC; UKRC Reg. Ind. Couns.

Star System: * Introductory course only • ** 2-3 yr pt-time course to Cert/Dip level •
*** Professional development for trained counsellors
For added help, see section 'Essential Information for Students', page 1

318

SENSORY SYSTEMS TRAINING,   0141 424 4177
162 Queens Drive, Queen's Park, GLASGOW, G42 8QN,
No response received to our enquiries for 2000. Entry details as of Nov 1998

*   **1) NLP Practitioner Training**

*   **2) NLP Master Practitioner**

UNIVERSITY OF STRATHCLYDE,   0141 950 3359
Counselling Unit,Faculty of Ed, Jordanhill Campus, Southbrae Drive, GLASGOW,
G13 1PP,
Diploma, Certificate and Post-Diploma advanced training events. In-house/tailor-made
training is available

♿ Facilities for physical disability and learning impairment available

*   **1) Certificate in Counselling Skills**

Duration	1 year, part-time, introductory 5 day week + 2x3 day blocks + 9 Mondays
Entry	No formal qualificiations; selection on written statement

***   **2) PG Diploma in Counselling (BAC Acc)**

Duration	1 year, full-time (420+ hrs)
Entry	Post graduate/post experience, written statement, personal reference & interview; ongoing counselling experience essential

***   **3) PG Diploma in Counselling (BAC Acc)**

Duration	2 years, part-time, 1-8pm, 1 day/week & introductory 5 day week + 2 weekends
Entry	Post graduate/post experience; selection on written statement; personal reference & interview; ongoing counselling experience essential
Apply To:	Heather Robertson, Administrator

SHE, JAMES WATT COLLEGE OF FURTHER & HIG,
                                                01475 724 433

Finnart Street, GREENOCK, Renfrewshire, PA16 8HF,
No response received to our enquiries for 2000, entry details as of Nov 1998

*   **1) National Certificate: Introduction to Counselling Skills**

**   **2) Higher National Certificate: Counselling**

---

*Star System: * Introductory course only • ** 2-3 yr pt-time course to Cert/Dip level •
*** Professional development for trained counsellors*
For added help, see section 'Essential Information for Students', page 1

319

COUNSELLING TRAINING INITIATIVES LTD,(CTI)　0115 944 7849
Galtee House, 1 Heanor Road, ILKESTON, Derbyshire, DE7 8DY,
Please see National Section for fuller details of courses offered

♿ No response received to our enquiries for 2000, entry details as of Nov 1998

COUNSELLING & TRAINING HIGHLAND,　　　　01463 712066
Room 23, Queensgate Business Centre, 1 Fraser Street, INVERNESS, IV1 1DW,
In-house and counselling/skills workshops also offered eg: Counselling Skills for those working with special needs

♿ As venues vary consideration is always given to special needs and access

* **1) Certificate in Counselling Skills** (Univ Strathclyde)

Duration	120 hrs, 1 weekend + day/fortnight
Entry	Selection by application form
Apply To:	Pam Courcha/Sue James, Counselling Tutors

** **2) Diploma in Person-Centred Counselling** (Univ Strathclyde)

Duration	2 years, weekends (450 hours)
Entry	Selection by interview
Apply To:	Sue James

INVERNESS COLLEGE,　　　　　　　　　　01463 236 681
3 Longman Road, Midmills Building, Crown Avenue, INVERNESS, IV1 1SA,
No response received to our enquiries for 2000, entry details as of Nov 1998

* **1) Introduction to Counselling Skills**

* **2) Certificate in Loss & Bereavement**

* **3) Certificate in Counselling Skills** (HNC)

* **4) Certificate in Counselling Theory** (HNC)

CENTRAL SCHOOL OF COUNSELLING & THERAPY,
0800 243463
80 Paul Street, LONDON, EC2A 4UD,
See National Section entry for full details.

Star System:　* Introductory course only ● ** 2-3 yr pt-time course to Cert/Dip level ●
*** Professional development for trained counsellors
For added help, see section 'Essential Information for Students', page 1

320

PERTH COLLEGE OF FURTHER EDUCATION,   01783 621171

Crieff Road, PERTH, PH1 2NX,
No response received to our enquiries for 2000. Entry details as of Nov 1998

*   **1) Introduction to Counselling**

*   **2) Coping with Loss**

*   **3) Extended Counselling** (SCOTVEC Unit)

UNIVERSITY OF DUNDEE,   01382 344 442

A.K. Bell Library, York Place, PERTH, PH2,
No response received to our enquiries for 2000, entry details as of Nov 1998

1) Counselling for Beginners

2) Introduction to Counselling

3) Further Counselling Skills

CENTRE TRAINING INTERNATIONAL SCHOOL OF HYPNOTHERAPY AND PSYCHOTHERAPY   01772 617663
FAX: 01772 614211

145 Chapel Lane, Longton, PRESTON, PR4 5NA,
See National Section entry for full details

Star System: * Introductory course only • ** 2-3 yr pt-time course to Cert/Dip level •
*** Professional development for trained counsellors
For added help, see section 'Essential Information for Students', page 1

321

ABERDARE COLLEGE, 01685 887500

Cwmdare Road, ABERDARE, Mid Glamorgan, CF44 8ST,

No response received to our enquiries for 2000, entry details as of November 1998

* **1) Introduction to Counselling Skills** (OCN accred)

* **2) Stage 1 Counselling Skills** (A framework for professional development in Wales) (WJEC)

* **3) Stage 2 Certificate in Counselling Skills** (WJEC)

COLEG CEREDIGION, 01970 624511

Llanbadarn Campus, ABERYSTWYTH, Dyfed, SY23 3BP,

Some courses are also run from the Cardigan campus, please contact the College for details.

♿ Parking, access, lift, additional support in study centre

* **1) Intoduction to Counselling** (CSCT/AEB)

Duration	30 hours, 2hrs/one evening, 15 weeks
Entry	No formal qualifications. An interest in people and a desire to work with change, growth and development.

* **2) Certificate in Counselling Skills** (CSCT/AEB)

Duration	1 year, 75 hours, evenings
Entry	Open, subject to interview and reference
Apply To:	Penny Murfin

** **3) Advanced Certificate in Counselling** (CSCT/AEB)

Duration	1 year, 150 hours, afternoon and evening sessions
Entry	CSCT Certificates in Skills/Theory equivalent (via APL), subject to interview
Apply To:	Yvonne Bates

** **4) Part-time Diploma in Therapeutic Counselling** (CSCT/AEB)

Duration	215 hours, 1 year including 6x1 day workshops
Entry	CSCT/AEB Advanced Certificate and interview or APL

* **5) Certificate in Counselling Theory** (CSCT/AEB)

Duration	75 hrs, 1 evening/week, 1 year
Entry	Open access
Apply To:	Penny Murfin

---

*Star System: * Introductory course only • ** 2-3 yr pt-time course to Cert/Dip level •*
*** Professional development for trained counsellors*
For added help, see section 'Essential Information for Students', page 1

322

CARMARTHENSHIRE COLLEGE (CCTA),   01554 748319/748000

Faculty of Health, Social &, Child Care Studies, Ammanford Campus, AMMANFORD, Dyfed, SA18 3TA,

 ♿ Limited access for disabled people, please enquire at the college

* **1) Introduction to Counselling Skills Leading to an Intermediate Award** (EdExel/BTEC)

Duration   20 weeks, 3 hrs, 1 morning afternoon or eve/week (90 hrs)

Entry   Preference given to those working in a setting where they are using counselling skills, but open to anyone with an interest

** **2) Advanced Certificate in Counselling Skills** (EDE

Duration   30 weeks, day release + a weekend residential (240 hrs)

Entry   Completion of 4) or equivalent and selection by interview/selection day

** **3) Higher Diploma in Counselling**

Duration   2 years, day release + 2 residential weekends (450 hrs)

Entry   Completion of 5)/equivalent; selection by inetrview/selection day

Apply To: Simon O'Donohoe, Counselling courses tutor

* **4) Bereavement & Loss Counselling**

Duration   30 hrs total daytime

Entry   Advanced Certificate in Counselling Skills/equivalent; selection by interview

* **5) Counselling in the Workplace**

Duration   30 hrs total, daytime

Entry   Advanced Certificate in Counselling Skills/equivalent; selection by interview

* **6) Couples/Relationship Counselling**

Duration   30 hrs, daytime

Entry   Advanced Certificate in Counselling Skills/equivalent; selection by interview

UNIVERSITY OF WALES, BANGOR,   01248 351151

Serials Acquisitions, College Road, BANGOR, Gwynedd, LL57 2DG,

No response received to our enquiries for 2000. Entry details as of Nov 1998

*** **Diploma/MEd in Counselling — Modular Course**

*Star System: * Introductory course only • ** 2-3 yr pt-time course to Cert/Dip level •
*** Professional development for trained counsellors*
For added help, see section 'Essential Information for Students', page 1

323

BARRY COLLEGE,   01446 743519

Colcot Road, BARRY, South Glamorgan, CF62 8YJ,

In-house/tailor-made training. Also workshops in counselling/counselling skills

♿ Wheelchair access, 'Earshot' — support for the hearing impaired. Learning support service.

*   **1) Introduction to Counselling** (Integrative) (OCN)

Duration	24 hrs part-time day or evening (Sept, Jan and March)
Apply To:	Sarah Penny

*   **2) Certificate in Counselling Skills** (CSCT/AEB)

Duration	1 year, 2.5 hrs/week, daytime or evening (75 hrs) (Sept start)
Entry	Open access

*   **3) Certificate in Counselling Theory** (CSCT/AEB)

Duration	1 year, 2.5 hrs/week daytime or evening (75 hrs) (Sept start)
Entry	Open

**   **4) Advanced Certificate in Counselling Skills and Theory** (Integrative) (CSCT/AEB)

Duration	150 hrs part-time day or evening (Sept start)
Entry	Completion of CSCT Certificates in Counselling Skills and Counselling Theory. APL route available.
Apply To:	Sarah Penny

**   **5) Diploma in Therapeutic Counselling Psychodynamic OR Humanistic** (CSCT/AEB)

Duration	215 hrs part-time day or evening (Sept start)
Entry	Completion of CSCT Advanced Certificate in Counselling Skills and Theory. APL route available.
Apply To:	Sarah Penny

***   **6) Diploma in Supervision** (CSCT/AEB) (Integrative)

Duration	150 hrs part-time day or evening (Sept start)
Entry	Qualified to diploma level in counselling Psychotherapy; In ongoing supervision for min 2 yrs since qualifying; Working as supervisior or able to take supervisees during the course.
Apply To:	Sarah Penny

Star System: *Introductory course only • ** 2-3 yr pt-time course to Cert/Dip level •*
*** Professional development for trained counsellors*
For added help, see section 'Essential Information for Students', page 1

324

BRIDGEND COLLEGE,   **01656 766 588**

Cambridge Road, Bridgend, BRIDGEND, Mid Glamorgan, CF31 3DF,
No response received to our enquiries for 2000, entry details as of Nov 1998

*   **1) Basic Approaches to Counselling** (South East Wales Access Consortium)

*   **2) Counselling Skills & Theory** (South East Wales Access Consorium)

**   **3) Advanced Certificate in Counselling** (BTEC)

LLANDRILLO COLLEGE,   **01492 546666**

Student Services, Llandudno Road, Rhos-On-Sea, COLWYN BAY, Clwyd, LL28 4HZ,
No response received to our enquiries for 2000, entry details as of November 1998

*   **1) Introduction to Counselling Skills** (NWACC/Open College)

*   **2) Foundation Certificate in Counselling Skills** (Liverpool Univ)

**   **3) Advanced Certificate in Counselling** (Liverpool Univ)

***   **4) Advanced Postgraduate Diploma/MEd in Counselling**

PEMBROKESHIRE COLLEGE,   **01437 765247**

HAVERFORDWEST, Dyfed, SA61 1SZ,

♿ Good access, incorporating reserved parking spaces/lift, for people with mobility difficulties. Happy to discuss other needs

*   **1) Introduction to Counselling Skills** (College Certificate)

Duration	4 full days (20hrs), or 8 half days, part-time (20 hrs)
Entry	

*   **2) Certificate in Counselling Skills** (WJEC)

Duration	15 full days (75hrs), plus directed study, over 4 months
Entry	Those using counselling skills at work and/or those who have attended an introductory course; selection by interview

**   **3) Combined Certificate in Counselling Skills — Foundation**

Duration	15 days (60hrs), plus directed study, over 4 months
Entry	Must have completed a minimum of 60 hrs counselling skills and personal development training; selection by interview

continued...

*Star System: * Introductory course only • ** 2-3 yr pt-time course to Cert/Dip level •*
*** Professional development for trained counsellors*
For added help, see section 'Essential Information for Students', page 1

325

** 4) Diploma in Counselling (CTI/OCN)

Duration	2 yrs, 1 day/week (330hrs + directed study). This course if offered alternate years
Entry	Completion of a minimum 120hrs relevant prior training; se;ection by interview
Apply To:	The Information Officer

COUNSELLING TRAINING INITIATIVES LTD,(CTI) 0115 944 7849

Galtee House, 1 Heanor Road, ILKESTON, Derbyshire, DE7 8DY,

Please see National Section for fuller details of courses offered

♿ No response received to our enquiries for 2000, entry details as of Nov 1998

CENTRAL SCHOOL OF COUNSELLING & THERAPY,
0800 243463

80 Paul Street, LONDON, EC2A 4UD,

See National Section entry for full details.

UNIVERSITY OF WALES COLLEGE, 01633 432520

Dept of Health & Social Care, Alltyryn Campus, Alltyryn Avenue, NEWPORT, Gwent, NP9 5XR,

Also offers in-house & tailor-made short counselling skills and related courses.

♿ Lifts, toilets, wide doors, tutorial support, a student services dept. Special needs should be openly discussed with tutor prior to interview

* 1) Introduction to Counselling

Duration	6 weeks, part-time, evenings; twice yearly
Entry	Open access

** 2) Modular Masters Scheme: The Counselling Pathway Part 1
Postgraduate Certificate in Counselling Skills (Wales Univ)

Duration	1 year, whole day or 2 years evening study
Entry	Professional qualifications and/or degree & experience in the helping field. Some exceptions; selection process, interview & references; applicants must be over 25
Apply To:	Mike Simmons

Star System: * *Introductory course only* • ** *2-3 yr pt-time course to Cert/Dip level* •
*** *Professional development for trained counsellors*

For added help, see section 'Essential Information for Students', page 1

326

**   **3) Part 2 Post Graduate Diploma in Counselling** (Wales Univ)

Duration	1 year, whole day or 2 years evening study
Entry	2) above/equivalent ie. 250 hrs training, 70 hrs supervised counselling practice. 70 hrs self-awareness/personal therapy work; porfolio for evidence of this work from those from outside; selection by interview & references; over 25 years
Apply To:	Lynne Lewis

***   **4) Part 3, Masters in Counselling** (Wales Univ)

Duration	1 year, whole day + 6 months for dissertation completion, cognitive specialism
Entry	Course 3) above or equivalent; selection interview, selection procedures & references; over 25 yrs old
Apply To:	Frank Wills, Deputy Head of Dept

SOUTH WALES COUNSELLING,   029 2070 9358

Albert Road Methodist Church, & Community Centre, Albert Road, PENARTH, South Glamorgan, CF64 1BY,

No response received to our enquiries for 2000, entry details as of November 1998

**   **Certificate of Higher Education in Counselling** (University of Wales, Cardiff)

SWANSEA COLLEGE,   01792 284000

Tycoch Road, Sketty, SWANSEA, SA2 9EB,

In-house and tailor-made training

♿ Lifts to all floors, ramps, car parking, learning support, individual assessment of needs and appropriate support

**   **Professional Development Certificate** (PDC) in Counselling Skills (Edexcel)

Duration	35 weeks, 4hrs/week over 2 years + residential weekend each year
Entry	Those who have completed 60 hours basic training or equivalent and have or will take up supervised skills use outside college. Over 21. Selection by interview
Apply To:	Ms J Atkinson

Star System: ** Introductory course only* • *** 2-3 yr pt-time course to Cert/Dip level* •
*** Professional development for trained counsellors
For added help, see section 'Essential Information for Students', page 1   *327*

WELSH CENTRE FOR COUNSELLING PSYCHOLOGY,
01792 295498 X 4734

Institute of Health Care, Studies, Univ of Wales,Swansea, Singleton Park, SWANSEA, SA2 8PP,

No response received to our enquiries for 2000. Entry details as of Nov 1998

*   **1) Advanced Counselling**

*   **2) Certificate in Counselling** (WNB; Univ of Wales Swansea) Part 1

**   **3) Diploma in Counselling** (Univ of Wales Swansea)

**   **4) Art Therapy & Person-Centred Counselling**

***   **5) Advanced Diploma** (with dissertation)

***   **6) MPhil in Counselling** (Wales Univ)

***   **7) PhD**

*Star System: * Introductory course only • ** 2-3 yr pt-time course to Cert/Dip level •*
*** Professional development for trained counsellors
For added help, see section 'Essential Information for Students', page 1
328

INDEX BY SUBJECT

INDEX BY INSTITUTION

INDEX BY INSTITUTION